Dance and Somatics

Dance and Somatics

*Mind-Body Principles of
Teaching and Performance*

JULIE A. BRODIE *and*
ELIN E. LOBEL

McFarland & Company, Inc., Publishers
Jefferson, North Carolina, and London

All illustrations, unless otherwise noted,
were created by Sarah Gill-Williams for this book.

LIBRARY OF CONGRESS CATALOGUING-IN-PUBLICATION DATA

Brodie, Julie A.
Dance and somatics : mind-body principles of teaching and
performance / Julie A. Brodie and Elin E. Lobel.
p.   cm.
Includes bibliographical references and index.

ISBN 978-0-7864-5880-6
softcover : acid free paper ∞

1. Dance — Study and teaching — Psychological aspects.   2. Dance —
Philosophy.   3. Mind and body.   I. Lobel, Elin E.   II. Title.
GV1589.B76 2012   793.307 — dc23   2012003634

BRITISH LIBRARY CATALOGUING DATA ARE AVAILABLE

On the cover: Dancer Pamela Newell © 2012 Michael Slobodian

Manufactured in the United States of America

*McFarland & Company, Inc., Publishers
Box 611, Jefferson, North Carolina 28640
www.mcfarlandpub.com*

To our children:
Adriana, Brodie, Evi, and Juleon
And our parents:
Bruce and Colleen Brodie, and Barton and Sharon Clark

Acknowledgments

We would like to thank the following people and institutions for their assistance and support: Alexander Lobel, Michael Hufnagel, Kenyon College Department of Dance, Drama and Film, Towson University, Jean Blacker and the GLCA New Directions Initiative, and James Costello.

Table of Contents

Preface: Somatics in Dance*

No real intellectual, emotional, or artistic growth can take place save as it is built upon a foundation of innate capacities and impulses."— H' Doubler 1957, 58

This book presents ideas about how dance educators can incorporate information found in somatic practices into their teaching of dance technique and why this is important for dancers today. It also relates somatic approaches for teaching technique to scientific principles supporting and explaining these pedagogical choices. Training in somatic techniques is an effective means of improving dance students' efficiency and ease of movement. However, dance educators do not always have the resources to implement separate somatics courses within their curriculums or to incorporate this body of knowledge into their technique classes. Others may already be incorporating somatic work into their classes by means of repeating their own training experiences, but may wish to do so from a more developed base of knowledge.

While we recognize that it has been a growing movement over the last several decades to include somatic work in the dance technique class or for dancers to study somatic techniques outside of class to enhance their skills, we are interested in the underlying concepts that make this work appealing and helpful to dancers. With this in mind, this text introduces fundamental principles that are central to many somatic practices and provides possible models for integrating these ideas into the dance technique class. This text is intended to be helpful for teachers of any dance style and level, not just higher education modern dance, as these Somatic Principles can be applied to all forms of movement and are important to recognize at all levels of mastery. Hopefully teachers and students will explore the material in this text together, but dancers wanting to improve their performance can certainly also utilize these ideas on their own.

The path to this book began years ago, when we started dancing together as children studying the Royal Academy of Dance ballet technique. We both pursued careers as modern dancers before finding our way into academe and have continued to explore alternative training methods since. Lobel is a professor of kinesiology, as

---

*Portions of this Preface previously appeared in the *Journal of Dance Education* (Lobel and Brodie 2006a) and are reprinted by permission of the authors and the publisher.

well as a Certified Laban Movement Analyst/Bartenieff Fundamentals practitioner and a Certified Feldenkrais practitioner. She teaches motor development, learning and control, as well as dance. Brodie is a dance professor with research specialties in kinesiology and Labanotation. She is currently enrolled in the Laban Movement Analysis/Bartenieff Fundamentals Certification Program, holds a black belt in karate, and is still dancing and choreographing. She attributes much of her long career as a mover to her training in various somatic techniques, including the Alexander Technique, Bartenieff Fundamentals, and yoga. We bring to this book our positive experiences with dance training and what we have learned from our less positive encounters, as well as what we have gleaned from our other explorations as movers and teachers.

Eight years ago, we were discussing our experiences with somatic learning and ways we have addressed its integration in our own classes. We found that what stood out were the commonalities between the various somatic practices that we have explored — the "ah-hah!" moments of realizing that inhibition and direction in Alexander Technique are similar to the non-doing and mental imagery used in Ideokinesis and Feldenkrais. Or that the Bartenieff Fundamentals' arm circles or knee drops are done in many somatic techniques with slight variations. It was this kind of thinking that originally inspired our article "Integrating Fundamental Principles Underlying Somatic Practices into the Dance Technique Class" (Brodie and Lobel 2004). Because of the clarity of this approach, the *Journal of Dance Education* (*JODE*) asked us to guest-edit a special issue devoted to the practical application of somatic principles in the classroom (Lobel and Brodie 2006b). We began to realize that the interest in this topic warranted further exploration and development, so we continued to flesh out our initial ideas through workshops, writing, and any other means of long-distance collaboration.

One challenge we have encountered has been finding ways of making the body of somatic knowledge more accessible to dance educators without minimizing the value of certification in specialized areas. We think we can best honor the depth of each field and the certification process by addressing the fundamental principles of somatic techniques and movement in general. Hopefully, focusing attention on what is universal can create a bridge between certified practitioners and potentially uncertified dance educators to pass somatic ideas on to students. It also may help students lucky enough to have specific somatic training with transferring their new experiences to dance technique and performance.

We have found that bringing awareness to the interdisciplinary principles of **breath**, **sensing**, **connectivity**, and **initiation** can assist dance students at all levels and with diverse learning styles in fulfilling their movement potential. Focusing attention on these processes can increase sensitivity, awareness, and responsiveness while moving. This state of consciousness can, in turn, improve dancers' alignment and efficiency in addition to enhancing their class-taking and performance skills (Feldenkrais 1972; Fitt 1996, 304; Lessinger 1996).

Throughout the book, we strive to demystify somatic thinking by explaining what is happening in terms of current scientific research when possible. Because somatic work is, by definition, based in the body and is about each individual's unique experience, it can be difficult to write about and explain without sounding vague or cultish. The phenomena seen and experienced can frequently be described in physiological terms, however, and we feel this is important to recognize, both to validate the skills and intuition of somatic practitioners and to help us in using these ideas to educate dancers. This recognition refers not only to the Somatic Principles we identify, but also to pedagogical approaches embraced by somatic practitioners that we can employ in the dance classroom. In addition, we want to reinforce the importance of students having a basic working knowledge of anatomy, physiology, and kinesiology in order to achieve a greater depth of understanding of the moving body. As such, we include this information as it arises in the context of each support principle. As Thomas Hanna said, "The somatic viewpoint seeks to understand life, first of all, by taking notice of the physical forces that have shaped the body of life.... Far from demeaning the phenomenon of life and robbing it of its significance, such a viewpoint leads to the discovery that life, in its manifestation as *the soma, takes advantage of these universal laws and uses them for its advancement*" (Hanna 1993, 38).

To begin, the introduction defines what we mean by "somatics" and "somatic techniques." In addition, it presents the underlying Somatic Principles that we have identified and some preliminary suggestions for ways to implement this material into classes. In Chapter 1, we take a closer look at pedagogical choices we make, or teaching strategies that are also aligned with somatic wisdom. Issues such as verbal, tactile, and visual feedback, pacing, transfer of concepts to dance technique, differing learning preferences, and methods and reasons for utilizing guided exploration and discovery are addressed.

In Chapters 2 through 6, we examine each Somatic Principle in depth. **Movement experiences** to support the suggested class structure are provided for each topic, as well as relevant scientific information. These movement experiences are written in the second person to facilitate the ease with which they can be implemented into classes. Our intention is never to be prescriptive or sound commanding, as this is contradictory to the somatic approach. Users of this book should feel free to adapt the language as needed to fit the situation and their own teaching style. **Teaching tips** are directed more specifically to instructors, providing additional information related to the particular movement experience and/or the content of the chapter, but they can also be used by a student or dancer using this book independently.

The final chapters of this text present additional ideas for the exploration, development, and integration of this material. Chapter 7 examines the concept of developing one's own practice as a means of enhancing dance training, including suggestions for how to realize this approach from both the teacher's and the learner's perspective. We have also chosen to include a chapter with specific applications of the Somatic

Principles to dance technique (Chapter 8). The Conclusion contains resources to assist interested readers in following up on any specific technique or topic the book has broached. We also relate the feedback we have received from some of our students as a way of tying it all together and inspiring us to continue the journey to becoming more effective and insightful teachers of dance technique.

We have attempted to be as user-friendly and practical with this information as possible, but it is also important to us that this work is viewed as a philosophical approach to teaching and not just a how-to book. As such, we encourage you to spend time contemplating and physically exploring the concepts on your own before trying to incorporate them into your classes. Certain ideas, formats, and methods are bound to be more or less effective for you and for your students. We believe that teachers who experience bodywork with certified practitioners or explore basic principles thoroughly on their own can take the ideas and concepts they find most helpful and use them to enrich their approach to movement education. And students will be incited to further their work with somatic practitioners when they see and feel the results in their performance.

Introduction: The Fundamental Somatic Principles*

Beneath the level of our verbal, acculturated consciousness is a realm that we are only now beginning to perceive and trace out. I call it the somatic realm— somatic because it sees the human being and all living beings not merely in terms of bodily structure but in terms of bodily function, namely, movement.— Hanna 1993, xii

The term somatics has become fairly mainstream in the world of dance and performing art, and even beyond, in our contemporary self-help culture. Many dance teachers and performers draw upon and reference somatic theory, with more or less knowledge and experience supporting their use of these ideas. In reality, the somatic lexicon has become so intertwined with contemporary modern dance that for some it has become a basis of the technique itself. As somatic work is a powerful tool in creating efficient, expressive, and creative artists, one can only encourage this fusion. Others in the dance field may not have ready access to somatic practices, or may struggle with integrating somatic content into their teaching or performance of dance technique. Our hope is that this book provides dancers and teachers with background information, general concepts, and experiential activities drawn from somatic work to assist them with continuing this trend as effectively and appropriately as possible.

In this chapter, we create a working definition of somatics and introduce the fundamental Somatic Principles of breath, sensing, connectivity, and initiation that are central to many somatic practices. These four fundamental principles of breath, sensing, connectivity, and initiation were primarily culled from the following somatic disciplines: the Alexander Technique, the Feldenkrais Method, Laban Movement Analysis/Bartenieff Fundamentals, Body-Mind Centering, and Ideokinesis, although other somatic practices and practitioners are referenced as well (Alexander 1932; Bainbridge-Cohen 1993; Bartenieff and Lewis 1980; Feldenkrais 1972; Fitt 1996; Hackney 1998; Hanna 1979; Swiegard 1974). While, strictly speaking, Pilates training, yoga, and the martial arts are not always considered to be somatic disciplines, we have chosen to include ideas from these forms given their widespread popularity among

---

*Portions of this Introduction previously appeared in *Journal of Dance Education* (Brodie and Lobel 2004) and are reprinted by permission of the authors and the publisher.

dancers and dance educators. It also seems appropriate and helpful to include yoga and the martial arts based on the influence of these older, Eastern forms on more current somatic thinking.

Definition of Somatics

Derived from the Greek word *soma*, meaning "the living body in its wholeness," the term *somatics* is credited to Thomas Hanna (1979, 5–6) and references processes inclusive of the entire being — body, mind, spirit, and the environment in which they coexist. This work rides on a belief that the soma is a changeable, fluid entity that responds to both external and internal stimuli (Hanna 1979). The focus is on the individual experience; how we feel as opposed to how others perceive us or how we think we are being perceived. By increasing internal sensitivity or listening, we can become aware of habitual ways of moving and responding and arrive at new movement possibilities (Feldenkrais 1972; Hanna 1979). In this manner, somatic thinking emphasizes the process, rather than the product.

Utilization of Principles Rather Than Techniques

The many somatic practices provide differing points of view, but they have at least three elements in common. They all:

1. Deal with "Truths" about the way the body works and moves. Human movement and body/mind (Bodily) wisdom are fundamental to life itself. It stands to reason that there are basic concepts or principles supporting all movement and movement re-education systems. In other words, there is no copyright on concepts like breath, connectivity, sensing self and the environment, and initiation — they are innate components of the living organism.

2. Believe that awareness is the first step toward change. Once a person can sense what he or she is doing and experiences new options, he or she can make choices, and lasting change becomes possible.

3. Have common goals: improving alignment and efficiency to enhance physical functioning and artistic capacity.

Focusing attention on these fundamental aspects of the living experience and on the manner in which we embody them can help us identify our tendencies and maximize our movement potential.

The exciting part is understanding and experiencing the many different approaches to getting at the same end result. In her article "Matching," Elizabeth Behnke (1995) reminds us of Don Johnson's distinction between principles and tech-

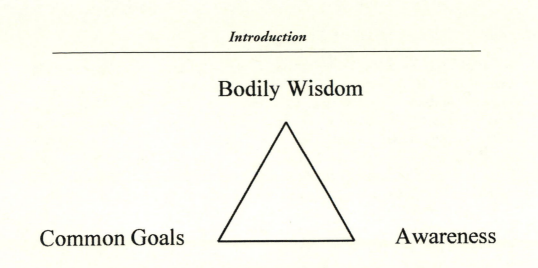

Figure I.2 Triangle of Commonalities among Somatic Techniques.

niques in somatic education: "Principles are fundamental sources of discovery that enable the inspired person continually to invent creative strategies for working with others, whereas techniques are specific methods arising from such principles" (Behnke 1995, 317). It is the identification of these Somatic Principles that we believe is most important and useful for dancers and dance educators and that makes our approach unique.

Why Integrate Somatics and Dance?

Shifting the focus from product (skill acquisition) to process (what is actually happening in the body) can promote optimal functioning and help prevent injury (Alexander 1932; Bartenieff and Lewis 1980; Hackney 1998; Swiegard 1974). However, it is all too easy for dancers and teachers alike to get caught up in trying to master class material, and certainly, the emphasis needs to be on dancing, not on theories for how to dance best. How, then, can dance educators encourage process-oriented learning and moving without disrupting the flow of class?

Bringing awareness to the bodily processes of breathing, sensing, connecting, and initiating can help students reconnect the mind with the body within the context of technique class. Again, these are not new ideas. These concepts are addressed in various existing somatic techniques, which have long been recognized as a potent resource for dancers (Batson 1990; Green 2002; Myers 1983). However, identifying and isolating fundamental principles or bodily processes common to many somatic practices can provide teachers with a method for applying and integrating this body of knowledge into the dance technique class. Additionally, applying these principles within the dance technique class facilitates the transfer of learning (Magill 2007; Schmidt and Wrisberg 2008). Even when dance students have access to separate somatics courses, they do not always know how to implement their new insights into their dance technique classes and performance situations. In order for the learner to integrate movement information and awareness gleaned from somatic training, they must have opportunities to transfer that knowledge to the target context of dance technique class or performance.

In addition to being vital components of the movement experience, focusing on these fundamental Somatic Principles helps occupy the conscious, judgmental aspect of the mind and can assist in achieving a state of quiet consciousness more conducive to optimal learning and performance. The various somatic techniques are founded on an underlying belief in the wisdom of the body — they just utilize different approaches to access that wisdom (Hanna 1979). Essentially, directing attention to breathing, sensing, connecting, or initiating enables the body to take full advantage of its own innate knowledge. Timothy Gallwey (1976), author of the performance enhancement text *The Inner Game of Tennis*, discusses it in terms of Self 1 and Self 2, in which Self 1 is the "teller" and Self 2 is the "doer." As he notes, "Self 1 does not trust Self 2, even though it embodies all the potential you have developed up to that moment and is far more competent to control the muscle system than Self 1.... By thinking too much and trying too hard, Self 1 has produced tension and muscle conflict in the body" (12). This movement pattern of increased tension and inefficient muscular coordination decreases movement potential, so it is important to find methods for quieting the voice of Self 1.

Four Fundamental Principles Found in Somatic Disciplines

Breath. This first principle is central to all aspects of life and movement. Mabel Todd (1937, 217), author of *The Thinking Body*, said of the diaphragm: "Like the equator, it is the dividing line of two great halves of being: the conscious and the unconscious, the voluntary and the involuntary, the skeletal and the visceral." As such, it connects the mind and body in the most immediate fashion. Changes in emotional and/or physical states are reflected in the breath, and embodiment practitioners attest to the breath's ability to work in the opposite direction as well (Alexander 1932; Mayland 1995; Speads 1995). This speaks to the importance of the breath in promoting overall health and relaxation, in addition to controlling the effects of the sympathetic nervous system in times of stress. In other instances, the role of the breath in connecting to the core and in finding the flow of movement is emphasized (Bartenieff and Lewis 1980; Hackney 1998; Todd 1937). This is vital to dancers working to achieve their full functional and qualitative range.

Sensing. Sensing both self and the environment can assist with being fully present in the moment, opening the door to increased responsiveness. Attending to information provided by the exteroceptive systems (vision, audition, touch, and smell) provides the proprioceptive system with information necessary for accurate and appropriate reaction to stimuli (Hackney 1998; Moore and Yamamoto 1988; Schmidt and Wrisberg 2008). Frequently, dance students rely primarily on visual information from the mirror to detect and correct errors in their movement skill performance. However, in application to dance performance, the visual system should really be used to navigate and negotiate space, people, and objects in the environment. Providing students with the opportunity to experience how their exteroceptive systems inform them about the environment and how that information influences movement can help redirect the learner's attention from product orientation to process orientation. Placing focus on the environment is therefore reinforcing the innate functions and interactions of all the exteroceptive and proprioceptive systems (Hackney 1998; Kandel, Schwartz, and Jessel 1991; Schmidt and Wrisberg 2008). We have separated the topic of sensing into two chapters; one on the subject of kinesthesia and the other about the visual system and other modes of sensing to help clarify the

Figure I.3 Somatic Principle of Breath (Evi Brodie; photograph by Marcella Hackbardt).

differing, yet overlapping roles of the exteroceptive and proprioceptive systems.

Connectivity. Connectivity within the body and into the ground is necessary for movement control, power, and efficiency. Connectivity implies understanding, on a kinetic level, the forces acting on the body and the body's structural potential to resist, yield, or amplify these forces in movement (Bartenieff and Lewis 1980; Hackney 1998; Hamill and Knutzen 1995). Discussion and exploration of the physical laws of movement are included in order to clarify these forces and ways of responding to

Left: Figure I.4 Somatic Principle of Sensing. *Top:* Figure I.5 Somatic Principle of Connectivity (both images of Evi Brodie; photographs by Marcella Hackbardt).

them. Different somatic practices address this concept of connectivity in different ways: primary control in Alexander Technique, lines of movement in Ideokinesis, total body connectivity patterns in Bartenieff Fundamentals and Body-Mind Centering, and the powerhouse in Pilates, to name a few (Alexander 1932; Bainbridge-Cohen 1993; Bartenieff and Lewis 1980; Hackney 1998; Silver 2000; Swiegard 1974). The developmental patterns that support our progression from birth to maturity and our ability to navigate the pull of gravity are part of all of these approaches to connectivity (Fiorentino 1981; Haywood and Getchell 2009; Mills and Bainbridge-Cohen 1990).

Initiation. This last principle is vital to accurate and efficient performance of a movement. Directing the learner's focus to where the movement originates and how it sequences through the body increases the likelihood that the kinetic chain will be completed as desired (Bartenieff and Lewis 1980; Hackney 1998; Hamill and Knutzen 1995). Therefore, precision in initiation and sequencing can lead to greater biomechanical efficiency in movement as well as a heightened sense of expressive capacity. The motor learning and development concepts related to intention provide

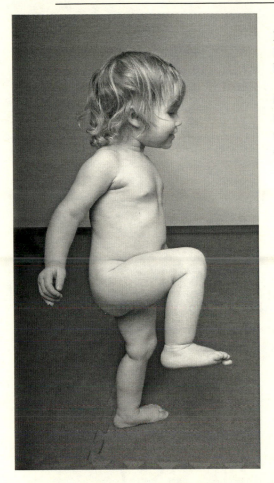

Figure I.6 Somatic Principle of Initiation (Evi Brodie; photograph by Marcella Hackbardt).

a conceptual framework for understanding and selecting from the various initiation techniques or ideas employed in somatic work.

Conclusions

It is important to remember that the four Somatic Principles of breathing, sensing, connecting, and initiating do not exist in isolation in the human body—all are occurring simultaneously and are intimately connected (Hackney 1998). For example, breath can be used to explore connectivity and initiation, or sensing the environment can initiate movement and alter the breath. Only for simplicity and clarity are each discussed individually. Eventually, the classroom approach should also emphasize the interconnectedness of these bodily processes. The ultimate goal is that students are able to discern which techniques for connecting the mind to the body are most effective for them in given situations, allowing them to shift fluidly from one to another while dancing.

It is equally important to recognize that there is no substitute for a meaningful experience in a somatic technique with a trained practitioner. However, not all dance educators and students have ready access to trained practitioners, even if budgetary and curricular restraints are irrelevant. In addition, different somatic approaches work for different people. Extracting and understanding the common themes (or truths about the organization of the body) for inclusion in dance training can enable the dance educator to take advantage of this body of information in order to address the individual needs of diverse learners. For students, applying new information and experiences directly to dance technique assists with the transfer of these somatic concepts.

The ultimate goal of focusing on breathing, connecting, sensing and initiating while dancing is to increase awareness, and it is that awareness that opens the door to making new choices. When they are present in movement, dancers are making choices informed by the kinesthetic sense and the external environment, not based on habit, feedback from the mirror, or verbal commands. Presence in movement is a consciousness of posture, motion, and state of being (Alexander 1932; Feldenkrais 1972; Fitt 1996). This manner of moving and learning enhances artistic as well as technical growth. As Elsa Gindler (1995, 6) said, "When a task is executed thoughtfully, and when we are contented with ourselves in the doing, we experience consciousness. By that I mean consciousness that is centered, reacts to the environment and can think and feel." Likewise, being conscious of movement results in a thoughtful and satisfying performance.

The following introductory movement experiences introduce the four fundamental Somatic Principles explored in depth in subsequent chapters.

MOVEMENT EXPERIENCE ONE: BREATH

a. Lie on your back, arms and legs extended, and palms up. Bring your awareness to your breath. Notice areas of the body contacting the floor; how air enters and exits; where in the body the breath flows; the rhythm of your breathing; movement of the body with each breath. Notice sensations arising in the nose, mouth, chest, abdomen, and limbs. Feel the path of air traveling from the nose, to the lungs, then filling the abdomen. Reverse this path on the exhalation, emptying the abdomen, then the lungs, and allowing air to escape through the mouth. Send the breath to any areas in which tension is sensed. Have you made any discoveries about the breath cycle? Is the exhalation full and complete? Is there a pause between the exhalation and the next inhalation?

b. Roll to the fetal position and connect the hands to the floor to assist with coming up to a cross-legged position. Place your hands on your belly and ribs: send attention to the motion in the sagittal plane. Move your hands to the sides of ribs: direct attention to the lateral motion in the frontal or vertical plane. Round forward, placing the torso on the knees: pay attention to the expansion in the back. Press to downward-facing dog (weight on hands and feet, chest pressed through the shoulders, and coccyx reaching toward backward high): feel the softening of the external muscles and the hollowing in to the center with each exha-

Figure I.7 Three-Dimensional Breathing.

12

lation. Walk back and hang; then roll up. Take a moment to experience the breath while standing. Sense the movement of the breath in all three dimensions.

MOVEMENT EXPERIENCE TWO: SENSING

a. Take a moment to sense and feel where you are in the space. Scan the environment with your eyes. What do you see? Where are you in the room? Begin to notice the textures of what you are seeing. Notice any objects in the room. Notice the shapes and forms of the objects and people in the environment. Notice the depth of the surfaces. Let your gaze travel to the ceiling. Notice the texture, depth, and form of the ceiling. Let your gaze travel to the ground. What do you see?

b. Now let your visual scanning of the environment lead you into walking. As you are moving through the space, continue to take in your environment. What are you seeing? Parts of your body, others, objects, surfaces? Explore the phenomenon of really seeing while you change directions, levels, and timing. Notice the visual information that is stationary and the visual information that is moving. As you continue to move, shift your attention to the sounds in the room. What do you hear? Do you hear yourself, others, the sound of movement? Continue moving through the space, and shift your attention to what you smell. Notice the changes in smell as you move and pass by others. Continue to move through the environment and shift your awareness to touch. What are you touching? What is touching you? Your clothes, the ground, the air? How is the air moving around you as you pass by others?

c. Now use your awareness of touch to meet and greet others in your environment. As you move near someone find a way to communicate with each other briefly through touch. Start by connecting with your hands, but then begin to explore communicating with different body parts and body surfaces. Touches may be brief and light, but be fully aware of the body parts in contact. What can you convey and sense with the hands, the feet, the head, or the back surfaces of your bodies? Conclude your exchange, and communicate in the same manner with the next person you move near to in the environment. Staying with your partner, develop this communication through touch into a conversation through touch by responding to the tactile information your partner is giving you. Try not to judge or pre-plan the conversation. Stay focused on what you perceive, and allow your responses to be spontaneous. Find an ending, separate, and have another touch conversation with someone else in the environment. Continue this exploration of communicating and conversing via touch with others in the environment. Now take this touch conversation to the floor. See a place in the room and move toward it, separating from your partner. Relax into the ground facing down (prone). Take time to sense how you are touching the floor. Which parts of you are contacting the ground? Take a moment to feel, see, and hear where you are in the room. Does the room seem the same or different than when you began this experience by scanning the environment with your eyes?

Figure I.1 "Somatic Principles" (Karen Snouffer).

MOVEMENT EXPERIENCE THREE: CONNECTIVITY WITHIN THE BODY AND INTO THE GROUND

a. Start prone. Explore pushing with your arms. Try both, then one at a time. Take time to yield before the push, and feel how the force of pushing ripples through the body. Allow the pushing to move your body through space, as well as changing your orientation in space by rolling, sliding, rotating. Then repeat the process with your legs.

b. While still on the floor, try locomoting through space by pulling with the arms, then the legs. Begin by reaching both hands toward a specific point in the space. Grounding your hands on that point, try pulling your body toward it. Imagine that you are holding onto a rope, trying to pull yourself out of quicksand. How can you pull with the feet and legs? Progress to exploring different combinations of pushing and pulling with the arms and legs. Does the experience differ when coordinating the limbs on the same side of the body (homolateral) rather than the limbs on opposite sides of the body (contralateral)? Try incorporating different facings, levels, and dynamics. Gradually bring the energy inward until you find yourself standing quietly. Notice any changes in your sense of your body — its connections internally and into the earth.

MOVEMENT EXPERIENCE FOUR: INITIATION

a. Start standing: explore how you can move within your own space and through the environmental space, initiating movement from a distal end such as the fingertips, toes, head, or tail (coccyx region). Notice how the movement sequences through the body when it is initiated from a distal end.

b. After exploring initiation from different distal ends, shift your attention to initiating the movement from a mid-limb joint (elbows and/or knees). Try the homolateral knee and elbow and then the contralateral knee and elbow. Again, notice how the movement sequences through the body. Now, try initiating movement from the proximal joints (hips and shoulders), and attend to how the movement sequences through the body.

c. Let the core initiate movement within your own space and through the environmental space. How does it sequence through and out of the body? Let the initiation lead the whole movement. Continue to explore initiating movement from the core, making it smaller and smaller until it resolves into stillness. Take a few moments to reflect on where you are now. How do you feel and what do you sense?

Teaching Tip: These guided discovery movement experiences can be done separately but also can be done consecutively (one through four) as a discrete movement exploration class based on the four fundamental principles found in somatic disciplines.

1

Pedagogy

Strategies for Teaching and Learning Based on Somatic Principles

In how you learn is the secret of how you unlearn. It is in how we learned to do things that the real answers of how to reorganize ourselves lies.—Keleman 1979, 25

While the four fundamental Somatic Principles and related activities are more concrete tools that dancers and teachers can utilize for class design and performance enhancement, the underlying pedagogical approaches in somatic work are at least as important to recognize. In this chapter, we consider these teaching strategies and why they are effective, even necessary, in creating new movement options for students in dance technique class. One possible model for integrating somatic principles into the dance studio will also be presented. This information is included at this point in the text so that these pedagogical approaches can inform and support thorough exploration of the four fundamental Somatic Principles in the ensuing chapters.

Guided Exploration and Discovery: Methods and Reasons for Utilizing

Feeling is not always reliable, as has been noted by Alexander (1932, 42) in his classic text, *The Use of the Self.* What we are accustomed to feels correct, although it may be far from the most efficient use of the body. Most dancers have experienced being positioned in the "right" alignment and how foreign that place seems. In order to encourage a new sense of the body and its movement possibilities, it is particularly important to provide movement experiences that deviate from traditional dance activities. It is difficult, if not impossible, to discover and accept new choices with movement that is already ingrained in the neuromuscular pathways (Swiegard 1974). A new sensitivity can begin to be established with guided exploration activities that isolate breathing, sensing, connecting and initiating, allowing time for individual discovery and attention to internal sensation. Focusing on these four aspects of movement in an improvisatory setting can help the dancer reenter the body and retrain the kinesthetic sense. With practice, then, the same methods can be used to reevaluate movement patterning in more traditional or set exercises.

The use of exploratory movement activities can also help dance students decrease their reliance on the mirror. Alignment and movement corrections derived from visual information from the mirror will probably not produce lasting changes or transfer to dance performance (Magill 2007). In addition, overreliance on the mirror may actually interfere with the ability to attend to kinesthetic cues (Feldenkrais 1972; Fitt 1996). Exploratory movement activities allow the dance student to relearn how the exteroceptive and proprioceptive systems can and should work together. The exteroceptive system involves sensing the external environment (Kandel, Schwartz, and Jesell 1991). It includes the classic five senses of seeing, hearing, smelling, tasting, and touching. The proprioceptive system involves sensing the position and movement of the body in space and relies on information from receptors in the muscles, joints, and skin (Kandel, Schwartz, and Jessell 1991). Both exteroception and proprioception are discussed in detail in Chapter 3, but for now suffice it to say that ideally a symbiotic relationship exists between the two systems. Information from the environment works with feedback from the body, enabling dancers to detect and correct movement problems (Coker 2009; Magill 2007; Schmidt and Wrisberg 2008). This is beneficial to the dancer, as feedback corrections based on the exteroceptive and proprioceptive systems can be utilized in performance situations (Magill 2007).

Exploratory activities tend to be led verbally. This method permits each student to have his or her own experience with the concept because the dancer is not invested in mimicking a visual form. This individuality of experience should be encouraged and honored throughout the class, even when executing specific, choreographed material. Each body is unique, and dancers must learn to solve movement problems to the best of their own ability and based on their own experience. Encouraging this approach in traditional technique as well as in exploratory activities can aid dancers in the integration and retention of new ways of moving. In addition, discovering and embracing one's own movement choices speaks to the artistry, not just the skill, involved in dance.

In her *Dance Magazine* publication about the body therapies (an early term for somatics) and modern dance, Martha Myers (1983, 21) noted the importance of language in teaching: "Language conditions our mental habits and thought processes just as movement conditions our physical habits. The two interact on unconscious and conscious levels. Language is, therefore, integral to the sensations we experience." As there is little, if any, modeling involved in the exploratory activities, clarity of language is instrumental in guiding them effectively. For example, instead of merely telling students to think about their breathing, their attention can be drawn to the three-dimensionality of the breath. Being specific and providing suggestions for how to sense these dimensions (see Movement Experience One, Introduction) can help students feel more comfortable and may open the door to new discoveries.

Feedback: Verbal, Visual, and Tactile

Wording has perhaps even more important implications when it comes to corrections. A lack of understanding can lead to misdirected and/or excessive effort, and then students will frequently revert to former movement patterns (Alexander 1932; Feldenkrais 1972; Fitt 1996; Gallwey 1976; Schmidt and Wrisberg 2008; Swiegard 1974). When giving verbal feedback during the dance technique class, asking directed questions, providing images, or suggesting desired kinesthetic sensations may be more beneficial than a command-style correction (Fortin, Long, and Lord 2002; Gallwey 1976). For instance, a problem with shoulder tension might be addressed by bringing the learner's awareness to that area through questions: "What sensations are you experiencing in the shoulder region as you lift the arm overhead? Explore moving the arm through its range. Does the shoulder feel different in other positions?" Or by providing an image: "Feel as though soft, warm mud is sliding down the upper back as the arm lifts." Or through kinesthetic sensation: "Try to sense the connection of the scapula into the back as the arm lifts." All of these methods recognize the importance of awareness in enacting change and empower students to find their own solutions to the problem, rather than just saying, "Get your shoulders down!" These various approaches to feedback also honor the fact that different dancers learn in different ways.

We will discuss the visual element in depth in Chapter 4, but it should be noted here that if a mover can really and truly see what he or she is doing in comparison to a desired action, this may be one of the most effective means of creating change. Visual feedback tends to get a bad rap in somatic work because of the tendency to overrely on modeling and the mirror. However, we have already noted that our kinesthetic sense can be unreliable when it comes to changing habits (Alexander 1932; Feldenkrais 1985). If a student can see what needs to be done, giving the nervous system a clear image, he or she has found an extremely efficient and effective means of both learning material and finding ways of circumventing habitual patterns. The key is that, once discovered, time and attention must then be directed to feeling the new ways of moving to help retrain the kinesthetic sense.

Teaching Tip: Videoing class can be

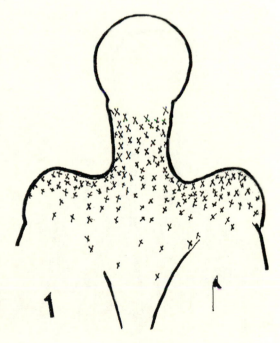

Figure 1.2 Shoulder Tension.

a useful tool for students to get a clearer sense of what they are actually doing in posture and movement. It can be especially helpful at the intermediate level, where students tend to want to "do" more than refine. Video can be taken of students performing everyday actions, such as walking, changing direction, stepping up and down, sitting and standing, and even picking up and carrying a backpack. This video can be compared with a video of class. It can be revealing to see how the same patterns carry over from pedestrian to extraordinary actions. Videoing midsemester can also be helpful, especially when the video is analyzed prior to a conference with the teacher to discuss progress and goals for the remainder of the semester.

Tactile feedback is also a useful tool. Touch can be particularly helpful in bringing awareness to a part

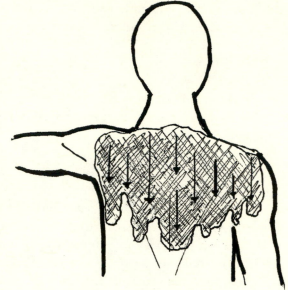

Figure 1.3 Mud Image.

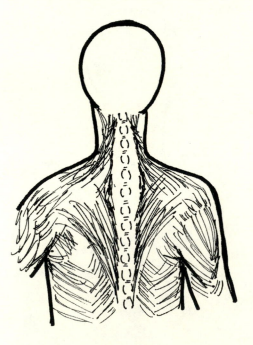

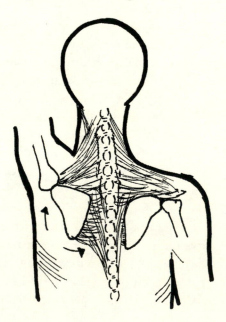

Figure 1.4 Scapula Rotation.

that is lacking sensation or a movement pattern that is off the radar. Unless a neurological deficit is present, all parts of the body have sensation, and the basic movement patterns or coordinations are part of the developmental process (Kandell, Schwartz, and Jessell, 1991). However most of us have areas of our bodies that we do not attend to as much as other areas for one reason or another, or movement patterns that are less utilized. Touch can reawaken sensitivity, helping to release unwanted tension or revealing hidden expressive capacity (Feldenkrais 2010). Manually guiding students into a new position or taking them through an unused motor pattern can also help students discover new movement possibilities, but these methods must be used with caution as the results may not be repeatable by the students (Buchanon and Ulrich 2001; Schmidt and Wrisberg 2008).

Movement Experience: *Assisted X Roll*: The X Roll is commonly used in technique classes as a way of reinforcing contralateral connections and clarity of distal initiation in the body (see Chapters 5 and 6). From a supine X position (in which the body is lying on the ground with the legs and arms extended making an X shape with the whole body), reach one hand across the body. Counter-tension in the leg on the same side will create a spiral in the body. Eventually allow the arm to "win," so the body releases into a prone X position. Continue the roll in the same direction, with the opposite arm reaching back and across the body until it "wins" and initiates a roll back to the supine X. Next, send the leg across, repeating the same pattern of reaching and counter-tension, creating a spiral that leads into a roll, but with initiation from the lower body.

Figure 1.5 Assisted X Roll (left to right, Julie Brodie, Kora Radella, and Balinda Craig-Quijada; photograph by Marcella Hackbardt).

Many times, students struggle with clarity of the spatial reach and with establishing the counter-tension that fosters the contralateral sense of connectivity. Students can work in groups of three, giving tactile feedback to help with these issues. While one dancer lies in the X, another can assist with the initial motion of the arm across the body, providing a gentle pull to the reaching hand. The third party reinforces the counter-tension by providing gentle traction to the leg, creating a diagonal pull. When the partner releases the foot, the person in the X should be encouraged to ride the hand initiation into the roll, releasing into the floor, but with a sense of easy spatial reach through the limbs. Repeat with the other arm and both legs. The sense of diagonal connection can also be established while the roller lies motionless in the X. The manipulating partners can provide gentle traction to the opposite arm and leg, placing their hands mid-limb (at the elbow and knee) or distally (at the hand and foot).

Passive versus Active Techniques

When change is physically enacted by someone else, a technique is considered to be passive, while in an active technique the change is created by the mover and not the instructor (Schmidt and Wrisberg 2008). For example, traditional massage would be a passive technique, while a student moving through a Feldenkrais Awareness Through Movement (ATM) lesson would be engaged in an active technique. Some somatic techniques employ a combination of passive and active work, like the Alexander Technique, where the student is able to passively experience new options during table manipulations, but is then actively engaged in moving through simple actions like sitting, standing, and walking while the instructor provides hands-on feedback (Feldenkrais 1981; Vineyard 2007).

One of the criticisms of passive guidance techniques is that movement produced by someone else uses different motor commands and muscles, making it feel dissimilar when the action is produced by the learner themselves (Magill 2007; Schmidt and Wrisberg 2008). Because of the complexity of kinesthetic input, the perception of motion is affected by how the motion is produced. In other words, a passive technique will create a different kinesthetic sensation than what is created when moving actively through the same pattern. However, passive work is still useful for directing attention to the sensations that arise from going through new movement patterns, and it emphasizes the quality rather than the outcome of movement. As with visual learning, in order to retrain the kinesthetic sense, passive tactile input must be reinforced by spending time and placing attention on feeling the new ways of moving when they are produced actively.

In addition, the neuromuscular pathways that are programmed for accomplishing a given action will not be altered by passive techniques. In order to circumvent habitual ways of carrying out a movement, this patterning must be addressed. It is the initial decision to move that sets the sequence of nervous stimulation and muscle contraction into play. In a passive technique, this initiation from the motor cortex does not occur, so there is no change to the following neuromuscular pattern. Only by augmenting passive manipulation with active repatterning can lasting change occur (Rose and Christina 2006).

It is interesting to consider visualization in these terms. Many would initially categorize imaging or Ideokinesis as a passive technique, just because movement is not involved. However, because change is being enacted by the mind of the mover, it is active by definition (Coker 2009). Neuromuscular repatterning is occurring by visualizing action, which allows the body to begin reprogramming for the most efficient execution of that movement (refer to Chapters 4 and 6 for a more thorough discussion on the neuromuscular effects of visualization).

Changing a Part Affects the Whole

As teachers and students we cannot just spot-fix, but must look at the use of the whole being or self in movement. We are a kinetic chain, so an adjustment or correction in the placement of one body part will affect the rest (Hamill and Knutzen 1995). In addition, it is important to recognize that the habitual way of doing something, at least initially, fills some need — whether it is physical, emotional, and/or aesthetic. Somatic work is based on the concept that the body, mind, spirit, and environment are all integral to the whole being. Our posture and ways of being or moving in the world reflect a summation of our physical and emotional genetic tendencies, our life experiences, and cultural standards. For example, consider a dancer with slumped shoulders. This common problem could be the result of a physical defect (scoliosis), an emotional problem (depression), a social issue (large breasts), or some combination of these factors. Without a clear understanding of the deeper issues at play, addressing the problem with external correction will not be as effective.

Movement Experience: *Self Image Drawing:* With a partner and large sheets of paper, trace each other (or just have students draw a smaller version of themselves). Color in your body using shades you feel are representative of your bodily experience. Consider where you hold tension, places that hurt or feel pleasurable, areas that are sensitive, parts that are more or less mobile or powerful or expressive. What parts do you really enjoy about your body, and what parts do you wish were different and why? Which parts do you know really intimately versus parts that are relatively unknown, and do these correspond with areas you have left blank in your drawing?

Teaching Tip: This activity can be used to start students thinking more globally about their bodies, not just as instruments of dance. This can be the foundation for a more in-depth self-image narrative. Activities like these also provide the teacher with valuable information about students' perceptions of themselves and possible physical limitations to take into consideration.

A Take-home Assignment (Teachers can feel free to use this as it is or to modify it as they wish): Write a self-image narrative about your life as a mover and a dancer. Reflecting on the body drawing done in class, discuss which aspects of your self-image and movement repertoire you value and which aspects you devalue? Also in your narrative include information about your movement background, your dance experiences, and what you perceive to be your strengths and weaknesses. Please mention any health issues or previous injuries that are pertinent. How do you hope to grow as a dancer this semester, and how do you envision your narrative continuing into the future? What kind of experiences do you hope to have in class? Do not limit yourself to these questions. If you feel so inspired, write poetry, draw, or include a quotation or a memorable childhood experience — whatever you want to share that captures the essence of you as a mover in some way.

Application and Integration of Common Themes in the Dance Class

No single method exists for approaching the integration of somatic concepts into the dance class (in fact, it would be very un-somatic of us to suggest this!). In the following chapters, many ideas and activities will be presented with the hope that they will provide a starting place for teachers unsure of how to begin. Or perhaps they will spark new ideas or provide new material for those becoming tired of their "tried and true" activities. The fundamental principles of breathing, sensing, connecting, and initiating can provide a framework for utilizing and accessing many diverse somatic approaches. For example, in one model utilizing concept teaching, students could be introduced to the four fundamental Somatic Principles gradually over the course of the semester. As Jan Erkert (2003, 30) states in *Harnessing the Wind: the Art of Teaching Modern Dance*, "Every day in every class, a dance teacher works on everything. But focusing attention on one principle or concept, such as spiral, shifting weight, or confidence, yields much deeper results. Identifying a principle to teach each day gives clarity to movement patterns, class structure, and corrections."

Perhaps one of the fundamental principles is selected as the focus of each class, and during the warm-up, students are led through guided explorations designed to increase awareness of that particular bodily process. For example, breathing can be explored early in class via nontraditional, experiential activities (see Chapter 2 for sample movement experiences). Once familiar with the concept, dancers are then encouraged to apply the information to their work in more complicated combinations. In this case, dancers attend to their use of breath in technical exercises and in the culminating phrase of the class. New awareness of the breath can be further reinforced in the cooling-down phase of the class, encouraging retention and integration of the experience while also placing attention on the need for a recuperative phase within the class.

Transfer of Concepts to Dance Technique

Once a fundamental movement concept has been introduced and explored, that concept should remain the focus of ensuing activities to optimize transfer. In studying the integration of Feldenkrais into dance technique classes, Fortin, Long and Lord (2002) recognized that the transition from their Awareness Through Movement activities to the more technical parts of class was "a delicate moment, exactly for this reason: it focuses on the interface between sensorium and motorium. For the teachers, this transition coincided with a passage from verbal to visual guidance" (172). One solution to this potentially awkward transition is to move from the exploratory activity into a "set" standing combination. Because the students are familiar with the phrase, their attention can still be directed internally, focused on whichever movement concept they have been experiencing (Schmidt and Wrisberg 2008). The students are applying any new sensations to dance movement while vertical and working against gravity, but with little visual guidance and maximal concentration on the sensation of the movement, not on learning the steps. Transferring the newly learned sensations to "dance movement" while vertical and working with gravity is key to enhancing motor performance, as dancers rarely perform solely lying down (Magill 2007; Schmidt and Wrisberg 2008). Teachers can then move into new technical and locomotor combinations, easing into visual guidance while still reinforcing the concept of the day.

Backward teaching is another way of structuring class that works with the somatically driven dance experience. In backward teaching, the teacher creates the final combination or phrase first and then deconstructs it, looking for specific movements or actions that may be most challenging for students. These components are then woven into the earlier parts of class so that when students get to the last phrase it is less intimidating. By doing this, the students have already established the neuromuscular pathways for sections of the final phrase. This structure allows them to learn it faster, learn more material, and be freed up to focus on other aspects of the dance experience. Teachers should realize when utilizing this method that they do not just have to weave in specific steps. It may be kinds of coordination patterns, qualities, or initiations that are practiced throughout class leading up to the grand finale.

Teaching Tip: Concept teaching and backward teaching are effective for students, and they also are helpful tools for teachers when planning classes. We all experience burnout or blocks from time to time. Selecting a concept and then building a class around it or creating a fun phrase and then using it as fodder for the rest of the class can help circumvent these teaching challenges.

Somatic-Inspired Teaching Philosophies

The use of guided explorations suggests a deeper philosophical belief in the innate wisdom of the body and in the importance of student driven learning — taking responsibility for enacting one's own changes and finding one's own way of moving. A teacher is not telling students exactly what movements to do or asserting that there is a right or a wrong way to perform a movement. This aspect of nonjudgement distinguishes somatic instruction from traditional dance technique, where student performance is frequently critiqued.

In addition to allowing students to have ownership in finding and shaping their own unique artistic instruments, this somatic approach provides a sense of freedom from style-based criteria for judgment. Many students struggle with being told one correction by one teacher only for it to be contradicted by a different teacher. For example, opinions about how the arms and hands are to be held will be very different coming from a ballet teacher rather than from a Cunningham modern dance teacher. If the student's understanding of the carriage of the arms is founded on his or her individual experience of the connection of the humerus, scapula, and back to provide full range of motion, stylistic adaptations may be less confusing and frustrating. Students may also then feel empowered to take or leave the suggestions being provided from different sources.

Another distinguishing somatic philosophy is the need to slow down. We all have a sense of when we have done something to the best of our ability — when we do not and we rush through, it creates stress and dissatisfaction. Slowing down allows us to find alternative ways to achieve a particular skill, and we can pay attention to the sensations resulting from moving in these new ways (Feldenkrais 2010). Moving slowly may also reveal weak areas in a motor program. Lester Van Tress, a piano instructor, had his students practice playing their recital pieces in slow motion, attesting that the places where they faltered were the same spots that would cause problems under the stress of performance. By working through these spots slowly and by bringing awareness to them, the weaknesses were resolved (Van Tress 1976).

In the early stages of learning, we have to consciously think about and process every moment of every movement. Eventually, with repetition, the basics of the movement become ingrained in the neuromuscular pathways and dancers can rely on muscle memory to complete actions without attending to every detail (Rose and Christina 2006). This memorization is a good thing, as it enables the dancer to pay attention to new information that further refines the movement. At an advanced level, slowing down brings attention back to the basics of the motor program, and by making it conscious again, the dancer is obliged to reevaluate how he or she is choosing to move. While overthinking is detrimental in a performance situation, this process of slowing down improves a dancer's ability to discern, refine, and choose what they are doing while in the rehearsal phase (Schmidt and Wrisberg 2008).

Somatic thinking also honors the importance of rest as part of the learning process (Feldenkrais 1972). This concept of balancing exertion and recuperation is imbedded within most somatic techniques and is supported by motor learning research that indicates that distributed practice is preferred to massed practice (Hackney 1998; Magill 2007; Schmidt and Wrisberg 2008). Providing a resting phase that is as long, or even longer, than the active phase during motor learning encourages skill acquisition and retention and assists in injury prevention (Arnheim 1980; Clippinger 2007; Rose and Christina 2006; Vincent 1978; Watkins and Clarkson 1990). The lineage of this model can be traced as far back as the inclusion of Shavasana, or the resting (corpse) pose, placed between other Asanas in yoga practices (Iyengar 1979, 2005).

Traditionally, dance class does not allow much time for this recuperative stage of the learning process, with the class structure revolving around repetition and over-load to build capacity (Nettl-Fiol 2008, 97). Teachers might do well to reconsider this practice, building opportunities for rest within the class structure. This may require dancers and teachers alike to reconsider how they are defining rest. As a culture, we tend to think of rest as a time of doing nothing and even associate it with a period of non-productivity. In somatic thinking, rest is a time of non-action, but this does not mean nothing is being done. As noted by Batson and Schwartz (2007, 50), "In resting, a student is encouraged to observe themselves with attention to residual sen-sations, novel organization of the self-image, and a general state of open awareness to their present experience. From within this reduced activation, a recalibration of self-organization occurs that allows for more freedom of choice when reactivating movement."

Teaching Tip: Teachers might play with incorporating times for rest at different points in the class. Class can begin and end with time for rest. If class starts with a movement experience, allowing time for self-sensing before and after the guided exploration may set students up for more effective integration of the concept into later work. In a large class, teachers might experiment with using the "down time" as one group is working for the other students to engage in active rest. This active rest might consist of the kind of self-sensing described above, engaging in watching peers, or even visualizing the phrase material.

The concepts of nonjudgment, slowing down, and respecting the role of rest in training all place an emphasis on the process of the experience rather than the product of the experience. There is a focus on the whole person — the uniqueness of each being, with the inner experience being just as important, if not more so, than the outer image. The goal and the challenge are to maintain this orientation in the context of set combinations or choreography as well as movement explorations or improvi-sations.

Somatic belief in the wisdom of the body also provides a different perspective on "errors." Rather than viewing challenges as problems that need to be fixed, this belief engenders an approach that the body will learn and discover its own best solution when permitted. This does not mean that students are unguided or left to flounder, but that they are not saddled with judgment or too much external input from the teacher. Sometimes teachers feel that if they are to do their job well, they need to be providing corrections and comments after each performance of a combination. Frequently, if students are allowed to work through the material several times before receiving feedback, their performance will grow and they will self-correct. Providing feedback too soon and/or giving too many directives can overengage the analytical mind and actually frustrate attempts to get the movement "in the body." It is also interesting to note that giving verbal feedback or corrections is more effective when it is asked for by the learner, assuming the learner has sufficient experience with the movement skill (Magill 2007; Schmidt and Wrisberg 2008).

Creating Conditions for Learning: Classroom Environment

The classroom environment created by both teacher and students is equally important to the process of creating change. If a classroom environment is perceived as safe, where students have freedom to explore and permission to make mistakes, there will typically be less ambient environmental and internal bodily tension. With less tension, the body can sense what needs to be done. As part of this safe and supportive atmosphere, teachers need to be sure to respect differences in sensitivity, anxiety, and learning preferences. Take, for example, a student struggling with performing an inversion. Once insecure in his or her ability to find a suspension point when upside down, it becomes next to impossible to accomplish. However well intentioned, stopping the whole class and directing everyone's attention to the poor student attempting the inversion will probably not work well for the sensitive or nervous dancer. Providing different suggestions (to the entire class or while peers are otherwise occupied) that focus the mind on sensation rather than "correct" execution may be more helpful and can be tailored to individual need. A very visual dancer may respond well to imaging the inversion before doing it or to seeing how another student is achieving success with the action. A kinesthetically focused performer may do best with trying the preparation slowly, feeling what is happening in terms of connecting the hands to the floor and shifting the center of gravity. Regardless of individual differences, the body can sense and adjust to imbalances if the movement is not over-analyzed or corrected to the point of freezing up the performer.

Feedback versus Reinforcement

When considering the classroom environment being created, it is important to distinguish between feedback and reinforcement. Positive reinforcement can be a useful tool in establishing a nurturing and supportive environment, particularly with beginning levels. General comments like "Great job!" or "Much better!" can go a long way toward boosting student confidence and morale, which can in turn help students take more chances, try harder, and trust their innate abilities more. However, this kind of "cheerleading" does not actually enhance specific skill acquisition. For comments to be used as feedback, they must be more specific (Coker 2009; Magill 2011), for example, saying to the class, "On the next try notice that Jill is succeeding with that roll and getting back up quickly because she is really using her head-tail connection. That makes her more compact so she can go in and out of the floor efficiently." This comment not only gives Jill specific, positive feedback, it also provides valuable information to the rest of the class.

Differences Between Somatic Techniques

Examining distinguishing features of the somatic techniques themselves may give us additional thoughts on their integration into technique class. Some somatic work is done as a group learning situation, while other techniques are designed to be taught one-on-one. Feldenkrais Awareness Through Movement (ATM) lessons, for example, are designed to be an individual experience within a group setting. Alexander work, on the other hand, is done through private lessons. As such, Feldenkrais ATM sessions are led verbally, while Alexander sessions involve a great deal of hands-on work. Dance classes are almost always group sessions, so the techniques employed in group somatic work such as verbal cueing may transfer more readily. While valuable ideas can be derived from the Alexander class, they may require more adaptation to be effectively transferred to technique classes. Despite the challenges, finding ways of bringing hands-on or more individualized feedback into the classroom may open up new teaching possibilities and help with addressing the different kinds of learners in the class (Bell 1996; Lessinger 1996).

Movement Experience: ***Hands on Dégagés***: Have students perform a quick, but relatively simple dégagé combination. Various images can be applied. Repeat the same combination (either in the same or the next class session) with a partner. One student places a hand on the back of his or her partner's neck, lengthening the spine gently. Trade roles and discuss or journal about the different sensations that occurred in the experience.

Artistry in Movement or Performance Quality

Most somatic techniques discuss efficiency in movement and finding a neutral place as a means of improving performance, but many do not systematically address artistry or movement quality in detail. Laban Movement Analysis/Bartenieff Fundamentals is one of the few somatic techniques that includes performance quality as a core component. In his book *The Mastery of Movement,* Laban (1980) outlined specific qualities of movement that can be identified and explored to enlarge the expressive capacity of the performer. While improving movement performance in general will lead to improvements in artistry, dealing with artistic expression directly is important for the fully realized dancer.

Laban identified some basic qualities that can be seen and felt in the performer, such as the weight of the movement, the flow of the movement, the time of the movement, and the focus or space of the movement. For each of the basic qualities or efforts of performance, as he named them, there are two opposites that describe the range or endpoints of the continuum. The quality of weight has a range from strong to light effort or quality, while the flow of a movement can go from bound to free. The manner in which a movement exemplifies the quality of time can vary from quick to sustained, and the focus of the performer's moving can be from a direct, pinpointed focus to a more global or even soft focus (indirect spatial focus). It is beyond the scope of this book to go into detail regarding the combinations and permutations of Laban's effort work but even so, much can be gained by accessing the basic qualities of movement as outlined in Laban Movement Analysis/Bartenieff Fundamentals (Bartenieff and Lewis 1980; Hackney 1998; Laban 1980).

Movement Experience: *Walking Through the Efforts*: Begin locomoting through the space in any way you wish. Continue moving through space, changing the directions by traveling forward, backward, sideways, and diagonally, and then explore changing the level to high, medium, or low. Keep traveling through the space while changing the quality of how you move, such as skipping lightly, galloping strongly, walking with ease or resistence, quickly or slowly. Keep moving and experiment with changing your focus from pinpointed to all-encompassing (direct and indirect space effort). Notice which aspects of the walk came more easily to you. In particular, which qualities were easiest to access in the moment. For an extension of the Walk, pick one of the qualities that came easily (time, space, weight, or flow). Explore the range of that particular quality, for example from quick to sustained. Now pick one of the elements that was more challenging and explore the range of that quality.

Teaching Tip: The Movement Experience Walking Through the Efforts can be used as a warm-up for class and can be either teacher-directed, in which the teacher calls out the elements to be explored, or student-directed, as a follow-the-leader form in which the students call out which efforts they want to move through. With the student-directed approach to organizing the walk, it is helpful to go through the efforts and their breakdown into opposite ends of the spectrum before starting the movement experience. This can be done either verbally or in writing so that everyone knows and understands what the options are prior to the experience.

Movement Experience: *Polar Opposites Effort Solo*: Begin standing and take a moment to sense and feel yourself. Decide on an effort quality, and begin moving with this quality in mind. Continue for up to a minute, exploring all the ways in which you can move with this quality. Stop moving, and consider the opposite end of the effort continuum, so if you used lightness now use strength. Move with this quality for a minute. Continue exploring until you have moved through all of the following effort qualities: light/strong, sustained/quick, free/bound, direct/indirect. Select a pair of opposing qualities and create a brief solo using a few movements that exemplify these quality pairs. For example, six movements that range between light and strong. Divide the class into two groups. Have one group show their solos while the other group observes, trying to identify which effort pairs the performers picked. Switch groups and repeat.

Teaching Tip: These effort qualities can be explored from a different perspective, using a set phrase rather than improvisatory material, depending on the needs and interests of the class. Students can learn a very basic phrase and then be divided into groups. Each group can be given an emotion to portray through the set phrase by altering the effort life of the material. After working on the phrase, each group can show its version to the rest of the class. The observers can provide their interpretation of the feeling of the phrase and then determine the effort changes that helped convey this emotion.

Set Movement Exercises and Experiential Movement Activities

The previous movement experiences illustrate another distinction among somatic techniques: the use of set exercises versus experiential activities. The Bartenieff Fundamentals Basic Six are set movement sequences used to address the body aspect of the Laban Movement Analysis System (Bartenieff and Lewis 1980; Hackney 1998). Pilates also has set exercises (Silver 2000). These established movement patterns can be easily included in the technique class, particularly in the floor work combinations. While this inclusion is valuable and a nice resource for material, teachers should be sure that students have time to work through the underlying principles before layering in the need to keep to a certain rhythm or dance aesthetic. For example, allow time to work through femoral flexion before including thigh lifts in a floor combination. Then be sure to reference the femoral flexion involved in standing activities and provide opportunities to rediscover the release in the hip socket and underlying core support when in this different orientation.

Other somatic techniques, like the Alexander Technique and the Feldenkrais Method, do not utilize set movement sequences. The ideas, images, and even some of the more pedestrian actions used in these techniques can still be brought into the dance classroom, however. For example, the monkey position in Alexander can be used in a combination to warm up the back, or the Feldenkrais pelvic clock could be integrated into a floor phrase early in class. The monkey is a standing position with the hips and knees slightly flexed and the back extended with its normal curves present. The arms hang with the pull of gravity, giving the stance an ape-like appearance. From this position, a neutral spine may be more easily sensed because the tension has been taken off of the hip flexors. The most basic description of the pelvic clock lesson

Figure 1.6 Monkey Position (Balinda Craig-Quijada; photograph by Marcella Hackbardt).

is to begin lying on the back with legs bent and feet flat on the floor, hip width apart. Begin by tilting the pelvis forward and back corresponding to 12 and 6 on a clock face. The lesson continues with tilting side to side (corresponding to 3 and 9 on the clock face) and then progresses to half circles and full circles moving clockwise and counterclockwise (for a more detailed explanation refer to Feldenkrais 1972, 115–129). This activity might be used as a way to mobilize the lower spine and to engage the pelvic floor muscles.

Teaching Technique Versus Exploring Fundamentals

Teachers employing explorations and somatically based approaches may run into some resistance or skepticism on the part of their students, at least initially (Nettl-Fiol 2008, 92). It is common for students to view improvisation and less codified work as outside the realm of technique class. Even when

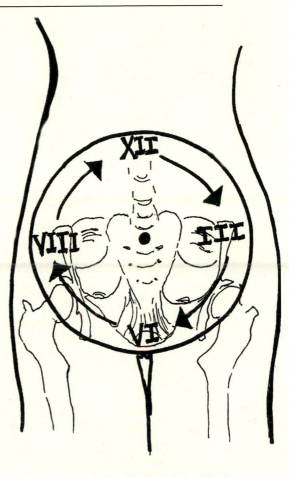

Figure 1.7 Feldenkrais Pelvic Clock.

they see their growth in these areas, they may not recognize how this work relates to their overall dance training. Many students are so indoctrinated with the product-driven ideal that spending time exploring their own movement seems much less important than working on increasing the height of a développé, for instance. Even if it is not deemed less important, it may be seen as completely unrelated.

In the Russian martial art system called Systema, students are not taught forms or set techniques. They train with basic principles, such as the importance of being relaxed, breathing, and using the energy provided by an opponent rather than resisting (Vasiliev and Scott 2006). In karate, students learn set defensive/offensive patterns, but then are taught to employ many of the same principles as in Systema (Wedlake 2005). While many find it satisfying to master set material in karate, these students may have difficulty in an actual combat situation, because it is not a predictable set-up and response situation. With time, and as the underlying principles become clearer, the transfer to open situations can occur. On the other hand, Systema students with no established vocabulary may find the open-ended practice situations daunting until they develop their own movement vocabulary based on the principles and what works for them as individuals.

We face the same difficulties in dance training: Should we drill vocabulary first and then focus on the movement principles? Or should we provide the basic principles and only later apply it to set movement? Some contemporary teachers feel strongly about teaching from principles and using improvisation to experience these principles without being bogged down by a teacher's style or the need to learn steps (Bales and Nettl-Fiol 2008; Erkert 2003, 15; Green Gilbert 2006, 118). However, in truth, dancers also need to practice their ability to learn choreography and specific dance skills if they are to have as many dance options open to them as possible. Finding a middle ground can be tricky. While the best solution will depend on the specific situation and necessarily involves many variables, considering the skill level of the class may be helpful.

Teaching Different Skill Levels

When making choices about how and when to address Somatic Principles, the level of sophistication of somatic thinking and teaching needs to match the dance level. While somatic wisdom can be embedded in classes of all levels, it is probably best not to dwell on the philosophical components until further along in training. Pacing and the openness of improvisations also need to be considered at each level and with each class.

Beginning dancers need to master the basic skills involved in dance but can be learning them within a somatically congruent framework. These students are working on gross motor skills and will probably not be able to attend to details about quality initially. However, by including work that is based on the foundational Somatic Principles and by teaching with a somatically infused approach, these beginning level students may be able to avoid some of the pitfalls of more traditional training methods, such as working with excessive tension or developing less efficient coordination patterns. Beginning level students should be introduced to improvisation or exploration early on so that creativity and ownership are seen as part of the dance experience. As with the martial arts example, however, these explorations need to be very delineated and not too complicated so that beginners with little established vocabulary do not feel uncomfortable or lost. The class pace should also move along so that maximal ground can be covered, allowing students to feel a sense of mastery and improvement. This approach means not taking too much time for corrections or commenting on what is being taught and why.

Intermediate dancers tend to be eager to learn new, more advanced skills, but need to also start refining the basics. Getting these students to slow down and attend to the "how" and not just the "what" can be challenging. Again, embedding the somatic material within "dancier" combinations can be one way of addressing this issue. Taking too much time to discuss and give feedback may still disrupt the flow of class, and dancers may lose energy and enthusiasm. At this point, however, specific corrections need to be provided. Teachers can play with group feedback, peer-teaching, and individual correction that is related to the whole group. Journaling is another efficient method for giving feedback that can be particularly effective at the intermediate skill level. Explorations and improvisations can be more involved at this stage, and while clarity and expectations are important, more freedom can be allowed. Students will tend to be more accepting and interested in an improvisation if they understand the goal or purpose of the activity.

It is at the advanced level that the artistry of dance really comes into play. As more sophisticated movers, advanced dancers need to spend more time on the subtleties of their movement. These students are more willing and eager to take a step back to really examine how they are executing movement and not just what they are able to achieve. This mentality creates a learning environment ripe for deeper somatic exploration and self-evaluation. Slower-motion or self-paced work can be explored, as can more open-ended improvisations.

Teaching Tip: "Noodling," or lying on the floor and moving as desired, can be a good way for dancers to assess where they are in the moment, both physically and mentally. It can provide a chance to consciously bring the mind and the body together, increasing awareness and allowing time to follow the needs of body. This kind of "shape flow" action, as it is called in Laban Movement Analysis, is therefore valid and valuable (Hackney 1998). It can be included in a dancer's self-practice or used as a way to start or end class. Teachers should be aware that this kind of undirected self-sensing is different than asking dancers to make intentional choices in improvisation. Both are valid, but they have different objectives and the open-ended nature of noodling may initially be difficult for beginning dancers who are just discovering and becoming comfortable with their own physicality.

Movement Experience: *Sample Improvisation Adapted for Differing Skill Levels. Beginners:* Face a partner and decide who will lead and who will follow. Leaders, do any movements you wish, only go slowly enough so your partner can follow you, and do not turn around and lose your partner. Followers, mirror your partners' actions as accurately as possible. When instructed, change who is leading. With practice, students can change leaders on their own until it becomes difficult to tell who is leading. *Intermediate:* Begin with mirroring. Then one person move as desired while their partner watches. Other person respond to the movement. Make it into a movement conversation. *Advanced:* Begin with a movement conversation. Gradually add physical contact.

Teaching Tip: Journaling can be a good way of providing feedback and checking in with individual students without disrupting the pace of class. As with class planning, journal assignments should be level specific. Novice dancers will need more structure in order for their journal assignments to be as useful as possible. With experience, dancers may be more able to journal in a free-flow fashion about what is most important to them from their class experiences.

Conclusions

In all movement education, whether it be dance, the martial arts, or some other system, we need to recognize different learning and teaching preferences and find some balance that can work for both the students (emphasis on the plural) and the teacher. In reality, dance teachers rarely are working with a blank slate. If running their own studio, teachers may have the pleasure of being a student's first dance instructor more frequently. Even in higher education, teaching beginning level classes is often easier and more gratifying than the intermediate level class where teachers and students may butt heads about previous training and preconceived value systems of what is dancing or dance. Teachers need to recognize how frustrating this process of relearning can be, as often it involves taking a step back in terms of technical difficulty. Students need to be reminded of the importance of being open to change and new ways of approaching movement. With time, patience, and mutual respect, common ground can be found between pushing forward with learning new material and with exploring movement principles.

Application of Fundamental Principles to Technique and Culminating Movement Experiences:

a. Try transferring the principle explored at the start of class to a set standing warm-up. Shift the emphasis of an established back and torso phrase, for example, to breathing, initiating, connecting, or sensing the environment, depending on the goal for that class. Face away from the mirror to bring awareness to bodily sensations, and for sensing the environment, face a partner. Really see your partner as you do the combination.

b. Next try attending to the principle being explored in new technical and locomotor combinations. Keep in mind that certain kinds of phrases may naturally engage some of the fundamental principles more readily than others, encouraging the transfer of this information to dance technique. For example, breath is easily accessed in combinations involving swings, falls and suspensions, or sharp accents. Connectivity may be most helpful in adagios requiring balance, combinations with quick direction shifts, or material with significant level changes. Sensing the environment can be applied to locomotor or partnering phrases requiring navigation of groups or individuals, or a phrase can be performed in silence to emphasize visual, auditory and kinesthetic awareness of other dancers in the space. Gestural phrases may particularly benefit from initiation analysis. Try focusing on initiation in a floor combination, alternating

Figure 1.1 "Pedagogy" (Karen Snouffer).

between peripheral and central initiation. Then extend this concept into a standing phrase exploring both sequential and nonsequential movement.

c. In the previous suggestions, the Somatic Principles of breathing, sensing, initiating and connecting were applied to dance technique in isolation. However, all of the principles coexist and are important in the execution of any given movement phrase. Once all principles have been explored and applied in more technical combinations, the following activity can be used to facilitate the integration of information: learn a simple dance phrase and repeat it four times. With each repetition, focus awareness on one of the four principles of breathing, sensing, connecting, or initiating. Notice how the experience differs in each version. On the fifth trial, make choices about how to approach the phrase, selecting which concepts to apply to the various movements according to your unique needs as a dancer. Students should be given ample time to explore and make choices, especially in this final phase.

2

Breath

Bridging the Conscious and the Unconscious

Each act of creativity has its conception in inspiration, a pause—the space in which potential is manifest—and a birth/death as the created act is "expired" and allowed to emerge. When we don't breathe fully in or out, we are withholding ourselves from full participation in both our living and dying, receiving and giving, as they express themselves from moment to moment.—Hartley 1995, 202

Respiration is a natural and continuous function of living beings. It is the first and last thing we do on this earth. So why focus on something so innate? Breath supports life and movement and thus is of vital importance to a dancer. Full breathing supports health in general, and many of the somatic techniques direct attention to breathing as an inroad for enhancing function and ease in movement (Alexander 1932; Calais-Germain 2005; Dowd 1990; Feldenkrais 1972; Fitt 1996; Hackney 1998; Hartley 1995; Todd 1937). Breathing is largely an involuntary process, but with the potential for voluntary input (Carola, Harley, and Noback 1992). For this reason, it can be thought of as a meeting place for the conscious and unconscious control of movement, making it an important resource for those interested in increasing awareness of habitual ways of moving and responding to their environment.

We can see that the importance of breath in movement techniques far predates contemporary somatic work. Both yoga and tai chi are centuries old and utilize techniques for enhancing respiration (Iyengar 1979; Jou 1998; Liao 1990; Siaw-Voon Sim and Gaffney 2002; Yang 2005). In yoga, the practice of pranayama (breath control) is one of the supports for a full practice by the Yogi (Iyengar 1979, 2005, 2010). In tai chi, breathing techniques arise in the practice of both form and meditation (Yang 2005). In the martial arts, the *kiai,* or yell emanating from the breath, is used as much as a mechanism to access the core strength of the body as a way to intimidate opposition (Wedlake 2000, 64–65). In all of these ancient forms, proper breathing is considered to enhance performance as well as being central to overall health and well-being.

In more current practices (many of which drew on the foundations built by yoga and the martial arts) we still see that breath is a founding principle (Alexander 1932, 1969; Bainbridge-Cohen 1993; Bartenieff and Lewis 1980; Feldenkrais 1972; Hackney

1998; Johnson 1995). F.M. Alexander wanted to improve his speaking voice. He discovered that the misalignment of his head and neck and his habitual shallow breathing under stress inhibited the fuller use of his vocal apparatus, in addition to affecting the overall use of his body (Alexander 1932). Moshe Feldenkrais, a Judo Master and founder of the Feldenkrais method, also focused some of his lessons on the function of breathing (Feldenkrais 1972, 1984). In both Body-Mind Centering and Bartenieff Fundamentals, breath support is considered a necessary prerequisite for core support, flow, and artistry in movement (Bainbridge-Cohen 1993; Bartenieff and Lewis 1980; Hackney 1998). Mabel Ellsworth Todd also included respiration as a key topic in her book, *The Thinking Body* (1937, 217–246). We can go on and on with examples, but the point is that historically somatic techniques have used awareness and focus on the breath to elicit change within the respiratory system as it functions under both voluntarily and involuntarily control (Johnson 1995). This change, in turn, influences the whole organism and the ability to perform optimally.

Movement Experience: *Running with the Breath in Mind.* Run in a circle with relaxed breathing, allowing your arms to hang easily at your sides. After about five laps, inhale and hold your breath while running five more laps. Let the air go and continue running while your breathing returns to normal. When ready, exhale all the air in your lungs and try to run five more laps. Compare the three scenarios and consider the importance of breath to any effortful activity.

Overview of Systems and Anatomy Involved

Breathing includes both external and internal phases of respiration. The external phase of respiration is the exchange that occurs between the air and blood within the lungs. The lungs provide oxygen from the external environment that is absorbed into the blood and carried via the circulatory system to all the cells of the body (Calais-Germaine 2005; Carola, Harley, and Noback 1992; Kandel, Schwartz, and Jessell 1991). The internal phase of respiration is the exchange of this oxygen-rich blood with these working cells. The cells absorb oxygen from the blood and, in return, give up carbon dioxide and other byproducts of metabolism. Carbon dioxide is transported back to the lungs where it diffuses out of the blood and is exhaled (Calais-Germaine 2005; Carola, Harley, and Noback 1992; Kandel, Schwartz, and Jessell 1991). More oxygen is brought on board again. Metaphorically, our respiration connects us to our external and internal environments. As Hackney (1998, 61) says in her book *Making Connections*, "With every breath we connect and have an exchange with the environment outside of ourselves. The fuller our respiration, the more each and every cell of our bodies is dialoguing with the world."

External respiration is the result of inhalation and exhalation of air through the lungs, and it is this phase that we are aware of when we breathe. Air enters and exits the lungs through the mouth and nostrils, which connect in a common space called the pharyngeal cavity (Calais-Germaine 2005; Linklater 2006). This cavity leads to the trachea or airway tube. The trachea branches off into two bronchi, with one feeding each lung. The bronchi then branch off into smaller bronchioles, which eventually lead to the alveoli. It is at the alveoli, or little air sacks surrounded by capillaries, that the exchange of gases between air and blood occurs. Carbon dioxide leaves the capillaries and enters the alveoli to be exhaled, while oxygen moves from the alveoli into the oxygen-depleted blood (Brooks and Fahey 1985; Calais-Germaine 2005; Carola, Harley, and Noback 1992; Todd 1937).

The lungs are made up of five lobes: three lobes on the right and two on the left because of the heart's location on the left side of the chest cavity. These lobes of the lungs are made of smooth muscle fibers and tissue that is innervated involuntarily and is therefore under unconscious control. Each lung is encased by a plural membrane, which acts as a fluid-filled sheath protecting the lobes themselves. The lungs interface with the trunk or torso via this plural membrane that attaches to both the diaphragm and the intercostal muscles (the muscles lying between the ribs). Inhalation and exhalation, or the actual air exchange, only occurs within the five lobes of the lungs (Calais-Germaine 2005; Carola, Harley, and Noback 1992; Mareib 1992). However, muscular contraction or holding of either the diaphragm and/or muscles acting on the ribcage can influence air exchange by changing the amount of volume available for the lobes to expand and contract (Calais-Germaine 2005).

The diaphragm is the primary muscle of respiration, and it also separates the two cavities (chest and abdominal) within the trunk of the body. This thin muscle membrane is made up of two portions lying predominantly in the horizontal plane, but it arcs upward into the chest cavity in a dome shape. As the diaphragm contracts, it flattens out, moving down in the abdominal cavity. The action of the diaphragm moving down toward the pelvic floor pulls the lungs downward thus expanding the volume available, and air enters (inhalation). As the diaphragm relaxes and resumes its dome shape, the volume of the chest

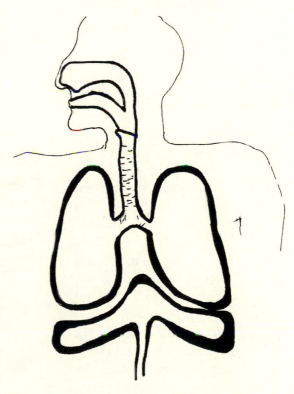

Figure 2.2 The Airways and Diaphragm.

cavity is decreased, compressing the lungs, and exhalation occurs (Brooks and Fahey 1985; Calais-Germaine 2005; Carola, Harley, and Noback 1992; Mareib 1992; Todd 1937).

Though the diaphragm lies in the horizontal plane, it is unequal in distribution, having more of its surface area in the back than the front due to its attachments (see Figure 3.3). It connects to the front surface of the body near the bottom aspect of the sternum and on the back surface of the body near the third lumbar vertebra. Because of these attachments, it is easier to feel the motion of the diaphragm itself on the back of the trunk. The motion of the abdominal cavity resulting from expansion of the lungs makes it easier to feel the diaphragmatic action indirectly on the front of the trunk. The diaphragm also attaches to the inside of the six lower ribs, where it inter-digitates with fibers of the transversus abdominus muscle (Calais-Germaine 2005; Carola, Harley, and Noback 1992; Todd 1937).

Movement Experience: *Child's Pose Breath Awareness.* Assume child's pose. Reach around and place your hands on your back. See if you can feel the action of the diaphragm and expansion of the lower back as you inhale. Relax and extend your arms. Now focus on the sensation of the breath expanding your belly. Notice your abdomen gently pressing on your thighs as you inhale. Allow each exhalation to be full and complete.

Teaching Tip: It is interesting to note that the posterior attachment of the diaphragm is near to the origin of the powerful hip flexor, the psoas. Todd, (1937, 10) theorized that in our evolution from sea to land the development of the lungs and diaphragm would have occurred around the same time as the development of the psoas. We needed to be able to differentiate the upper from the lower body in order to push off at the same time that we needed the ability to breathe air. The location of the two muscles and proximity of their attachments makes the breath an especially useful tool in accessing the psoas muscle. The psoas lies deep in the body, close to the spine, so it is difficult to

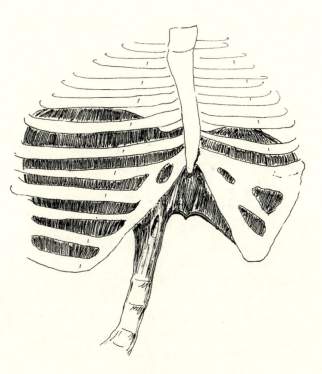

Figure 2.3 The Diaphragm.

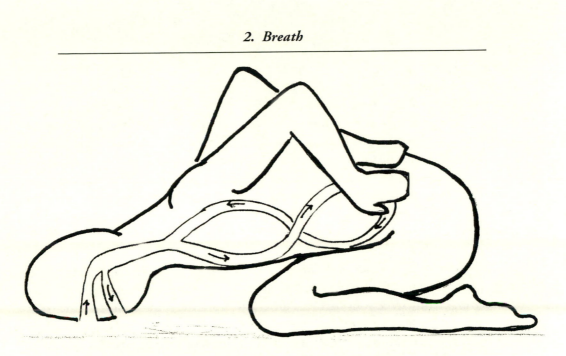

Figure 2.4 Child's Pose Breath Awareness.

feel its engagement. Students who overuse the superficial hip flexors (the rectus femoris, in particular) can find it difficult to let go of their habitual muscle use in order to go deeper to the more efficient psoas muscle. Applying these ideas to the Femoral Flexion exercise (Basic Six Thigh Lift) from Bartenieff Fundamentals, focusing on the breath can help in two ways (Bartenieff and Lewis 1980; Hackney 1998). Initiating the flexion action at the end of the exhalation right before the contraction of the diaphragm seems to help students with initiating contraction of the psoas muscle, perhaps because of the proximity of the muscular attachments. In addition, the hollowing of

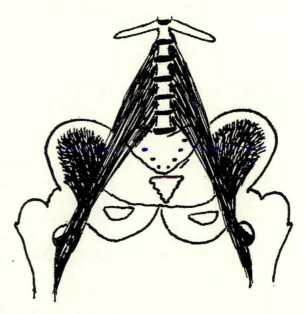

Figure 2.5 The Psoas Muscle.

the abdominal cavity that occurs with exhalation makes it easier to feel and access this deep muscle consciously.

While the diaphragm muscle creates an internal force acting on the lungs through its upward and downward motion in the center of the body, the muscles that act on the ribcage are an external force acting on the lungs (Calais-Germaine 2005; Carola, Harley, and Noback 1992). The ribcage is composed of twelve pairs of ribs, ten fixed and two floating, the sternum and the spinal column. While all of the ribs are connected posteriorly to the twelve thoracic vertebrae, only the fixed ribs are connected anteriorly to the sternum via the costal cartilages (Biel 2010). The vulnerable floating ribs are so called because they have no anterior attachment. The flexible, yet protective, bones of the rib cage are connected through the intercostal muscles as well as by the costal cartilages, which influence the shape of the cage itself. The ribs move more via these costal cartilages attaching to the sternum, yet they also move posteriorly at their attachment to the spine (Calais-Germaine 2005; Carola, Harley, and Noback 1992; Todd 1937).

Movement Experience: *Finding The Ribs.* With a partner, palpate (touch) as many ribs as possible. Feel the intercostal spaces between the ribs, as well as the bones themselves. Gently trace your partner's lower ribs from the spine around to the front as far as possible. See if you can find the floating ribs. Then palpate the costal cartilage leading to the sternum on the ribs just above. Place hands alternately on the chest, sides, and back of the trunk, and notice the movement of the ribcage during respiration. Change roles and repeat, then share your experiences.

Teaching Tip: This activity can be done side-lying if students are having difficulty tracing the bones. The soft tissues will drop in this position as a result of the pull of gravity. Be sure that students differentiate between palpating bone and the intercostal space, as these will provide different experiences. Additionally, be sure to have students trace the ribs all the way from attachment to attachment (sternum to spine). Noticing which ribs they have trouble tracing all the way around can create an opportunity for students to discover a fuller sense of their own ribcage as a container.

The external intercostal muscles assist the diaphragm in normal breathing. As the diaphragm contracts for inspiration, the external intercostals also contract, lifting the ribs up and out to increase the volume of the thoracic cavity even more. As the diaphragm relaxes up during exhalation, the external intercostals also relax, so the ribcage resumes its normal state and the volume available for air is reduced (Calais-Germaine 2005; Todd 1937). It is relevant that inspiration is active, but exhalation is a passive process involving only the relaxation of muscular contraction when in a resting state.

In addition to the intercostal muscles that lie in two layers between the ribs, numerous other muscles in the trunk, head, and neck form attachments on bony aspects of the ribcage, thus indirectly influencing the volume available to the lungs for respiration (Biel 2010). Most of these muscles only need to be used for their respiratory action in situations of effort, when larger quantities of oxygen are needed (Calais-Germaine 2005). The labored (or forced) breathing we experience during and after exercise is the result of calling these muscles into play (Calais-Germaine 2005; Fitt 1996). They allow the ribcage and the abdomen to both expand and contract more fully when needed.

Any unnecessary tension in these accessory muscles will influence the ability to breathe easily and fully at rest or during exercise. If, for example, there is tension in the neck and shoulder region, the contraction of these muscles may interfere with the ability to exhale fully, as they will essentially hold the ribcage up. Without a full exhalation, less carbon dioxide can be expelled, and less fresh, oxygen-rich air can enter and be available to the muscles of the body (Brooks and Fahey 1985; Mareib 1992).

As the nose and throat are the two direct entryways into the trachea, the nostril and throat cavities also influence the amount of air taken into the lungs (Calais-Germaine 2005; Linklater 2006). At one time or another we have all experienced difficulties in getting enough air when the nasal passages are inflamed due to illness, such as a cold. The status of the mouth, tongue, and throat can likewise influence the amount of air taken into the lungs. Any shortening in the back of the neck or tension in the jaw muscles inhibits the flow of air. This situation is frequently reflected in vocal tone and projection (Linklater 2006).

Most of us naturally breathe through the nose at rest and through the mouth during exercise. The nose helps filter impurities out of the air and also brings the air temperature closer to the body temperature (Calais-Germaine 2005). Larger volumes of air can be moved more quickly through the mouth, however. Yogis and many martial artists advocate breathing in through the nose and exhaling through the mouth (Iyengar 1979, 2005; Yang 2005). In Eastern philosophy this cycle is referred to as "in through the heavenly door, out through the earthly window" (Huang and Wurmbrand 1990, 16). In this technique, the benefits of filtration and air warming are matched with the ability to exhale deeply. Outdoor winter athletes know the advantage of this manner of breathing, as cold air rushing into the lungs can be painful. Others encourage only nostril breathing, asserting that while it takes getting used to, nose breathing can ultimately result in greater breath control and overall deeper breathing (Iyengar 1979, 2010; Yang 2005). It is valuable to experiment with both mouth and nose breathing.

Movement Experience: *Nostril Breathing.* Either seated or lying down, block one nostril with a finger. Experiment with breathing through one nostril alone and then change to the other. Notice which one is easier and which nostril feels more open; notice if your belly is expanding more easily with one nostril or the other. Rest, and then see if you can inhale more completely, expanding the belly out.

Repeat breathing through one nostril and then the other, but use the opposite hand to close the nostril (i.e., close the left nostril with the right forefinger and vice versa). Experiment with the amount of force used on the inhalation and exhalation. Be sure to have Kleenex on hand for this one! Rest, and notice if the air feels as if it moves more freely through the nasal passages now.

Repeat breathing through one nostril, and notice where the tongue is in the mouth. Press it up against the inside of the upper teeth for a few breaths and release

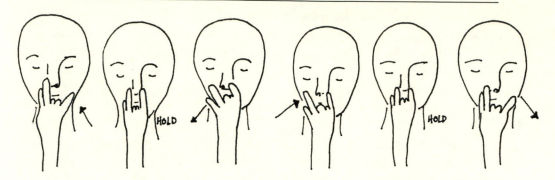

Figure 2.6 Movement Experience: Nostril Breathing.

it down toward the inside of the lower front teeth for a few breaths. Rest as needed. Note how the air moves through the nasal passages, and how much of the sensation of the breath can be felt through the nasal passages into the throat. Another variation on this movement exploration is to try generating a hum while pressing one nostril closed.

Teaching Tip: This movement experience can be used to facilitate awareness of differences in the use of the two nasal passages and to create a fuller picture and sensation of how air travels into the body and is affected by the use of the head, neck, jaw, and throat. Bringing awareness to the nose, throat, and jaw is useful for opening up the airway into the lungs. Students can either sit with their legs crossed or lie on their backs with their legs extended. Having students lying on their backs as much as possible in the beginning reduces the overall muscular tonus of the body and helps free the mind to concentrate on the task at hand. However, sitting up can be very useful when your students have more experience with somatic techniques or to bring variety to the learning situation.

The Nervous System's Control of Respiration

The brainstem, specifically the medulla oblongata and the pons, are primarily responsible for the unconscious control of respiration. They apparently establish a baseline breathing rate that provides for adequate oxygen at rest (Carola, Harley, and Noback 1992). Many other sensors within the body also react when more oxygen is required, as during exercise or in situations of stress (Carola, Harley, and Noback 1992; Kandel, Schwartz, and Jessell 1991). For example, some receptors respond to increases in carbon dioxide in the blood, others to increased acidity due to lactic acid that is a byproduct of muscular activity. When stimulated, these receptors cause an increase in the rate and depth of breathing. They act on the medullary rhythmicity area, which in turn excites the inhalation and exhalation phases of respiration through muscular contraction of the diaphragm, the external intercostals, and other accessory breathing muscles as they are needed. Receptors within the bronchioles themselves are a localized regulator of breathing rate, responding to increases in carbon dioxide. This response vasodialates the bronchioles, effectively reducing resistance to air flow in and out of the lungs (Calais-Germaine 2005; Carola, Harley, and Noback 1992).

The Parasympathetic and Sympathetic Nervous Systems and Breathing

The parasympathetic and sympathetic nervous systems are the parts of the autonomic nervous system that maintain homeostasis or balance within the body (Carola, Harley, and Noback 1992; Kandel, Schwartz, and Jessell 1991). The autonomic nervous system is a motor system under involuntary or unconscious control that regulates the internal visceral organs including the heart, intestines, glandular function, dilation of the eyes, and breathing. The sympathetic nervous system is responsible for the fight or flight response, which readies the whole self for immediate action, whereas the parasympathetic nervous system is responsible for relaxation and rest of the whole self (Carola, Harley, and Noback 1992; Kandel, Schwartz, and Jessell 1991). Together, the sympathetic and parasympathetic systems balance each other out, sometimes working one at a time and other times working in a coordinated manner to ensure the overall regulation of the human system. The actual autonomic response and its effect on breathing depends on the stimulus, or stressor, that caused it. Stressors, as defined by Hans Selye, are "factors that cause homeostatic imbalances in the body that result in adaptation by the body" (Selye 1976, 7).

The sympathetic and parasympathetic nervous systems do not directly affect the muscles acting on the lungs or the lobes themselves, however they provide a background level of stimulation to the body, which affects the quality and the action of breathing (Carola, Harley, and Noback 1992). The sympathetic nervous system affects breathing through the presence of circulating adrenaline. Adrenaline, combined with any buildup of carbon dioxide in the blood, makes the smooth muscle tissue of the bronchiole tubes dilate. The sympathetic response also shunts blood to the lungs, readying them for an increased workload. As such, the sympathetic nervous system's influence on breath results in an increase in the volume of air expelled and taken into the lungs in relation to the action being performed (Calais-Germaine 2005; Carola Harley, and Noback 1992). We all know that when stressed, either physically or emotionally, our breathing rate increases and the action becomes more effortful. The parasympathetic nervous system's influence on breath results in the potential decrease in the volume of air taken in and expelled from the lungs in response to relaxation of the human system. As the stressors are removed, our breathing returns to normal.

Voluntary and Involuntary Control of Respiration

Breathing, specifically the external respiration phase of taking air into the lungs and expelling air out of the lungs, is under both conscious and unconscious control of the nervous system. As noted above, there appears to be a general pattern of breathing for all humans that is rhythmical and spontaneous in nature (Calais-Germaine 2005; Carola, Harley, and Noback 1992). This general pattern of unconscious breathing is called the normal rate and represents the tidal volume needed for basic life functions that do not require large amounts of energy, such as sleeping, reading, rest, and easy, light-paced walking (see Figure 2.5 Tidal Volume). Breathing rate at rest is approximately twelve to fifteen inhalations per minute depending on the individual's physical build and health (Calais-Germaine 2005; Carola, Harley, and Noback 1992). During exercise, the breathing rate and the volume automatically increase as the accessory muscles are called into play and the inspiratory and expiratory reserve lung capacities are accessed. The lungs empty more completely, which allows more air to enter on the next breath. This, combined with the increased breathing rate, provides the additional oxygen needed for the working muscles. Our emotional states also influence our breathing, and again, these adjustments are involuntary (Calais-Germaine 2005; Carola, Harley, and Noback 1992). It is fortunate we do not have to think about breathing in order for it to transpire, and in fact, we cannot voluntarily stop breathing altogether even if we try. Parents know that a child holding his or her breath will independently and automatically start breathing, even if he or she makes it to the point of "turning purple."

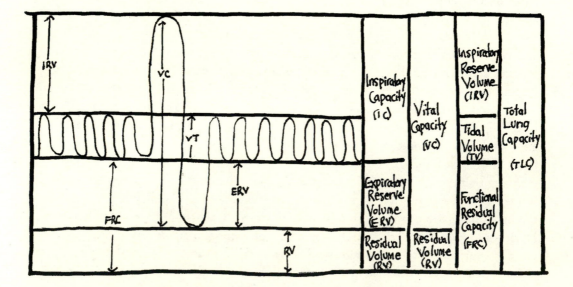

Figure 2.7 Respiratory Tidal Volume.

48

It is important to recognize that we can consciously control aspects of our breathing, as seen in the previous example. In some instances, thinking about breathing too much can actually interfere with a normal and healthy rhythm (Schmidt and Wrisberg 2008). However, at other times awareness and control can be used to advantage. As we have seen, physical and emotional stressors alter the breath, but the reverse is also true. Countering the involuntary impulse to breathe faster and shallower, in particular, can be helpful in calming the sympathetic response. Voluntarily changing the rate and/or depth of our breathing can help us control our responses to stressful situations, or help us discover habitual holding patterns in the muscles associated with respiration. It is for this reason that the breath is considered to be the meeting place for the conscious and the unconscious. Awareness of these habitual ways of responding to stress and patterns of tension can be the first inroad to change (Todd 1937).

Types of Breathing

There are two basic ways in which to breathe — by moving the chest and by moving the diaphragm (as reflected in motion of the abdomen). Most breathing is a combination of movements of the chest and the diaphragm, but motion of one or the other can be emphasized more strongly by consciously shortening and lengthening the muscles of either the chest or the abdomen (Calais-Germaine 2005). Diaphragmatic and paradoxical breathing illustrate the two basic relationships between the movements of the chest and the movements of the abdomen during inhalation and exhalation.

Diaphragmatic breathing occurs when the abdomen pushes (extends) out on inhalation, causing the upper chest to sink and lower toward the pelvis. The abdomen pulls in toward the spine (contracts) and the chest rises in the direction of the head on exhalation. In diaphragmatic breathing, the natural role of the diaphragm is encouraged. Because the diaphragm pulls the ribs downwards and outwards, both actions can be explored separately emphasizing one dimension or the other. It is thought that diaphragmatic breathing reduces stress and is related to the parasympa-

Figure 2.8 Movement Experience: See-Saw Breathing.

49

thetic nervous system (Calais-Germaine 2005; Carola, Harley, and Noback 1992; Kandel, Schwartz, and Jessell 1991).

Paradoxical breathing occurs when the abdomen flattens toward the spine during the inhalation, and the chest expands. During exhalation the abdomen pushes forward while the chest lowers. Paradoxical breathing is thought to be related to the sympathetic nervous system, and thus, the fight or flight response (Calais-Germaine 2005; Carola, Harley, and Noback 1992; Kandel, Schwartz, and Jessell 1991). Both diaphragmatic and paradoxical breathing can be used to create a see-saw like motion of the abdomen and chest (refer to Figure 2.8 See Saw Breathing).

Movement Experience: *See Saw Breathing of Chest and Abdomen.* Draw your attention to your breathing. Notice what is moving when you inhale and exhale: is it your chest, your abdomen, or both? Inhale and push out your abdomen and exhale and let it relax. Continue this pushing out of your abdomen on the inhalation and letting it relax on the exhalation. Try to do less and go slower. What happens in your chest while you do this? Continue this while trying to reduce your effort more and more. Rest.

Try the same thing, but this time expand your chest while you inhale and then let it relax on the exhale. Continue this movement many times trying to use less effort and going slower.

Now put the two actions together like a see-saw (teeter totter). When the abdomen is pushed out, the chest is relaxed, and when the chest is expanded the abdomen is flattened. Coordinate the breath so that the exhalation occurs first with abdomen extended and chest flattened. Then reverse this movement pattern, expanding the chest with the exhalation and flattening the abdomen. Reduce your effort and go slower. Rest a minute or two.

Repeat the same thing, but go a bit faster until you are moving the chest and abdomen independently of your breathing. The chest is up and abdomen down, abdomen up and chest down, quicker and quicker. Rest.

Try again, only this time take a big breath in and hold it while you move the abdomen and chest in a see-saw motion. Rest whenever you need to and then begin again. After you have tried it a few times, rest. Notice how you feel now.

Breathing Patterns and Movement

How we use ourselves and move has a profound impact on our breathing, and how we breathe is equally important to how we move. The purpose of this chapter is not to prescribe particular methods of breathing, but rather to increase awareness and to present options that may facilitate the discovery of new movement choices. Shallow breathing, not knowing when or how much to exhale, and the holding of breath all inhibit motor performance and motor skill, thereby reducing efficiency in movement. If the body is not getting enough oxygen, it cannot function optimally. Incorporating movement experiences to open awareness around the rate and depth of breathing, the cycle of inhalation and exhalation, and habitual holding patterns can facilitate different breathing and movement options for dance students.

Additionally, breath is functionally related to the fundamental state of the biological system. Unrestricted, regular breathing relieves anxiety and tension, alters nervous and emotional states, and reduces fatigue (Brooks and Fahey 1985; Carola, Harley, and Noback 1992; Mareib 1992). Although we can consciously control some aspects of external respiration, overtaxing conscious control may be disadvantageous in general to the student of dance (Schmidt and Wrisberg 2008). Making yourself breathe differently can create its own stress and can actually be uncomfortable. In this regard, breath movement experiences that encourage awareness rather than enacting change may provide a useful model for dancers and teachers accustomed to overcontrolling their movement patterns through consciously and continuously fixing parts of the body.

Teaching Tip: *Creating Situations for Change.* To strengthen the impact of movement experiences, attention should be directed to the underlying concept or principle throughout class. For example, class might begin with a brief breath exploration. Then between dance combinations at the barre or in the center of the room take a minute or two to draw students' attention to their breath again and have them notice the quality and the movement of it. Can they mentally go from doing their class activities to noticing their breath? Can they notice their breath without correcting it? Can they maintain awareness of breath while attending to their dancing? The ability to access movement principles during class in these three ways is important for dance students to practice and develop. Often students take class and are either far away in their thoughts or so heavily concerned with getting things right that they miss the opportunity to work on this aspect of attention. Being aware of movement on different layers is necessary to finding neutral and/or broadening movement choices.

Although it may appear counterintuitive, spending some time on breathing during technique classes can provide teachers and students with opportunities to discover breath-related habitual movement patterns and self-organizations impacting dance performance. One's perception of the pliancy of the ribcage as it is revealed through the motion of breathing can have a profound influence on movement. For example, this may be reflected in the ability to shape the torso in support of full expressivity. Breathing explorations can also be very useful for a student who appears to lack fluidity and connection between the upper and lower body. It might be obvious that working on force production and sequencing through the body would assist this student, but it could also be that the student's perception of their container (torso) as an integrated whole and its function in relation to breath is crucial to their upper-lower connectivity.

Movement Experience: *Pliés with Breath Awareness.* During pliés notice when you naturally inhale and exhale. Most people will exhale on the descent and inhale on the ascent. Exaggerate this breathing in the next repetition. Then experiment with reversing the breath cycle with each plié (inhale on the way down and exhale on the way up). Take a moment to give feedback about this switch. Reversing how breath supports an action we do frequently, and often without much awareness, can provide new insights into performance of the movement.

Some Common Movement Habits and Their Effect on Breathing

Increased general muscular tension, contracted abdominals, and a tight chest are holding patterns that impinge on breathing by reducing the movement available to the ribcage and diaphragm. We have seen that tension in the neck and shoulder region can result in shallow breathing. Holding the belly in, or overly contracting the abdominals, can be another culprit of shallow breathing resulting from both a cultural and dance aesthetic that emphasizes a flat stomach. Sometimes contracted abdominals are mistakenly associated with having a strong center for control of movement. However, the diaphragm muscle needs to be able to move fully through its range of motion to be most efficient. The only way for this more efficient use of the diaphragm muscle to occur is by allowing the abdominals to be less contracted and to change shape more fully throughout the breath cycle.

Movement Experience: *Diaphragmatic Breathing, Awareness through Touch.* This breath activity can quickly and easily help students experience a fuller form of diaphragmatic breath using their hands as a kinesthetic tool. Lie down on the floor with legs extended, placing one or both hands on the belly. To emphasize the impact of the abdominal musculature on breath do the following: breathe in, allowing the belly to protrude (for the sake of contrast and to fully experience what may be a foreign sensation, dancers may even need to consciously push the belly out initially). When you have mastered this, contract your abdominals and repeat the inhalation with this additional muscular engagement. Go back and forth between these two ways of breathing, noticing which one feels like it provides more air coming in and which one feels easier to do. Repeat all of the above but with the legs bent and the feet flat on the floor. If time permits, get up and walk while breathing with and without the sustained abdominal contraction.

Teaching Tip: The importance of the above activity is to highlight when the habitual contraction of the abdominal musculature interferes with a fuller breath and ease of moving. Experiencing for oneself the effect of abdominal tension on the breath creates a learning situation that arises from within each individual and can therefore be applied when needed. The point is to be able to choose and to return to a more neutral place easily. Questions will help students attend to how the breathing activities influence functional movement. For example, the following script might be used while students are walking: Does this feel familiar/different than the way in which you usually walk? Is it easier to walk now? Can you notice if you are holding in your abdominals strongly while you are walking?

Frequently in shallow breathers, the problem resides with the exhalation. If the exhalation is full and complete, more stale air is expelled, creating room for more fresh, oxygen-rich air to enter. The following activity can bring awareness to the length and quality of the exhalation and its effect on inhalation.

Movement Experience: *Awareness of the Exhalation.* Choosing a seated or lying down position, begin by noticing your breath. Can you feel and sense your breath without changing it? On the exhalation begin to count out loud to notice the duration of the air flowing out. After a full inhalation, you can begin counting, starting with the number one and continuing until the end of the breath is reached. Make it an easy counting, neither too fast nor too slow, not too loud or too soft. Repeat a few times, noticing if the number reached at the end of the exhalation is consistent or variable over a few tries. Repeat the above, but instead of counting, experiment with making an easy "hum" or "huh" sound a few times, paying attention to how long the sound can be sustained. Rest and notice the quality of the in and the out breath. Go back to the counting variation and see if anything has changed. Were you able to count for longer? Was it easier? Get up and walk around the room and notice if you experience yourself differently. Do you feel relaxed, bored, sleepy, refreshed, or ready to start class?

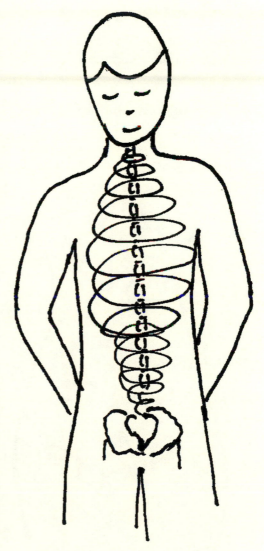

Another common movement habit influencing breath is the shortening of the neck that accompanies "forward head" syndrome. Alexander was far from alone with this problem. As living beings with many of our senses located anteriorly, we naturally tend to want to lead forward with our faces. Today's computer age only encourages this tendency to jut the chin and head forward from the rest of the spine. However, the neck is an extension of the rest of the spine. Shortening here has a negative impact on the organization of the whole being, starting

Figure 2.9 Imagining Spiral Breath.

with constriction of air flow in the throat and tension in the muscles attaching to the rib cage. A more efficient use is to let the head and spine lengthen up, and to allow stimuli from the environment to come to you, rather than trying to go to them (Alexander 1969; Linklater 2006; Todd 1937).

Movement Experience: *Spiraling Breath.* Sit in a cross-legged position, or whatever position is most comfortable. Bring awareness to the vertical energy of the breath: send breath up and down the spine with each inhalation. Imagine it spiraling around the vertebrae, up and out the back of the neck and down and out through the coccyx. Allow yourself to inhabit fully the vertical dimension, feeling the length and space created as the breath expands the lungs and thorax. Drop the chin slightly on the exhalation to increase the sense of length through the back of the neck. As the breath exits and the thorax empties, connect into the deep abdominals and experience the subtle lifting of the pelvic floor. Keep these engagements with the next inhalation, but not with tension.

Core Support and the Pelvic Diaphragm

The last part of the experience above indicates the role the breath can play in helping dancers access core support in the body and suggests the presence of a second

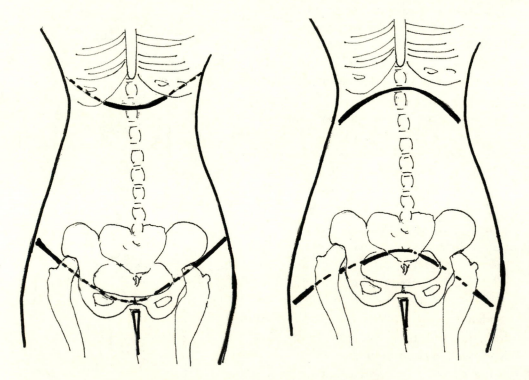

Figure 2.10 The Pelvic Floor and Diaphragm Mirror.

diaphragm within the body. The pelvic diaphragm, or pelvic floor, is the lower boundary of the pelvis, supporting the abdominal contents (Biel 2010; Calais-Germaine 2003; Franklin 2003). When healthy, the action of this pelvic diaphragm mirrors the thoracic diaphragm (see Figure 2.10 Pelvic Floor and Diaphragm Mirror). It is slightly domed up during expiration and descends as the intra-abdominal pressure increases during inspiration. These pelvic floor muscles form part of the core of the body, working with the deep back and abdominal muscles to support and help initiate movement on the deepest, most efficient level.

Movement Experience: ***The Pelvic Floor.*** The pelvic floor muscles can be difficult to sense initially, and they may need strengthening, particularly with aging or post-childbirth. The following images and ideas may be helpful: Imagine you are stopping the flow of urine; Kegel exercises like this one use repeated contractions to strengthen these pelvic floor muscles. To assist with accessing the pelvic floor while moving, imagine you are bringing the ischial tuberosities (sitting bones) together and up. Or try the image of a fountain shooting up from the pelvic floor, through the center of the body, and out through the head. Try curling the little toes of your feet, as this action frequently helps with sensing the muscles of the pelvic floor.

Core Support and the Transversus Abdominus

The transversus abdominus is another important muscle in establishing core support in the body. We have already discussed how exhaling can help dancers access the deep psoas and pelvic floor muscles, and the importance of not holding with the superficial abdominals for the sake of full diaphragmatic action. The natural hollowing of the belly that

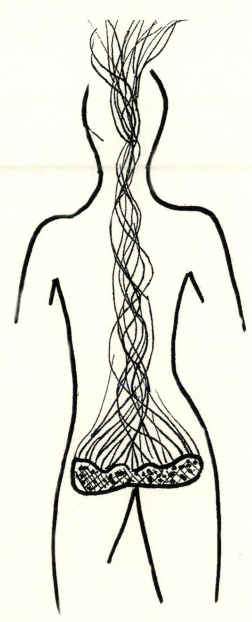

Figure 2.11 The Pelvic Floor Fountain Image.

occurs during exhalation can also help dancers with sensing and engaging the deep abdominal muscles, in particular the transversus abdominus. This muscle essentially wraps horizontally around the lower torso and helps stabilize the lumbar spine. Unlike the engagement of the rectus abdominus, the superficial "six-pack" muscle, the spine can articulate fully with use of the transversus abdominus. As with the psoas muscle, the fibers of the transversus muscle are physically related to the diaphragm, so the excitation of the diaphragm that occurs in breathing may actually assist with the engagement of the transversus muscle (Biel 2010; Carola, Harley, and Noback 1992). The following movement experiences will help students get a sense of the location and action of this important muscle.

Movement Experience: *Breath of Fire* (derived from Bikram yoga). Sitting on your shins, place your hands on your belly, where the action of the diaphragm can be felt. In short, quick bursts, exhale and inhale. Feel the connection of the breath to the core of the body. Do about twenty cycles, and then rest. Notice if your breathing changes and whether the Breath of Fire invigorates or taxes your body (Choudry 2000, 196–198).

Movement Experience: *Lifting The Head.* Lie on your back with arms and legs extended. Try lifting just your head a few times. Go as high as you can, easily and without strain. Rest. Fold your arms over your chest (as if to give yourself a hug); and lift your head a few more times to look at your feet. Notice how the rib cage moves in relation to your head lifting. Rest. Place your hands on your ribcage (one on either side) below each breast. Try lifting your head while you gently press your ribcage down and in the direction of your feet. Rest. Place your arms alongside your body and do the original movement of lifting your head. Notice the difference in how it feels compared to the first time you tried lifting your head.

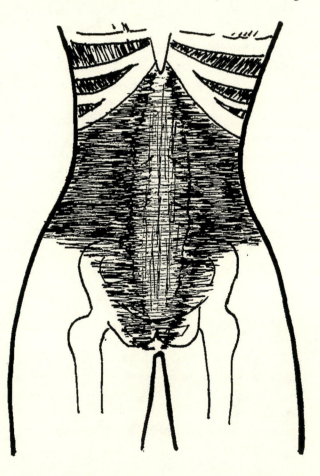

Figure 2.12 The Transversus Abdominus Muscle.

Breathing to Control Stage Fright, Release Tension, and Improve Movement Quality

Developing awareness of breathing patterns can provide insight into the emotional and physical state of the body, and changing these patterns can help us begin to change habitual ways of using the entire being. Consider the sympathetic fight or flight response. It evolved as a protective mechanism, increasing the body's respiratory and heart rate, shunting blood away from the digestive system to the muscles, and even narrowing the field of vision to focus all efforts on escaping imminent danger. In today's world, however, we are rarely actually in physical danger requiring these responses. The fight or flight response is elicited by situations of stress, for most of us, most of the time. Imagine having to stand before a huge audience to give a speech (chosen because this is more stressful for most dancers than dancing for a large audience). A pounding heart, fast and shallow breathing, and a dry mouth are hardly helpful to speaking, yet this is what our body does. While most of us have difficulty consciously slowing our heart rate, we can consciously slow and deepen our breathing. By doing this, we start to manage the sympathetic response, also known as stage fright (Brooks and Fahey 1985; Carola Harley, and Noback 1992; Kandel. Schwartz, and Jessell 1991).

With dance, there is a need for some sympathetic input to enable the dancer to fulfill the demands of a physically taxing performance situation (Coker 2009). However, adaptations resulting from emotional response and not physical need merely tax the system more than necessary. Breath awareness and control (and awareness that the situation is really not life-threatening) can lessen the emotional aspect of the response, making it more appropriate for the situation.

The ability of the ribcage and torso to make the appropriate shape changes while moving is critical to artistry in dance. As a dancer, one needs to be able to make many types of shape changes in the ribs and torso to accommodate movement. But it is also true that this dynamic relation of the ribs/torso and breath is an integral part of the art. We have only to look to two of the pioneers of modern dance, Martha Graham and Doris Humphrey, to see the importance of breath in the art form. Both built their movement techniques around the flow of breath, using it to enhance the contraction and release of muscular tension and to support the concepts of suspension, fall, and recovery. As Jose Limon said, "This region of the chest, the breath, is the fecund source of movement, and its range is limited only by one's inventiveness and imagination" (Brown, Mindlin, and Woodford 1997, 101).

Vocalization for and as a Result of Breath

Many somatic techniques use vocalizations as a way of accessing full breath support, and/or use the breath as a means of improving the ability to vocalize. Alexander

Technique, which developed as a way for F.M. Alexander to improve his speaking voice, incorporates activities like the whispered "ah" (Alexander 1932, 1969). In this exercise, the jaw is relaxed and the tongue is placed behind the front teeth. The breath is exhaled fully while whispering "ah" and attention is paid to the quality of the sound. When the exhalation is complete, the mouth is closed and the inhalation is not consciously initiated. The idea is that by focusing on the free flow of air in the exhalation, the inhalation happens automatically and easily. In Body-Mind Centering and Laban Movement Analysis/Bartenieff Fundamentals, students explore the voice's ability to create vibration in the different resonating chambers of the body by varying vocal tones. These areas of resonance correspond to the chakras of the body, and indeed, the incorporation of sound in mind-body connectivity can be traced back to ancient meditative practices (Iyengar 1979, 2005, 2010). Sound is produced by the flow of air through the vocal chords and relies on the body as a resonating chamber, so the use of sound provides audible feedback about the quality of breathing. Vocalization can simultaneously help to activate or raise awareness of all parts of the breathing apparatus (Linklater 2006).

Dancers are increasingly called upon to speak in contemporary work, so the importance of including vocal work in their training goes beyond the ability of sound to enhance the mind-body connection. In one somatically driven vocal training method, Catherine Fitzmaurice (1997, 1) uses what she terms "destructuring" and "restructuring" to bring efficiency and expressivity to actors' speaking. By inducing tremors in the body and replicating the effects of the sympathetic nervous system, students heighten awareness of the somato-sensory systems and their related emotional reactions to activation of the fight or flight response. The release of tension throughout the body that follows the tremor work carries over to the muscles of respiration. The restructuring involves learning to activate the external intercostals and the transversus so that the diaphragm is not overworked and can remain responsive to emotional impulses of the performer. While this level of consciousness in breath control is not required for most dancers, common themes emerge. Again we see the awareness of the breath as a powerful vehicle for accessing the core support of the body and for connecting the mind with the body, the conscious and the unconscious. As Fitzmaurice (1997) eloquently states:

> The diaphragm contains both un-striated and striated muscle and is responsive to both the autonomic and central nervous systems. It is therefore uniquely appropriate as a site to create (such) harmony, so that the healing of the culturally prevalent body/mind split is not merely a metaphysical, but is actually a physical and obtainable, goal which brings impulse and thought together as action [2].

Conclusions

Breath informs us about the state of the nervous system. Having students lie down both at the start and end of class to listen, sense, and feel how their breath is

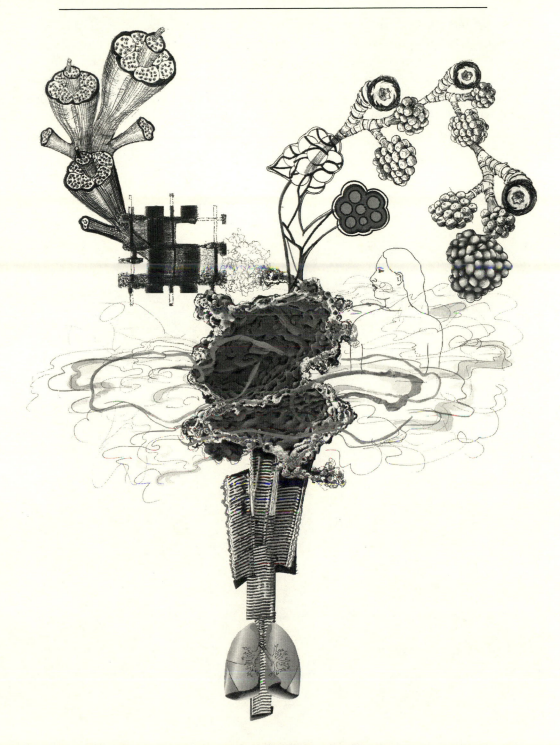

Figure 2.1 Breath (Karen Snouffer).

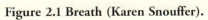

moving and moves them can be a situation for learning and change. First, the experience can be informative in that it is revealing of their psychological and physiological states in the moment, such as being tense, tired, nervous, or relaxed. Second, it introduces the principle of doing and not doing in movement. Dancers can choose to either observe their breathing without changing it or to alter it. Third, it can introduce and reinforce the principle that all movement, including the breath, is movement of the whole self and not fragmented parts.

3

Kinesthesia

The Sixth Sense for Dancers

You all want to know if you're right. When you get further on you will be right,
but you won't know it and won't want to know if you're right.— Comment given
to a student by Alexander 1969, 9

The importance of heightened sensitivity to balanced living and moving is a foundational principle among somatic techniques, and kinesthesia is a key player in the sensory system. Because the kinesthetic and visual systems are so prevalent in dance, we have divided the Somatic Principle of sensing into two chapters, devoting one to each of these sensory modalities. In this chapter, we look at ways that somatic work targets kinesthetic sensation as a tool for enhancing movement. We also examine interactions between vision, kinesthesia, and other modes of sensing the body and its relationship to the environment in this and subsequent chapters.

This chapter identifies the components of the kinesthetic system and explains common barriers to optimal use of the kinesthetic sense. In transcending these obstacles, we see how the components of kinesthesia can contribute to ease and efficiency of movement, and tools are suggested for teaching classes that utilize and emphasize the kinesthetic system. As part of this chapter, we consider the significance of establishing frames of reference for the learner because habit, and movement itself, influences our perceptions and interpretations of kinesthetic feedback. The methods that are introduced can help create a bridge between the classroom and the stage that can ultimately improve kinesthetic sensitivity in performance situations.

Defining Kinesthetic Sense

Kinesthesia is our ability to sense position and motion of the body in space (Magill 2011; Schmidt and Wrisberg 2008). While we all have kinesthetic abilities, kinesthesia, and our capacity to recognize and respond to kinesthetic feedback, does develop with age and experience (Haywood and Getchell 2009; Kandel, Schwartz, and Jessell 1991). As the central nervous system matures, or as we become more familiar with a skill set, our kinesthetic sensing improves (Magill 2011; Rose and Christina

2006; Schmidt and Wrisberg 2008). This improvement is of consequence to dancers and dance educators because kinesthetic input is needed for sensing and adjusting movement. This not only explains why beginners and children have a difficult time remembering and replicating dance initially, it also suggests the importance of kinesthetic training for more advanced movers wishing to improve their technical and performing skills (Hamill and Knutzen 1995; Fitt 1996; Kimmerle and Cote-Laurence 2003). When dancers move with more sensitivity to what is happening within their bodies and with less concern for the external image, their movement will not only become easier, safer, and stronger, it will also afford greater potential for expressiveness as well.

Overview of the Sensory System

On the most basic level, the sensory system can be divided into three categories. Exteroceptive, interoceptive, and proprioceptive input are differentiated based on the location of the receptors in the body and/or the location of the stimulus (Carola, Harley, and Noback 1992; Coker 2009; Rose and Christina 2006). The exteroceptors are the sensory organs responsible for seeing, hearing, tasting, smelling, and touching. These sensory organs are located near the surface of the body, and they receive and convey information about the external environment to the brain. The interoceptors are located deep within the body, and they respond to internal sensations in the vessels and the viscera (Carola, Harley, and Noback 1992; Kandel, Schwartz, and Jessell 1991). While they may produce sensations such as discomfort, hunger, or thirst, we are often unaware of interoceptive input. The proprioceptors are somewhere in between as far as their location in the body and the location of the stimuli to which they are sensitive. These receptors are associated with the musculoskeletal system and other sensory organs responding to movement and position of the body (Magill 2011; Rose and Christina 2006).

Components of the Kinesthetic System

The kinesthetic sense consists of the proprioceptive, vestibular, and haptic systems (refer to Table 3.1 Kinesthetic Sensory Systems). Together, these three systems aid us in our ability to act on and navigate through our environment and to participate in skillful movement activities such as dance (Magill 2001, 2007). Kinesthesia plays an important role in coordinated, consistent, accurate, and efficient movement as it permits dancers to feel and respond appropriately, matching what is happening in the body with desired outcomes and environmental stimuli (Coker 2009; Kandel, Schwartz, and Jessell, 1991; Magill 2007). We will examine this feedback system in

Sensory System	Location	Sensory Function
Proprioceptors	Muscles, tendons, and joints	Changes in body and or limb position
Vestibular	Inner ear	Position and motion in space with respect to gravity
Haptic	Skin	Interface between organism and environment

Table 3.1 Kinesthetic Sensory Systems.

more depth, but first let us look at the specific sensory organs contributing to the kinesthetic sense.

The proprioceptive system is made up of the Golgi tendon organs (GTOs), muscle spindles, and joint receptors. Collectively, the proprioceptors provide feedback about muscular contraction, force production, and joint position (Carola, Harley, and Noback 1992; Kandel, Schwartz, and Jessell 1991; Magill, 2007; Schmidt and Wrisberg 2008). They lie in the deeper tissues of the body (the muscles, tendons, joints, and the connective tissue covering of bones and muscles) and are sensitive to stretch, tension, motion, speed of action, and changes in position.

Golgi tendon organs lie in the musculotendenous junction and respond to tension. They cause their associated muscle to relax under conditions of tension, whether the tension in the tendon is created through muscular contraction or extreme stretch (Alter 2004). The sensory GTOs synapse with motor neurons that cause the muscle fibers to disengage when the tension threshold is reached. The reflexive relaxation of the muscle is a protective mechanism to prevent the muscle from tearing under situations of extreme duress. The relaxation occurs very quickly and subconsciously, but the information about the source of the tension and the response is relayed to higher brain centers where it joins with other kinesthetic input and can become available for conscious processing a bit later (Alter 2004; Carola, Harley, and Noback 1992; Kandel, Schwartz, and Jessell 1991). Engaging in a deep stretch activates the GTOs, and exemplifies how we can purposefully use these reflexes to our advantage. If the stretch is held, a moment of release occurs. We do not make this happen, but we become aware of the sensation afterward. Of course caution needs to be taken when stretching this far, but this experience, recognized by many dancers, may help to understand the action of the GTOs. More important to proprioception, GTOs provide information about the tension in muscles continuously, even when the reflex threshold has not been reached (Alter 2004; Carola, Harley, and Noback 1992; Kandel, Schwartz, and Jessell 1991).

Muscle spindles lie parallel to muscle cells within the body of the muscle and are sensitive to the speed of a stretch (Magill 2011). They are the source of the monosynaptic stretch reflex: when a muscle has been stretched rapidly, the spindles signal the muscle to contract (Alter 2004). Consider the classic knee tap doctors use to test reflexes. The strike to the patellar tendon stretches the quadracep muscle quickly, and it responds with a reflexive contraction that causes the lower leg to "jump." Again, this movement is an unconscious protective reflex, but the information from the spindles is relayed to the brain for further processing. We are aware of the tap and the leg jerk after it has occurred. Like the GTOs, spindles are constantly relaying information about movement of the muscles in which they are located, even when the reflex threshold has not been reached (Alter 2004; Carola, Harley, and Noback 1992; Floyd 2007; Kandel, Schwartz, and Jessell 1991).

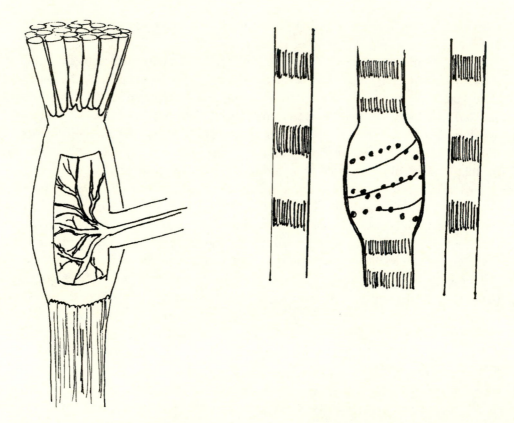

Figure 3.2 Golgi Tendon Organ and Muscle Spindles.

Teaching Tip: The stretch reflex has implications for technique beyond its contributions to the kinesthetic sense. In a precautionary sense, the stretch reflex is one reason ballistic stretching is not recommended. The muscle spindles are activated when bouncing, so contradictory signals are being sent to the muscle. In essence, you are trying to stretch a muscle being signaled to contract, which is not particularly effective and can result in torn muscle fibers. A slow, static stretch is a safer, more effective way to increase flexibility (Alter 2004).

The stretch reflex can also be used to our advantage, however. Many "wind-up" or preparatory actions are capitalizing on this reflexive contraction of the muscles to augment the voluntary effort applied during the actual movement. A pitcher, for example, pulls the arm back quickly before the actual throw. This preparation activates the stretch reflex in the shoulder and arm muscles, adding to the power of the pitch (Floyd 2007). In dance, the plié is extremely important as the preparation for jumping. Using a full, well-timed plié will assist dancers with finding ballon (suspension in jumping), as the stretch reflex initiated in the knee extensors and ankle plantar flexors will add to the push-off power. Pairing a dancer struggling to get in the air with a natural jumper can be helpful, as imitating the successful jumper's timing of the plié may resolve some issues.

Joint capsule receptors are sensitive to changes in the articular capsule surrounding synovial joints. There are several types of receptors involved in this feedback, but the important point is that we are very sensitive to the motion of our joints. Close your eyes and clench and then straighten your toes. You can feel which joints are moving, although the exact muscles activated will probably be less evident. In fact, information from the joint capsule receptors about position in space feeds directly into conscious awareness, unlike other proprioceptive input (Fitt 1996, 276).

The vestibular system of the inner ear provides information about our position and motion in space with respect to gravity through translation (forward and backward directional motion) and rotation (tilting and up/down directional motion) of the otoliths and semicircular canals (Kandel, Schwartz, and Jessell 1991; Rose and Christina 2006). The vestibular apparatus is responsible for many of the reflexes that compensate for disturbances in balance. Anyone who has had an inner ear infection can attest to its role in orientation and balance, as illnesses of this sort will result in dizziness and instability. In considering the role of the vestibular system in movement, the most common example is a cat always landing on its feet. While frequently somewhat less agile than cats, even humans going into a handstand and overshooting the vertical will usually be able to compensate. Unless we freeze with fear (understandably), the vestibular sense will guide us to find our feet, rather than falling on our backs like a board. The vestibular apparatus is also tied to other reflexes related to the eyes and skeletal muscles that we consider in the next chapter (Rose and Christina 2006).

Two kinds of receptors in different parts of the inner ear respond to different kinds of stimuli. Otoliths are tiny stones associated with the macula, one of the sensory receptors in the utricle of the inner ear. The macula respond to the position of the head in relation to gravity when stationary and to linear changes in speed and direction, not to rotational movement (Rose and Cristina 2006). As the head moves the stones follow, but with a slight delay due to inertia. When the stones follow the action, they brush against little hairs (cilia) in the macula. This movement of the cilia stimulates the receptor cells, and information about the position of the head is conveyed to the brain (Kandel, Schwartz, and Jessell 1991; Rose and Cristina 2006).

The semicircular canals are the site of another receptor: the crista ampullaris. Bony, ring-like structures, these three semicircular canals lie in all three planes, so they are sensitive to motion in all directions. Like the macula, the crista will also respond to linear motion, but they are specifically sensitive to rotational actions. Working in a fashion similar to the macula, inertia causes a gelatinous fluid in the semicircular canals to stimulate the cilia as the head moves in space. Distortion of the cilia depolarizes the crista, so the crista are responding to and providing information about changes in the velocity and direction of head movement (Kandel, Schwartz, and Jessell 1991; Rose and Christina 2006).

The haptic system (touch) relays information regarding the amount and type of pressure and areas of the body contacting the external world (Kandel, Schwartz, and Jesell 1991; Magill 2001, 2007; Schmidt and Wrisberg 2008). It should be noted that the kinesthetic haptic receptors are pacinian corpuscles and other mechanoreceptors that respond to

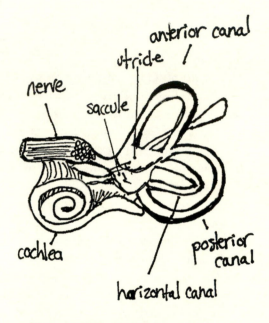

Figure 3.3 Vestibular Apparatus.

deep pressure. Haptic exteroceptors are more superficially located, and include thermoreceptors for sensing temperature, some mechanoreceptors for sensing light touch, and nociceptors for pain sensitivity (Floyd 2007; Kandel, Schwartz, and Jesell 1991; Magill 2007; Schmidt and Wrisberg 2008).

The various components of the kinesthetic system work together with the exteroceptive systems of vision, audition, touch, and smell. Somatic techniques emphasize all types of sensory input and its role in keeping awareness on the present moment and providing as much information as possible about the surrounding environment. As movers we do not necessarily identify individual receptor information as much as we rely on the integrated input that we call feeling and sensing. The brain puts all the kinesthetic and exteroceptive information together to provide as complete a picture of the body in space as possible. It is quite amazing how much input is constantly

Sensory Cells	Location	Sensory Function
Proprioceptive Cells		
Golgi Tendon Organ (GTO)	Musculotendenous junction	Changes in tension
Muscle Spindle	Muscle belly	Changes in speed
Joint Capsule Receptors	Articular capsule	Changes in motion
Vestibular Cells		
Otoliths and Maculae	Utricle of the inner ear	Translation
Crista Ampullaris	Semicircular canals	Rotation
Kinesthetic Haptic Cells		
Ruffini's Corpuscles	Skin (Deep)	Pressure and joint movement
Pacinian	Skin (Deep)	Deep pressure and vibration

Table 3.2 Specific Sensory Cells Contributing to Kinesthesia.

being processed to enable us to move and position our bodies as we desire and to respond accurately and appropriately to new incoming stimuli (Schmidt and Wrisberg 2008). Traditionally, a distinction was made between proprioceptive and kinesthetic information. This division has blurred in recent times depending on the field and the source (Magill 2007; Schmidt and Wrisberg 2008). For the sake of specificity, we follow the more traditional model and parse proprioception out from the larger topic of kinesthesia.

Open- and Closed-Loop Systems of Control

To understand the value of kinesthetic input, we need to understand its basic contribution to motor control. There are two main systems for controling movement, or ways in which the nervous system initiates and manages action. They are called open-loop and closed-loop systems (see Figure 3.4 Open and Closed Feedback Loops). Open-loop systems do not involve feedback from the sensory organs, while closed-loop systems do. In a movement that employs the closed-loop system of control, feedback from proprioceptors and other sensory organs is used to alter and refine the movement while it is in progress. The desired action is compared to what is actually happening, and necessary adjustments are made. Another distinction is that the motor program for an activity using an open-loop system of control is complete and

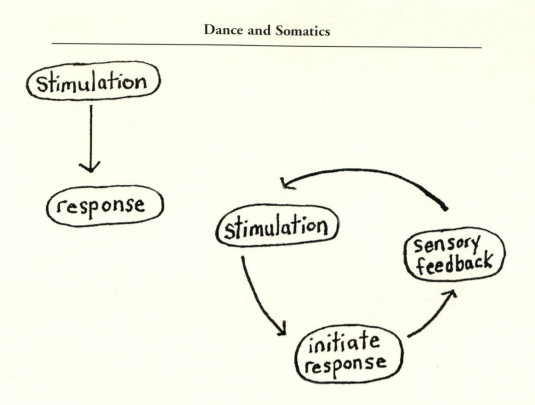

Figure 3.4 Open and Closed Feedback Loops.

requires no additional input. In contrast, a closed-loop system begins with an initial command to begin the action. The rest of the motor program is completed and controlled with the aid of sensory input (Magill 2001; Rose and Christina 2006; Schmidt and Wrisberg 2008).

Of course both open- and closed-loop systems are necessary for skilled activities, but thinking about how we are training with regard to these two systems can be helpful in improving movement through kinesthetic feedback. Open-loop systems are frequently activated for quick activities in which there is no time for adjustment, or when internal feedback is not needed to complete an action. Closed-loop systems require more time for the feedback to be applied to the motor program, and depending on how slow the action is, the kinesthetic input may or may not be conscious. Therefore to enact change, we need to circumvent any initial tendency to revert to the open-loop response; we need to go slow enough for the closed-loop system to be engaged (Coker 2009; Magill 2011; Rose and Christina 2006; Schmidt and Wrisberg 2008).

Barriers to Change

As we have seen, the kinesthetic sense is needed for accurate movement perception and for optimizing movement efficiency and expressivity — key issues for performers.

We all have kinesthetic abilities, but we often do not use this sixth sensory option optimally in dance and dance education. In addition to finding better ways to allow the kinesthetic sense to work for us in dance, we should also remember that the kinesthetic sense can be trained (Clippinger 2007; Hanna 1993; Magill 2007). Because it grows with maturity and experience, we need to take this into consideration just as we do strength, flexibility, endurance, and other training parameters. Breaking habits and moving with ease are some of the greatest challenges to dancers and dance educators. What can we learn from somatic wisdom? First let us consider some of the barriers that we may encounter when trying to enact change.

Trying too hard. Dancers tend to be doers. They train hard, and most have been brought up with the work ethic of "no pain, no gain." Not only can this attitude be dangerous because it encourages dancers to ignore their bodies' natural warning signals, but overworking can also make it next to impossible to sense and respond to the subtle kinesthetic cues being provided. Consider balancing in a precarious position. Most dancers will tense up in what they believe to be the correct position, gripping muscles in their determination to make it "stick." This tensing and holding makes it difficult for the body to make the many tiny adjustments necessary to keep the body in a balanced state and ruins the illusion of ease in the process.

Debauched kinesthesia or faulty sensory appreciation. Alexander coined the term *debauched kinesthesia* long ago to refer to the notion that we get used to what we are doing. This makes it hard to find new ways to move, even if those new ways are more efficient (Alexander 1932). If a student is used to hyperextending his or her knees, not doing so will feel "bent" initially. The proprioceptors in the region become desensitized and cease to respond to the misalignment when it is perpetual. This reaction is one reason why it is so difficult to break habitual ways of moving. In addition, our ability to attend to the sixth sense may be dulled by contemporary life. Our minds can become so occupied with sensing and acting on the external world that signals from the body are suppressed from consciousness.

Muscle memory. Students may confuse the terms muscle memory and proprioception or kinesthesia. To clarify, muscle memory can be thought of as a motor program for a particular movement action (Schmidt and Wrisberg 2008), while proprioception is feedback about the state of the body. Proprioception may be involved in muscle memory, as sensory feedback about the action is incorporated into the program, but they are distinct entities. Muscle memory can actually contribute to difficulty enacting change or finding new ways of moving because the performer will automatically revert to pre-programmed neuromuscular pathways when trying to achieve a given task. Motor programs are needed for us to be able to achieve complex movement sequences. Subcortical initiation of basic actions frees the brain up to respond to new stimuli and produce new actions. Therefore, we do not need to be aware of kinesthetic input to engage in the familiar, but the reality is that these actions are frequently not as efficient as they could be and could benefit from some kinesthetic attention.

Visual dominance and capture. As we discuss in the next chapter, the visual sense tends to dominate our attention. In traditional dance training, little is done to downplay this method: in fact it is frequently emphasized by reliance on the mirror, modeling, and demands for quick and specific skill mastery. One problem with this focus (joke intended!) on seeing is that it can override or interfere with the ability to attend to kinesthetic cues (Haywood and Getchell 2009; Lee and Aronson 1974). The visual should augment the kinesthetic, not overpower it (Magill 2001, 2007).

Maximizing Kinesthetic Input

Trust the body's wisdom: Get "out of the way." Kinesthetic sensing occurs on a variety of anatomical levels, from superficial to deep, from the skin to the muscles to the bones (Carola, Harley, and Noback 1992; Hackney 1998; Kandel, Schwartz, and Jessell 1991). In addition to working on different levels in the body, the kinesthetic sense also works on different levels of consciousness. The majority of the responses we make to kinesthetic input are subconscious and occur before we are even aware of the need for adjustment (Carola, Harley, and Noback 1992; Kandel, Schwartz, and Jessell 1991; Magill 2001; Schmidt and Wrisberg 2008). We are responding to a constant supply of sensory information at all times on an unconscious level. An intended action is initiated by the motor cortex of the brain. As the body responds, the kinesthetic sense is continually providing feedback, allowing for fine-tuning of the action. Often, this refinement needs to occur quickly, before the brain can even process what is needed, so it is not a voluntary adjustment to the action. In fact, once a movement pattern is established, overthinking or consciously controlling it can interfere in performance situations (Schmidt and Wrisberg 2001, 2008; Wulf 2007). This theme is common in somatic work — the concept of trusting the body's wisdom (Hanna 1979). Thinking too much or trying too hard can result in excessive tension in the body, interfere with natural reflexes, or delay reaction time (Magill 2007; Rose and Christina 2006; Schmidt and Wrisberg 2008).

In a recent Kenpo Karate black belt test, the students up for promotion were clearly nervous. They had been training their forms in slow motion: a wise choice, as we discussed in Chapter 1. However, after going through the first form at an excruciatingly slow pace, they were stopped by the examiner, a ninth degree black belt and expert in movement training. To their surprise, the examiner told the students, "Do it like your hair is on fire!" In analyzing the situation, he was clearly trying to get the students to trust their training and to "let it happen" in this pressured situation.

Teaching Tip: Another example of getting out of the way and trusting the body's wisdom (or not) can be seen in a simple locomotor activity. If you have beginning students skip across the floor, they will almost all automatically use opposition, or contralateral coordination of the arms with the legs. It is a cross lateral reflex. Just for fun, you can try bringing their attention to the relationship of their arms and legs. The next time across, many will struggle with what seemed so natural just moments before, with some students now exhibiting homolateral (same side) coordination of the arm swing with the skip. Of the students managing to maintain the original contralateral coordination, many will exhibit delayed timing due to the additional (unnecessary) processing being engaged.

Slow down. Not interfering with the body's natural feedback mechanisms is important and is one aspect to consider in training dancers who can tend to overthink and try too hard to make their movement "right." However, it is also vital to recognize that increasing kinesthetic awareness by taking time (slowing down) and shifting focus to the body is central to learning and/or relearning efficient and effective movement patterns (Alexander 1932; Feldenkrais 1972; Hackney 1998). To alter habits and in learning new actions, a closed-loop system of control may be better. This method entails going slowly enough that the actual state of body can be compared with the desired state to adjust or correct the movement along the way (Schmidt and Wrisberg 2008). Otherwise, dancers will tend to revert to what they are accustomed to doing. This method applies to both alignment and movement sequences accessed via an established motor program.

Stay relaxed. If a dancer can stay relaxed, the kinesthetic sense will be able to provide feedback about any imbalances or inaccuracies, and the motor program can then respond. If the body is locked, the input will not be complete, and subtle responses are impossible. Of course, staying relaxed is easier said than done when trying to balance in some precarious position or executing some demanding sequence, especially with an audience watching. This is where the awareness of tension itself becomes important, as well as the use of other principles such as breath.

Use less effort. Using less effort is related to staying relaxed, but it may resonate better for some dancers. All movement requires some tension or effort. The key is discovering just how much is necessary for a given action, which is the very definition of efficiency. In her book, *Move into Life,* Feldenkrais practitioner Anat Baniel recommends trying any given movement sequence with a 90 percent reduction in force (Baniel 2009, 98). Reducing the amount of effort makes it possible to feel and notice subtle signals from the body. If the background effort is too intense, we may only be able to notice dramatic signals from the body, such as pain. By reducing the background input, we can sense and respond in a more sophisticated manner that will not only improve movement quality, it can also help prevent pain and injury. Once the effort is reduced enough, the optimal amount of force can be discovered.

Fechner's Law, the Law of Noticeable Difference. This law explains the effectiveness of staying relaxed, reducing effort, and going slow. It states that in order to notice the difference between different sensory stimuli we need to lower the baseline stimulus activity. Reducing background noise within the body makes it possible to consciously detect kinesthetic differences (Feldenkrais 1972). To illustrate this concept consider the following: if you were carrying a heavy load would you be able to feel a fly land on it? Now consider the alternative: if you were carrying a feather would you be able to feel a fly land on it? The practical application of Fechner's Law for both teacher and student is that one needs to slow down and use less muscular effort in order to feel subtle differences in moving. With many stimuli competing for our attention, it is crucial to create the time and space in order to become aware of what is happening kinesthetically in movement.

Tools for Teaching Classes That Train the Kinesthetic Sense

In addition to the general guidelines of honoring Fechner's Law, getting out of the way, and letting go of unnecessary tension, specific techniques can be utilized to help train the kinesthetic sense. After all, it is easy to tell a student to relax or quit trying but harder for them to accomplish. Improvements that result from these techniques or activities will transfer to performance situations, as they address the overall functioning of the dancing instrument, not just the mastery of specific movement sequences.

Emphasize breath. As we have seen in Chapter 2, focusing attention on breath is a useful method for enacting change. Breath is an important teaching and performance tool for connecting the body and the mind, and it provides a link between the conscious and the unconscious. In this regard, it is related to the kinesthetic sense. Additionally, breath relaxes us so we do not interfere with our reflexive and unconscious kinesthetic adjustments, and it helps to lower the baseline stimulus levels mentioned above.

Stop the initial response. Dancers will revert to established motor programs when attempting to achieve a known action. We will discuss this mechanism and ways of dealing with it more fully in Chapter 6, but it seems relevant to introduce the concept of inhibition here. To circumvent going into an open-loop system that is not susceptible to kinesthetic feedback, think about the action, then stop before actually moving. Try to become aware of the instinctive, or habitual, response of the body to this command. Repeat several times without doing anything. Then try replacing this first, instinctive response to the movement command with something new — an image, thought, or direction for the body. This technique is utilized in Alexander work and it is a basic premise of Ideokinesis: voluntary action reinforces established neuromuscular pathways unless the initial response is inhibited **and** the body is given something new to do in place of the habitual movement pattern (Alexander 1932, 1969; Sweigard 1974).

Movement Experience: *Proprioceptive Sensing.* While standing, close your eyes and notice the minute adjustments that are constantly occurring to keep you upright. This is the proprioceptive system at work; it is important to train sensitivity to this sensory input that is easily masked. Try exaggerating these tiny, internal movements so they become barely visible. Return to "stillness" after several minutes. Notice if anything has changed in your alignment.

Movement Experience: *Hands-On Proprioceptive Shifting.* Now try the proprioceptive sensing with a partner: one person with eyes closed, the other person hands on your partner. See if you can feel the little movements occurring in your partner whose eyes are closed. When you sense a slight imbalance or adjustment, see if you can give a little energy in that direction. What happens? How little force can you use? Try putting your hands in different places: head, chest and back, ankles and feet. These two experiences are designed to bring awareness to proprioceptive adjustments in one's self and others and to encourage comfort with being off-balance.

Go off-center. Shifting away from the vertical alignment emphasizes the role of the vestibular apparatus in maintaining equilibrium. Training with off-center movement will help to increase sensitivity to vestibular input in all situations. Note the importance of being relaxed so that the kinesthetic sense can work optimally to adjust the body and rediscover balance when not upright.

Figure 3.5 Going Off-Center (Balinda Craig-Quijada, rear, and Kora Radella; photograph by Marcella Hackbardt).

Movement Experience: *Going Off-Center.* Try rising on the balls of the feet and tilting off-center with the eyes open, then closed. Balancing with the eyes closed is harder, but it will improve with practice. Next try standing on one leg and shifting the center of gravity off the vertical, counterbalancing as needed to stay upright. Open your eyes slowly, trying to maintain internal sensitivity while allowing the external environment to enter your consciousness.

CREATE FRAMES OF REFERENCE

Creating reference point(s) or frames of reference can be a useful method for assisting learners with changing habits. Every movement changes our inner architecture and muscular tone. Knowing and experiencing, both physically and cognitively, what is different and *how* it is different is vital to creating lasting change that will carry over into other situations. Too often dancers fleetingly find a new way of moving through a well-designed class or the perfect correction, only to loose the changes by the next class or even the next repetition of the action or phrase. This happens because they do not have the tools to recreate the experience or because they were unaware of what they did differently to begin with. Establishing frames of reference by changing the orientation of the body in space and/or the context for a given movement can provide dancers with the information they need to fully embody change (Coker 2009).

POTENTIAL REFERENCE POINTS

The floor or another object. Noticing how you feel in relation to the floor before and after an activity provides a frame of reference for how that movement or action changes your contact with the ground and how your verticality lines up with the supporting surface. "Body scans" are done in some form or another in most somatic techniques and involve taking the time to check in with the body's state in that moment of time. The following body scan can be used at the beginning and/or at the end of any movement experience or technique class. It allows information from the floor, as the frame of reference, to be compared, integrated, and assimilated.

Movement Experience: *Scanning the Body.* Lie on your back with your legs fully extended and about shoulder width apart and your arms lying by your sides. Close your eyes and begin to feel and sense which parts of your body are contacting the floor, lying more intimately on the floor. Do you feel the back of your heel touching the floor, the lower leg, the back of the knee, the thigh? Is the contact the same for the right leg and the left leg? Notice the differences in the contact. Try to just notice and not change anything. How much of the back of your pelvis is contacting the floor? Is the right half of the pelvis lying in the same manner on the floor as the left half? Which parts of the lumbar spine are making contact with the floor? Can you feel the contact of each vertebra as you travel up your spine in your mind's eye? Or are some parts off of the floor, such as your lower back? Do some parts of your spine feel lighter, heavier, or perhaps painful on the floor? How much of the surface of your back is touching the floor? Notice if there is any difference in the contact of the two shoulders lying on the floor. Which parts of your arms are contacting the floor? The hands, the lower arm, and/or the upper arm? Are the two arms lying in the same manner on the floor? Bring your attention up to your head and notice how it is contacting the floor. Can you sense the length of your cervical spine from your neck to your head? Can you sense and feel the midline of your body from your nose to your pubic bone? Take a moment to sense and feel the whole of you contacting the floor, including all of your parts from your toes to your head. What are you feeling and sensing while you are lying on the floor?

Most somatic techniques have a foundation in floor work because in addition to providing a frame of reference, the body can relax on the floor, as it does not have to fight against the pull of gravity. This can create transfer issues, as mentioned in Chapter 1, but the value of floor work is indisputable. The chair work done in both the Alexander Technique and Feldenkrais work are examples of using an object as a frame of reference rather than the floor. In Alexander work, the hands are placed gently on the back of the chair while leaning forward by creasing at the hips and keeping the back lengthened. This contact with the chair provides a frame of reference for the alignment of the spine while thinking about lengthening and widening the back.

Movement to extremes. This method also creates reference points for the student. By moving between opposite endpoints for a given action (i.e., flexion and hyperextension of the spine), one can then go to the middle or neutral point and experience what that place feels like with more clarity. Many somatic methods utilize this technique in order to recalibrate the system or reestablish a true neutral (Alexander 1969; Bartenieff and Lewis 1980; Feldenkrais 1972; Hackney 1998). As we have seen, many times our postural and movement habits skew our sense of

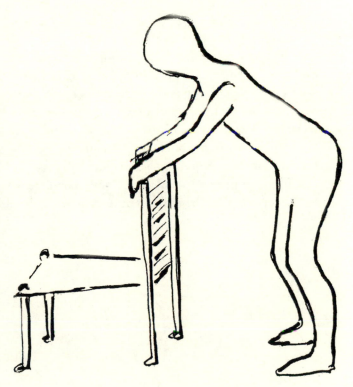

Figure 3.6 Chair as a Frame of Reference.

neutral to varying degrees. This difference is important because altering the baseline patterning for action is less efficient, and it can also make it difficult to have complete range of motion in movement.

Movement Experience: *Spinal Movement to Extremes.* To experience the concept of moving to extremes, start on all four limbs, or bearing weight on your hands and knees. Move through the upper back, middle back and lower back, going from hyperextension to flexion and then to neutral. Transition to standing, creasing at the hips with the hands on the knees. At this point, the visual sense can be integrated with the kinesthetic. Look to see if the sensation of the back as flat (neutral), flexed, and hyperextended matches up with what you see in the mirror. This movement experience is an example of when the mirror may be useful initially. However, you must be able to feel the difference rather than see the difference to have the experience transfer to performance situations. The movement to extremes can then be done upright, focusing on placement of the pelvis (although the spine still participates). While standing with your knees released, swing your pelvis forward and back, then find neutral.

Teaching Tip: This exaggeration of the pelvic alignment can be incorporated into traditional exercises or combinations. Build it into a plié sequence at the barre or a warm-up phrase for modern class. Swinging the pelvis to extremes and then finding neutral in this more traditional context will help with transfer. It also is a nice way to loosen and lubricate the hip joints.

Exaggerate habits. Exaggerating your tendencies is a similar concept to movement to extremes; it is yet another way to assist the learner with recognizing what they are doing, thereby making change possible. For example, imagine you are teaching class, and many of your students' shoulders are up to their ears. You give the correction to lower the shoulders and some students achieve this directive. However, a few minutes later the shoulders are tensed up again. Rather than continuing to draw their attention to dropping the shoulders, try asking the students to raise their shoulders higher during the whole combination and see what happens. This direction uses the extreme half of the movement to extremes idea. Refining the exaggerated action,

Figure 3.7 Movement Experience: Spinal Movement to Extremes.

trying to make it more "elegant" can heighten the level of awareness surrounding the habit even further. Becoming aware of habits by exaggerating them can actually create an opportunity for the learner to find the neutral point again. In this way, they are creating the change themselves by reestablishing internal sensitivity to the habitual action.

Provide variety. Providing variations on how to accomplish a given action can give the brain more options for creating efficient and effective pathways. This idea is part of why movement to extremes and exaggeration work. The proprioceptors that quit responding to a habitual stimulus are resensitized when moved through a full range, or to extremes. Changing the habitual ways we perform actions or trying new movements stimulates the sensory system, providing another way of increasing our kinesthetic awareness.

Movement Experience: *Interlace Fingers.* Try interlacing your fingers. Repeat this action. Chances are you did it the same way. Now consciously reverse the overlap. It will feel odd, even uncomfortable at first, but you are probably more acutely aware than when interlacing the normal or habitual way.

Teaching Tip: This premise can be applied to technique class as well. Look for opportunities to change routine or habit. For example, start with the left foot instead of the right, change the facing in the room, or in a lateral arm swing, alternate which arm travels in front of the other.

Manual guidance. Passive manipulation or guidance is another tool that can provide the learner with a frame of reference (Coker 2009; Schmidt and Wrisberg 2008). In this situation, someone repositions or guides the movement pattern while the learner just attends to the sensation of the action without actively trying to produce it. As suggested in Chapter 1, one of the advantages of passive guidance is that the learner is freed from the goal of producing the movement and has more attention available to sense the quality of the action. Remember that for passive work to transfer to performance one still needs to provide time for the learner to enact the movement or action themselves. As we have seen, kinesthetic input is complex, resulting from the accumulation of many types of sensory information. Because of this, actively doing an action is going to provide a different kinesthetic sensation than feeling the action someone else is producing (Coker 2009; Schmidt and Wrisberg 2008). This guidance can be applied to both learning movement and postural adjustment. For example, in the previous activity of moving to extremes with spinal flexion and extension, a partner can assist with adjustments to achieve the truly flat back, or neutral pelvis. This partnership can augment visual and active kinesthetic feedback in recalibrating the dancer's awareness.

External Kinesthetic
Feedback and/or Imagery

Providing sensory-based feedback and/or imagery may assist the student in repatterning or learning new neuromuscular pathways. Visualization is covered more completely in the next chapter, but utilizing feedback and images that are rich to the sensorium and that emphasize feeling rather than doing can help students access the kinesthetic sense. Chances are, these experiences and changes will be more lasting and transferable to performance than the mastery of set sequences or specific spot-fix corrections. For example, bring attention to the sensation of weight and release while doing leg swings on the floor, standing, traveling, and in a final phrase. Encouraging students to really feel the foot or leg and how it contacts the floor as it brushes through may be more beneficial than just telling students to go through first position.

Touch. The more that students have a sense of the whole body, the more kinesthetic input can be used effectively to enact change. Again, we need to remember that the body is a kinetic chain, and altering one piece affects the rest. Touch, either by oneself, a surface, or another person can be a wonderful inroad for increasing awareness of the wholeness, as well as the boundaries, of body (Franklin 1996). For example, in an attempt to increase awareness of the vertical alignment and to "awaken" the deep postural muscles, one can gently push down on one's own head. Tapping the skin will arouse the more superficial proprioceptors and give a sense of the outer border of the body.

Movement Experience: *Body Part Dance with Partner.* Find a partner and sit on the floor back to back. Start by feeling the breath through your backs. Use a very light touch, and move slowly. What do you sense and feel about your back? About your partner's back? Try to maintain contact with your partner's back at all times. One of you move, and the other respond to that movement, repeating

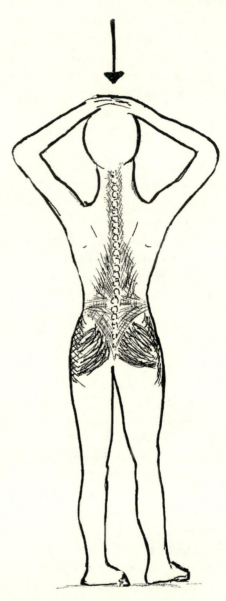

Figure 3.8 Awakening Postural Muscles.

this process over and over again. Remember to go slowly and gently. Gradually try to extend the movement to include the head and/or the arms. Go slowly, and make it smooth. See if you can change levels, maintaining contact of at least one body part at all times. When you and your partner feel more like one body than two, begin to travel through the space. Continue to stay connected via a body part or parts(s). Feel free to change levels while you are moving through the room. As you are traveling, you and your partner may want to connect with another pair. Once connected, you will need to figure out how to move as a group. Have a sense of being one organism, one living cellular unit, like an ameba. Sensing and feeling the connected body parts, change levels, then travel to meet another group to start this whole process over again. Once this has been repeated a few times, allow the group or groups to sink to the floor, maintaining contact. Gradually disconnect and roll away from each other to find your own place on the floor. Using the floor as a frame of reference, notice which parts are touching, contacting and lying more intimately on the floor. Roll to your side, get up, and take a moment to feel what it is like to stand now. Has anything changed? Do you feel different? What parts of your feet are feeling the floor?

Being "In the Moment"

As one of the issues we face in kinesthetic sensing is the overwhelming sensory input to which we are exposed, learning to be present in the moment is central to optimizing our kinesthetic abilities. Encouraging students to leave everything else at the door and giving them time to focus inward on their bodies can help set them up for a richer, more rewarding class experience. Again, focus on the breath can assist with this transition from external to internal sensing, as can guidance with a kinesthetically founded vocabulary or use of movement experiences that rely on sensory input.

Movement Experience: *Partner Touch Dance.* Person one, place your hand on your partner (person two). Person two, move one's hand to a new spot on your body. Person one place your other hand on person two. Release your first hand. Person two change the placement of the second hand. Continue.... Notice that you may lose sense of which hand is yours. In this instance, touch and the kinesthetic sense are being used as a way to circumvent our predictable movement choices — the mind is occupied with the task at hand as well as lots of sensory input, so there is less time to preplan or judge movement choices being made.

Conclusions

In looking at the various somatic techniques, one of the most basic throughlines is the concept of awareness as the gateway to change. Until dancers can sense and feel what they are actually doing in posture and movement, change is not possible. This awareness revolves around the ability to attend to the kinesthetic sense and apply the information in a variety of contexts.

Often dulled or ignored because of the overwhelming sensory and motor demands of class, kinesthetic sensitivity can be heightened and trained in dancers.

Figure 3.1 "Kinesthesia" (Karen Snouffer).

Self-discovery through movement experiences shifts the focus from the mastery of material/technique to what is actually happening in the body. Organic learning can then occur, as the individual discovers for himself or herself what is to be understood and taken from the experience, rather than "putting on" material. These pedagogical concepts that were discussed in depth in Chapter 1 are the basis of the kinesthetic activities presented here.

Allowing time for students to process what they are feeling and doing is important to create lasting change. Reverting back to what is "known" can happen when we move on from our new experiences of movement too quickly. This additional processing can be accomplished in various ways, including journaling during and after class, discussion as a group or with partners, or even through a moment of quiet reflection.

4

More Than Just a Mirror Image*
The Visual System and Its Relationship to Other Modes of Sensing and Learning

Seeing for some of us is limited to the general impression of that which is observed, whether it is nature, persons, objects, or events. In our rush, we dash from object to object, event to event, with little awareness of detail or the aesthetic qualities of that which is encountered. We look but we do not see. — Hawkins 1991, 21

Exteroceptive sensory information is integrated with kinesthetic input to provide us with a complete picture of the world and how we are moving within it. Seeing, hearing, touching, smelling, and tasting are all important components of the living experience, yet in the rush of day to day life, we can filter out many pleasurable and/or important signals coming from our surroundings. Somatic work frequently brings our awareness to these modalities of sensing as a mechanism of focusing the mind on the present moment, rather than worrying about what has already happened or might happen next. This chapter will examine the role of vision in learning and changing movement patterns. This is not to downplay the importance of other sensory systems, but humans tend to rely most on the visual sense (Magill 2011; Schmidt and Wrisberg 2008).

The question is, how can we help our dance students move beyond blank stares or eyes glued to the mirror to use vision as a powerful learning and performing tool? Many dance teachers address some aspects of vision in training already, but probably through more or less trial-and-error discoveries or through an intuitive sense of how vision works. Current information about the visual system can help dance educators target the role of vision in learning material, detecting and correcting errors, and enhancing performance. It is also important to recognize that vision does not work in isolation; it is tied to multiple systems working synergistically. The actual anatomy and physiology of vision is only part of what we need to consider in a holistic approach to the function of vision in learning and performing movement. In the processing of visual sensory input, other systems and modes of executing skilled movement are accessed. For this reason, the scope of this chapter will move beyond just vision to

*Portions of this chapter previously appeared in *Journal of Dance Education* (Brodie and Lobel 2008) and are reprinted by permission of the authors and the publisher.

examine its relationship to the vestibular and the proprioceptive systems, fight or flight responses, and the role of mental imaging in producing movement. With more knowledge, all aspects of the visual potential can be maximized, and informed decisions can be made about its use in teaching. For example, dance technique classes can reflect this component of training by exploring topics like performance focus, kinesthetic and environmental awareness, imagery in verbal feedback, and visualization techniques. Throughout this chapter, the movement experiences are intended to introduce students to the various components of vision being described and also to enhance appropriate interplay of the visual system with other components of motor learning that are involved in performing dance.

Traditionally in dance, visual information has been utilized in two primary ways: (1) learning movement by modeling the teacher and (2) making alignment and movement corrections based on two-dimensional visual information obtained from a mirror. Both of these uses of visual information have their place in dance training, but dance educators should temper their reliance on them based on several factors. Feedback from the mirror is only one method of noticing and adjusting movement performance. Research in the field of motor learning indicates insufficient evidence that movement corrections based on visual feedback obtained from the mirror can be utilized in the target context of a dance performance (Magill 2001, 222; Tremblay and Proteau 1998). While modeling is an effective way of learning, teachers must consider whether they are providing a clear image of the desired movement. Even with adequate demonstration, students may or may not perceive the movement accurately, or they may choose to focus on less important aspects of the movement image being presented. In addition, overreliance on visual cues may interfere with the ability to attend to kinesthetic cues and can contribute to the glazed-over stare or the eyes-glued-to-the-mirrors phenomena so often seen in dancers. For the purposes of this chapter, we dissect vision into its various components, but it should be noted that all visual components are operating at all times.

Two Systems at Work

Vision is an exteroceptive system that provides us with information about the environment so that we can respond appropriately (Kandel, Schwartz, and Jessell 1991). Much has been learned about visual contributions to motor development and skillful performance in recent years. For example, prior to 1968, only one visual system was recognized as being active in human vision (Trevarthen 1968). It is now known that there are two distinct visual systems that detect, integrate, and act on different kinds of information in the visual field (Brown, Halpert, and Goodale 2005). Each visual system has its own set of characteristics in terms of how it functions and operates to aid in human movement production, action, and balance. These two systems operate in parallel at all times (Kandel, Schwartz, and Jesell 1991; Magill 2001; Schmidt and Wrisberg 2008).

Focal and Ambient Visual Systems

The focal visual system is conscious and functions primarily to identify objects and their size and shape in the environment. It picks up visual information within the boundaries of the central visual field. Less efficient in low-level lighting situations, the focal visual system is the slower of the two systems (Magill 2001; Schmidt and Wrisberg 2008), which has important ramifications for our ability to perceive and react to visual stimuli in performance situations.

The ambient visual system is unconscious and functions primarily to detect objects and movements around us. Unaffected by low-level lighting situations, the ambient visual system is used primarily in locomoting through space, i.e., navigating through our environment (Coker 2009; Kandel, Schwartz, and Jesell 1991). Optical flow is yet another important aspect of vision related to both the peripheral visual field and the ambient system. Patterns of light reflected on the retina create optical flow (Magill 2007, 127). The changing angle of the pattern with time provides information about motion and position. Optical flow patterns that traverse by and to the eye permit us to regulate our motion, position, and timing in relation to our environment (Schmidt and Wrisberg 2008, 92–93).

Movement Experience: *The Focal and Ambient Systems and Optical Flow Patterns.* Start standing, seeing the space you are in without moving your head. After a minute or two, allow your head to move to see more of the space you are in, at this moment. Let this naturally lead you into moving any way you want in the space. While locomoting through the space, identify or name the objects and the people sharing the space with you. Really see the people and the objects in the room. What colors, textures, and shapes surround you? Continue to travel through the space any way you want, but meet and greet people you come near. Make eye contact, grasp hands and say hello, exchanging names. Every time you meet someone you have been introduced too say, "Hello, Evi," or whatever his or her name is. Keep doing this for a few minutes. Continue moving through the space, but now try not to touch anyone. Try moving more quickly without any contact with others. Now move faster, but use less space and continue to avoid touching others in the room.

Teaching Tip: To highlight the navigational component of this movement experience the instructor can do the following: narrow or reduce the size of the space, create obstacles, and vary the tempo from slow to fast. The first part of this activity is designed to engage the focal visual system, with its emphasis on object identification. When the emphasis shifts to moving through the space in the second part, the ambient system is coming into play. As another tier to this activity, a specific site can be des-

Figure 4.2 Optical Flow Patterns (Kora Radella, Balinda Craig-Quijada, Samantha Beckerman, and Shaina Cantino; photograph by Marcella Hackbardt).

ignated on the floor. When students come to this spot they must stand still and experience the motion of the other bodies around them. This is one way to increase the learner's awareness of optical flow.

Visual Dominance and Capture

The visual system is the dominant sensory modality in humans (Kandel, Schwartz, and Jesell 1991). We tend to rely on the visual sense, even when there may be other faster or more reliable sources of information available (Fitt 1996; Kamen 2001; Lee 1980). Visual information also captures our attention more quickly and longer than any other sensory information. Dominance and capture are problematic when other sensory systems have to compete with visual information for attention (Lee and Aronson 1974). Specifically, because the focal system accesses the conscious brain, use of this focal system for feedback about body position or movement can slow reaction time, may be less accurate, and can result in overthinking or overcontrolling movement (Magill 2007; Schmidt and Wrisberg 2008). While the focal system may be helpful in learning movement initially, allowing the kinesthetic and ambient visual systems to operate optimally can free up the focal visual sense for other uses in performance (Schmidt and Wrisberg 2008). Performers can train to become more responsive to their other senses and to direct their awareness effectively to enhance their performance. As such, we stand to gain from the application and transfer of this body of knowledge to the field of dance (Hamill and Knutzen 1995; Kandel, Schwartz, and Jesell 1991; Magill 2001; Schmidt and Wrisberg 2008).

Movement Experience: *Becoming Aware of Visual Dominance.* Stand with your eyes closed to return awareness to the proprioceptive sensing and the shifting your body is doing at all times in order to maintain upright posture against the pull of gravity. Because our vision is so dominant, we are not even aware of all of this movement with our eyes open. Our attention is captured by the visual input. With the eyes still closed, shift the weight from both feet to one foot, back to two feet and then to the other foot. Notice how difficult a simple weight transfer becomes when vision is taken away. Open your eyes slowly, trying to stay with your increased internal awareness as the external environment enters your consciousness via your eyes. This movement experience highlights the importance of increasing our awareness of the other senses and what they can contribute to balance and motion. This awareness is vital for dancers, who may, for example, be placed under blinding lights in performance situations.

Central and Peripheral Vision

The visual field is an approximately 180-degree workspace where visual information is detected by the optical sensory receptors (Magill 2007, 125). This visual field is broken down into the central and peripheral visual fields, terms more familiar to most than the focal and ambient visual systems (see Figure 4.3, Visual Field). The central visual field comprises approximately 90 degrees of the space in front of the retina, while the peripheral visual field accounts for the remaining 45 degrees on either side (Schmidt and Wrisberg 2004). In general, the central and peripheral visual fields correspond to the focal and ambient visual systems. The central visual field is related to focal vision, and the peripheral visual field is related to the ambient visual system. However it is important to note that the ambient system also operates in the central visual field (Magill 2001; Schmidt and Wrisberg 2004).

Movement Experience: *Partners Mirroring with Central and Peripheral Vision.* Pair up with someone, face each other, and decide who will lead first. Leader: move relatively slowly and without changing facings or fronts. Follower: focus your eyes on the body part(s) moving or capturing your attention most readily. After several minutes, the person following shift focus to look beyond your partner's shoulder. Keep mirroring for several minutes. Then switch leaders. Compare the two focal experiences. Most people will find that they can actually follow more accurately when not looking directly at the lead person. Engaging the peripheral vision and utilizing the ambient system provides more information more quickly than using the focal system to identify individual parts of a whole movement (Schmidt and Wrisberg 2008).

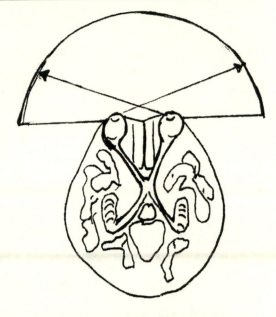

Figure 4.3 The Visual Field.

Interplay of Visual and Kinesthetic Systems

The value in training the other senses becomes clearer when we remember that visual information is not always correct or even the sensory information we are interested in using during dance class or performance (Magill 2007). Consider students tending to cue off of others rather than trusting themselves. The dancers being imitated may or may not be doing the movement "correctly," and even if they are accurate, the students busy following are probably not attending to how they are doing the movement as much as they are worrying about what they should be doing. As such, sometimes directing the learners' attention to other sensory information is more effective for enhancing performance (Schmidt and Wrisberg 2008).

Ideally, dancers learn to pair vision with kinesthetic input and use both optimally. As we saw in the previous movement experience, one way to achieve this pairing is to avoid fixing on a point(s). This allows a dancer to access both the proprioceptive and the ambient visual systems, which can sometimes provide more reliable and faster feedback (Magill 2007; Schmidt and Wrisberg 2008). However, when creating movement experiences to highlight use of the ambient and proprioceptive systems, it is important to remember that the ambient system is difficult to self-detect, except perhaps when traveling through space or when optical flow patterns within the environment are enhanced (as when other people are moving in the space, or when moving the head while standing). It is also important for dancers to practice "splitting" their awareness between bodily and visual sensory input to enable them to attend to both kinesthetic and environmental stimuli simultaneously.

Movement Experience: *Partner Pushing Hands: Conscious Pairing of Pro-*

prioception and the Peripheral Visual Field. Get a partner and stand approximately arm's length away from each other. Designate a leader and a follower. Touch palms with your partner so that your fingertips point toward the ceiling (hyperextend at the wrist joints), and relax your elbows down toward the floor. Slowly move your pairs of hands together in a circle going clockwise in the horizontal plane (the leader's side). While you are doing this motion, attend to the kinesthetic information you are receiving from

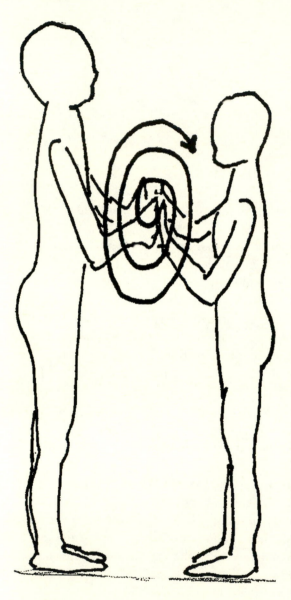

different areas of your body, such as your feet, knees, and hips, as well as your hands. Try to create as fluid and smooth a motion with your partner as possible, and focus on sensing with your whole body, not just your eyes. Try to experience the interplay between inner (you) and outer (partner). Stop and take a moment before you begin again in the counterclockwise direction. At the end of this exercise, take a few moments to share with your partner what you saw and/or felt during this exercise. Some possible points to discuss would be: Where were you looking? What did you see? Faces, the room, or both? What do we use to sense besides our eyes? How does feeling or hearing inform seeing?

Take a few minutes to walk through the space, focusing attention on specific body parts (feet, knees, ribs, etc.) without losing visual presence. Visual presence means being aware of the external environment as well as internal sensation. Notice if you can see the room and feel how you are walking at the same time. Try alternating, focusing attention on feeling, then seeing, then both together. Which is easier? This movement experience highlights the roles of proprioception and vision in movement production by utilizing a partner to simultaneously direct attention to these two sensory systems. This experience of dual awareness is then transferred to solo performance in walking.

Figure 4.4 Movement Experience: Partner Push Hands.

Vestibular-Ocular Reflex and Other Reflexes Affecting Movement Choices and Habits

The role of vision in regulating the righting reflexes that are so important for balance should also be considered in dance training. As we discussed in Chapter 3, the vestibular system of the inner ear senses the movement of the head. This component of the kinesthetic sense is actually connected to the involuntary muscles controlling the motion of the eyes (Kandel, Schwartz, and Jesell 1991). Upon detecting motion of the body and the head, the vestibular system signals the eye muscles to respond so that the eyes move, stabilizing the visual image (Rose and Christina 2006, 119; Todd 1937, 103). This response is sometimes referred to as the "doll's eye reflex," as the moveable eyes of a doll do essentially the same thing (Mareib 1992, 530; see Figure 4.5, Doll's Eye Reflex). Clearly this reflex is desirable so that the visual image is constant and not jumping around whenever we move in space. Of course we also can override this reflex to track objects in space — following the motion of others or our own body parts with the eyes (Rose and Christina 2006). Understanding this optic righting reflex and eye-tracking can assist us with analyzing tendencies and preferences in dance.

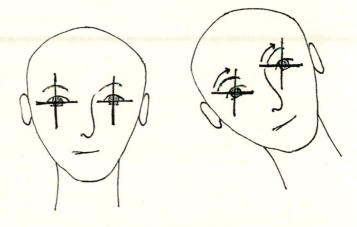

Figure 4.5 Doll's Eye Reflex.

Movement Experience: *The Vestibular-Ocular Reflex: Changing Focus While Moving.* Find a partner and face each other. Experiment with turning your heads, keeping your eyes fixed on each other. Then turn heads, tracking with the eyes so that your eyes are moving with your head. Now one at a time try turning your head and moving the eyes in the opposite direction. Have your partner watch to see if you are successful! Notice the tension that is involved in this action.

Rise on the balls of your feet. Look in different directions. Turn the head side to side, scanning the room. Look up and down. Tilt the head. Notice the difference between balancing with the eyes held constant as opposed to moving the focus. Go into an arch or upper back bend keeping the eyes forward. Try the action with the eyes following passively. Then think of leading the arch with the eyes. You might imagine watching a bug crawling up the wall onto the ceiling. Contrast these experiences. Perform a simple port de bra, or movement of the arms. Compare the experience of fixing the focus forward toward the audience or mirror with following the motion of the arms with the eyes. Watch each other in groups to see how the movement changes with the corresponding changes of the head and eyes.

Teaching Tip: Per the vestibular-ocular reflex, fixing the eyes provides dancers with increased stability. However, one of the goals of dance training is to prepare dancers to fulfill varied choreographic demands. Moving the head and eyes freely affects the quality and intention of an action, and should be a choice available to dancers without sacrificing balance. Therefore, it is important to train the ability to change focus in movement for greater expressivity and versatility.

It is the authors' hypothesis that when people concentrate on doing unfamiliar eye motions or using their eyes in new ways it can lead to dizziness and/or nausea. While we believe this hypothesis is particularly true with eye activities, any kind of truly new experience may evoke this kind of disoriented response. This phenomena has consequences for both the teacher and the dancer. Dancers can take solace in knowing that this reaction is normal and that it will probably dissipate as the action becomes more familiar. Not all students will experience negative physical reactions to new experiences, but students who do should be encouraged to rest for a few minutes and to get back into class when they feel ready. If discomfort persists, teachers might consider providing simpler variations of the movement experience, either in class or as homework, which will allow the student to participate more fully. Creating a bridge for dancers who have adverse reactions to particular kinds of explorations is extra work, but necessary. Unless issues are addressed, those students get stuck on the side of the classroom and are, in a sense, enabled in only participating in what they already can do or know.

Learning and Programming Movement

Modeling is an effective way of teaching movement. Many aspects of movement that are difficult to describe verbally can be conveyed through demonstration. Additionally, delaying the imitation and watching before doing improves learning (Schmidt and Wrisberg 2008, 233). The cognitive effort that goes into first watching and then recalling and reproducing movement improves the ability to retain movement, although it is more difficult and less successful initially than following along with the demonstration (Coker 2009).

We do not replicate movement by directing certain muscles. We create a mental picture of the desired movement based on the instructor's words or actions, and the brain programs the body to fulfill that intent (Schmidt and Wrisberg 2008). However, it is very important to keep in mind that "the result is successful in proportion to our power of interpretation and amount of experience, but most of all perhaps to the *desire to do*" (Todd 1937, 33). So teachers need to be mindful of the accuracy of their demonstrations and consider elements such as showing the movement from different angles. Care should also be taken to emphasize pertinent aspects of the movement. Of course modeling cannot be effective if students are not actively and willingly engaged in observing the demonstration (Coker 2009).

Movement Experience: *Flash Phrase for Learning and Programming Movement.* Students: Observe a relatively complex movement or dance phase three times, without any verbal directions. Take a couple of minutes to replicate what you remember. Focus on doing your own version, while staying as true to the original as possible. Individual interpretation is to be expected. The goal here is to heighten visual acuity and the ability to replicate movement without overanalysis. Sometimes it is more important to see the big picture without getting hungup on the minutia. As you are working on the phrase, shift your attention to how the phrase feels. View in groups. With practice, students can become more adept at picking up visual information quickly. Clearly this skill is important for aspiring dancers.

Visualization or Imagery

In visualization or mental rehearsal techniques, we are bypassing the eyes and are going right to the mental picture being used to program movement. Since it is not just what we see that is important, but the interconnections between vision and other modes of learning, imaging seems relevant to this discussion of the visual system and dance performance. The benefits of visualization or mental rehearsal have long been recognized in dance education (Dowd 1990; Franklin 1996; Sweigard 1974; Todd 1937). Visualization is based on the concept that, given the correct image, the mind will begin to establish neuromuscular pathways that correspond to the actual motor performance of the movement (Coker 2009, 201; Todd 1937, 281; Rose and Christina 2006, 284). Instead of the eyes generating the image and conveying it to the motor cortex as in modeling, the imagination generates the image. As with modeling, the success of the image will be dependent upon its specificity and accuracy. The richer the image, the more effective mental rehearsal will be in improving performance (Hardy 1997; Martin, Moritz, and Hall 1999).

Movement Experience: *Mental Rehearsal.* Lie down in the constructive rest position, supine with the legs bent and both feet on the floor. Cross your arms over your chest, and let the knees touch or rest against each other (Sweigard 1974, 215). Take a few moments to mentally rehearse or visualize your "flash phrase" from before with your eyes closed. Open your eyes, and consider whether you were mentally doing the flash phrase and watching yourself as if you were in a movie or if you were inside your body doing the flash phrase. Now do it again, but this time do the opposite. If you first visualized yourself externally, try it again as an internal visualization and vice versa. Which one was easier for you to do? Now, mentally rehearse or visualize the

Figure 4.6 Visualization of Being Grounded or Rooted (Julie Brodie in "Uprooted," choreographed by Kora Radella; photograph by Marcella Hackbardt).

"flash phrase" from inside your body (internal) and try to make the visualization even richer and more detailed than previously.

When you are done, open your eyes, stand up, and physically do the flash phrase. How has it changed for you? Take a few moments as a group to share your discoveries. For enhancing motor performance, internal visualization is perceived to be more optimal than external (Schmidt and Wrisberg 2008). Regardless of the type of visualization utilized, mental rehearsal, just like physical rehearsal, takes practice to become fully useful to the performer (Coker 2009).

Performance Focus

"Focus is to the mind what gravity is to the body — a basic force" (Koner 1993, 5). In addition to being sensory organs, the eyes and the manner in which performers focus their attention are vital to the ability to communicate and connect with the

Figure 4.7 Visualization of Movement Phrase.

audience. The concentration of the eyes and mind together create the different types of projection observed in performance focus. As part of this state, the eyes must really see, not stare. The eyes and the mind are working as one because the visual image is registering consciously, and it is this immersion in the experience that captures an audience's attention. Focus can be described in many ways, but for our purposes we will divide it into three categories: internal, external immediate and external horizon. Each has distinct qualities and functions in performance.

Movement Experience: *Performing with Different Foci.* Internal: Begin moving however you wish, but using an internal focus, and staying within your self-space. With this focus, the performer's attention is directed internally. There is little acknowledgement of the environment, other performers, or the audience. The eyes may be shut or lowered to begin with, but eventually try to change where the eyes look without losing the sense of solitude or isolation. This inward or "soft" focus may help dancers connect with internal impulses and sensations (Bartenieff and Lewis 1980). This focus can be a qualitative performance choice or a tool for enhancing kinesthetic awareness. As discussed, listening to the body by increasing awareness of kinesthetic feedback is just as important as being aware of the external environment.

External immediate: Continue moving any way you want, but shift your awareness to the environment immediately around you. Really see the room, the people around you, even your own body or the audience as it comes into your field of vision. Notice if or how this focus changes your movement. This focus is probably the most frequently used in contemporary modern dance. Experiment with attending to the environment without losing the kinesthetic awareness you engaged previously. This is what is sometimes referred to as "presence in movement," and it tends to give the movement a more natural or pedestrian quality.

External horizon: Now move through the space any way you want and project "out to the balcony." Look way beyond the confines of the room, beyond the stage, even beyond the audience. Feel as if you are able to see forever, like looking out over the plains or out to sea. Maintain a sense of the immediate environment, but focus on projecting beyond. Notice if or how this alters your movement. This focus is frequently used in ballet or traditional modern dance forms. It tends to give the movement a more presentational quality.

After exploring all three foci improvisationally, try layering them onto the "flashing" or other set phrases. Show in groups and see if your peers can notice the difference. Discuss the impact of each focus on their perception of the phrase.

Applications to Teaching and Performance: Food for Thought

Many components of the visual sense and other related aspects of learning and performing movement have been introduced separately up to this point. However, as already noted, nothing works in isolation. What follows are common issues or experiences students and teachers may have that reflect the complex interactions between systems involved in movement production. Synthesizing the information in relation to specific movement applications can be a practical approach to this topic.

Significance of performance focus. Performance focus is important artistically, as it alters the quality or intention of the choreography. But thinking about the kind of focus being used and really seeing also occupy the conscious mind. This is beneficial in performance so the attention does not stray; once performers start thinking about the fact that they are performing or start evaluating their performance, it can be detrimental. Daniel Nagrin's motto was, "The shortest distance to the audience is through the other actor" (Nagrin 1997, 44). In other words, the audience can tell if a performer is fully invested in what he or she is doing.

In addition, the ambient visual system and the kinesthetic systems can work optimally on the subconscious level if the mind is focused on focus, rather than judging or controlling actions. Making specific choices about performance focus can be an effective use of focal vision, engaging the conscious mind to allow the body to access its own wisdom, or nonconscious means of interpreting visual and kinesthetic cues (Gallwey 1976; Schmidt and Wrisberg 2008). This can be explained in terms of the Bliss-Boder Hypothesis: "Performance is sometimes impaired by instructions that encourage performers to engage in conscious activities demanding attention and controlled processing. This is particularly true for high-level performers who have developed many elegant, nonconscious processes for detecting and processing visual and kinesthetic information, along with very fast and effective processes for making corrections based on this information. If these individuals are forced out of these nonconscious modes of processing (by coaches' instructions, thoughts about not making mistakes, or whatever) and into the more conscious, controlled information-processing activities, their performance usually suffers" (Schmidt and Wrisberg 2008, 100).

Challenges inherent in taking the head off center and/or shifting visual focus. Understanding the vestibular-ocular reflex may help both students and teachers deal with reluctance to move away from vertical or to let the head and eyes follow the motion of the body in space. The unconscious, reflexive attempt to keep both eyes level becomes the dominant righting reflex, and this explains how difficult it can be to balance with the eyes closed or tilted off center (Fitt 1996). This points to the importance of training to increase awareness and sensitivity to all the sensory input we have available to us. Regularly including class exercises that employ eye tracking, tilting the body, and turning the head help build balance and confidence via kinesthetic feedback.

Additionally with regard to this reflex we should consider Todd's (1937, 103) statement from *The Thinking Body*: "While rocking the head as a delicately balanced weight, note how the eyes move automatically against the direction of the head and how their vision is kept focused on the horizon. The eyes and neck muscles are being adjusted at the same time by their primary reflexes through the labyrinthine mechanism. When an attempt is made to keep the eyes directed so as to move with the head instead of against it, the primary reflexes have to be interrupted, which at once brings a sense of strain and tension." This accounts for the tension experienced when trying to look opposite to the motion of the head as in Movement Experience: The Vestibular-Ocular Reflex: Changing Focus While Moving. It also has application in the classroom. As teachers we are all familiar with the "sneaking a peek out of the corner of the eyes syndrome." Teachers might encourage students to go ahead and look. Looking out of the corner of the eyes creates tension because it is working against the reflex to keep the eyes stable. Freeing up the head and neck then frees up the rest of the body (and the psyche), which contributes to a positive learning situation.

A final thought on the eye-head relationship: leading actions with the eyes changes the organization of the body. The eyes may reflexively want to stay stable as the head moves, but if the eyes move, the head will want to follow. The head leading the body in space is an organic and efficient response, as is clearly demonstrated by an infant looking up from a prone position, or by a cat stalking its prey (Alexander 1932; Todd 1937). Taking advantage of these reflexes, as well as recognizing the difficulties inherent in opposing them, is vital to effective movement/dance training.

Issues in absorption and retention of verbal correction. Visual information can be applied to movement correction and external feedback. This application may be particularly helpful when the kinesthetic sense is misleading, or "debauched" (Alexander 1932; Gallwey 1976). For example, physically bringing the rib cage forward in someone with excessive lordosis may give him or her the sensation of falling forward. Telling the student to bring the ribs forward or to stop arching back is ineffective because for him or her it feels right to have the ribs back. One way to address this is for students to really see what is happening. The mirror can be helpful in this situation, but then students must feel the new placement in order to transfer the correction to performance.

Teaching Tip: When providing feedback, several ideas emerge from this information regarding vision and learning. As teachers we should be aware of and vary our use of cue words, including whether they are based on sensory or cognitive information: for example, see and look (visual); feel and sense (kinesthetic); hear and detect (auditory); think and compare (analytical) (Coker 2004, 123). Corrections that utilize multiple sensory systems and ways of processing reach a greater variety of learners. Just as pairing kinesthetic, visual, and manual guidance techniques may be a more effective way of initially presenting material. Movement correction is an ideal place to employ verbal imagery that appeals to the different senses as well.

"Spacing out" or blank staring in class. Staring sometimes occurs when there is nothing interesting to capture visual attention, or when one kind of vision is being engaged for a long period of time. Applying Laban's concept of exertion and recuperation, when one focal system is being used for a period of time, care should be taken to switch to the other system (Hackney 1998). This switch can alleviate strain and rejuvenate focus.

Teachers can evaluate how a given type of activity is engaging vision. For example, stationary movement work (as at the barre) lends itself to using focal vision, as does gestural movement work. Center work that locomotes through the space relates to the ambient system. So if students are beginning to freeze up focally during barre work, taking a few minutes to move across the floor may help. Or if students are glazing over while moving through the space, having them consciously see where they are by noticing details about fellow students or the room can provide a break from the emphasis on ambient vision.

Teaching Tip: Sometimes the fixing of focus occurs when students are glued to the mirror or when their minds wander as a result of knowing movements well. To get away from the mirror, direct learners' attention to the space by having them notice the environment they are in during class. Periodically turning away from or covering the mirror is a good idea. In situations where students are dancing on autopilot, teachers can shift attention to the body by using kinesthetic cue words, such as feel the floor with your foot, or by bringing awareness to the other sensory systems, such as sounds, smells, touch, even taste. Revisiting performance focus and the importance of practicing concentration of the mind may also be helpful. The Bliss-Boder Hypothesis suggests that emphasizing performance focus is also beneficial for students working either too internally or too analytically (Schmidt and Wrisberg 2008). Another common scenario for staring is when students are learning "new" movement. Again, they may be focusing ineffectively. Encouraging a holistic view of the demonstration and directing attention to pertinent aspects of the movement may be useful in this situation.

Combating performance anxiety and narrowing of the visual field. In Chapter 2 we discussed the sympathetic nervous system and the flight or fight response (also known by performers as stage fright or performance nerves) in terms of the breath (Kamen 2001). The narrowing of the visual field that occurs with this response, or tunnel vision, evolved as a mechanism to block out all input but that needed to escape a threatening situation and survive. As with many of the physiological changes associated with the fight or flight response, this narrowing of the perceptual field is neither beneficial nor necessary in performance situations. The opposite is actually true: performers want to have as much information about the environment as possible (Schmidt and Wrisberg 2008).

We have considered the notion of breath control as a mechanism for lowering arousal level. Under stressful situations, the breath gets shallower and faster; the mind is affecting the body. The reverse is also true: if you can control your breathing, the mind becomes calmer too. We would like to propose that vision may work in the same way, although further study is needed. If performers consciously override the perceptual narrowing that occurs with performance anxiety, they may be able to lower their arousal level, which ultimately will enhance performance. Therefore, occupying the conscious mind with performance focus and reminding dancers to really see may actually help combat performance nerves, in addition to being important in the other ways already noted.

Conclusions

With more knowledge about how the visual system operates, including its interaction with other ways of sensing, learning, and performing movement, teaching strategies can maximize the visual potential. As Timothy Gallway (1976,7) says in *The Inner Game of Tennis*, "Images are better than words, showing better than telling, too much instruction worse than none, and (that) trying often produces negative results." This quote speaks to the role of vision in learning dance. Then, in perform-

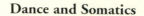

Figure 4.1 "Vision" (Karen Snouffer).

ance situations, the visual system should be used to navigate and negotiate space, people, and objects in the environment. Placing the learner's attention on performance focus and the environment is actually reinforcing innate functions and interactions of the exteroceptive systems and the proprioceptive systems (Abernathy 1999; Magill 2001, 223). Dance classes should reflect an awareness of the powerful role of vision in learning and performing movement, as expert performers utilize visual information more effectively than nonexpert performers (Abernathy 1999; Magill 2007, 283). In order to achieve this goal, teachers need to understand the relationship of the two visual systems to each other, to other modes of sensing and processing information, to verbal feedback, and to their effects on motor performance.

5

Connectivity to Self,
the Environment and Others

In tai chi, practitioners are considered to be either turtles or fish. A turtle swims by just using its limbs. A fish swims by using its whole body. Be a fish. —Wedlake 2005, 11

How often have you, as a teacher or a student, heard (or perhaps given) a comment about a dancer being disconnected? What does this really mean? Disconnected from what? Often when we talk about connecting or disconnecting in dance we are referring to the core-distal relationship, but other ways of connecting are also important in movement. Having a sense of the connections in the body and an ability to be grounded, or connected to the environment are needed for optimal control, power, and efficiency. Connectivity involves understanding the structural and functional capacity of the body to resist, yield, or amplify the forces at play in movement. This principle of connectivity is central to somatic work, as various techniques address it in some way or another and with many overlapping ideas (Alexander 1932; Bainbridge-Cohen 1993; Bartenieff and Lewis 1980; Feldenkrais 2010; Hackney 1998). However, it is in this arena that we see very specific ways of defining connectivity and a concurrent idiosyncratic use of language. Understanding both the similarities and differences between somatic techniques and approaches is helpful. The similarities reveal truths about the underlying developmental, structural, and functional organization of the body and its optimal coordination. The differences between somatic techniques is revealing of preferences and priorities that make certain methods resonate more or less with individual students and teachers.

In an attempt to parse out the topic of connectivity, we consider our potential to connect on three basic tiers: to ourselves, to the environment, and to others. In this chapter, we examine how the choices we make with regard to connecting on these different levels influence movement outcomes. As connectivity is intimately associated with forces in movement, physical laws governing motion are presented and related to the dancing body. Investigation of the developmental patterns that are at the core of connectivity assist with identification and exploration of different ways of experiencing connectivity and talking about connectivity with the goal of making this important movement fundamental more successfully applicable to dance technique.

We provide connectivity-based movement experiences on the floor, standing, traveling through space, and in partner and creative work to assist with transfer to class work. The goal with the material in this chapter is to give dancers choice in how to respond to forces that challenge connectivity, as this has direct implications for the execution of movement and its perceived intention.

Forces in Movement

As connectivity is related to our ability to make choices when responding to forces (either internal or external), it is helpful to first look at some of the physical laws dictating how forces act on the body. Not only does this knowledge base assist with understanding connectivity, it can be a rich source of class material to explore. First the origin of the force must be considered: whether it is generated within the body itself or externally, and whether it is an active or a passive force (Griffiths 2006; Hall 2003; Hamill and Knutzen 1995; Serway and Faughn 1992). For those who like a formula:

$$\text{Force} = \text{mass} \times \text{acceleration} \ (F = m \times a)$$

Internal forces. Internal forces are those generated by the body itself (Griffiths 2006; Hall 2003; Hamill and Knutzen 1995; Serway and Faughn 1992). The most obvious example would be the active force of muscles contracting to create movement. However, other forces are at play at all times, whether or not we are aware of them. Internal forces can be broken down further into two basic categories:

1. Active: Muscle contraction, which requires the input of energy. It is important to remember that maximal force is not always needed to accomplish a given action (Griffiths 2006; Hall 2003; Hamill and Knutzen 1995; Serway and Faughn 1992).

2. Passive: All tissue resists elongation. Taking into account the reciprocal pairing of muscles around joints, as one muscle group contracts, the opposing muscle group is stretched. Ligaments, muscles, tendons, and even skin provide passive force resisting movement initiated by the opposing muscles (Nordin and Frankel 2001). This is why static stretching is beneficial; if there is less resistance to an action because of increased flexibility, it reduces the effort needed and the risk of tearing the reciprocal muscle (Alter 2004; Clippinger 2007).

External forces. External forces are those that originate from outside the body (Griffiths 2006; Hall 2003; Hamill and Knutzen 1995; Serway and Faughn 1992). Again, they can be broken down into two main categories:

1. Gravity: In dance, we must always take the action of gravity into consideration. It is a constant factor in human movement: we can move against it, with it, or maintain a position by countering its effect. Gravity pulls any mass toward earth on a vertical

line from the point of support. The pull of gravity is proportional to the mass of the body or body part under consideration (Griffiths 2006; Hall 2003; Hamill and Knutzen 1995; Serway and Faughn 1992).

Movement Experience: *Gravity.* Flex at the hips and allow the arms to hang. The line of gravity goes through the center of the shoulder joints, and the arms naturally hang down. Any movement away from that hanging position of the arms requires muscular effort against the pull of gravity. Try moving an arm in any direction, and feel the engagement of the muscles as you experiment with moving away from the line of gravity.

Now lie on your back and lift one arm to the ceiling. Make concentric circles with the arm, gradually getting bigger and then smaller, going away from vertical and then back to it. Repeat with one leg, noting the pull of gravity when off vertical. Feel the balanced center point where the least muscular input is needed. Notice the difference in the pull of gravity between the arm and the heavier leg.

2. Applied load: An applied load is an outside force acting on the body (Griffiths 2006; Hall 2003; Hamill and Knutzen 1995; Serway and Faughn 1992). The force can be applied to the whole body or to part of the body. Examples would include getting pushed or lifted by another dancer. It could also mean initiating movement by pushing or pulling one of your own body parts (pushing the head to the side is an applied load to your head).

Movement Experience: *Applied Load.* While standing, lift one leg. Note the active and passive internal forces at play, and consider the external force of gravity pulling the leg back down. Now push your leg down with your hand to experience an applied load.

Newton's Laws of Motion

While physics formulas and definitions of forces may seem unrelated to dance teaching and technique, it can be helpful to break these concepts down and apply them to movement. "The most skilled dancer has learned how to work with and to use the laws of nature and physics, whether those ideas were openly introduced into training or an individual dancer intuitively used those laws" (Hays 1981, 2, as cited in Ranney 1988, 139). As teachers, we should not assume that all dancers will arrive at an intuitive understanding of how to manipulate these basic principles unassisted. As with the kinesthetic sense, sometimes the intuitive becomes clouded by efforts to imitate shape and form, rather than feeling and doing what is needed. Individual differences also affect outcomes (Coker 2009; Fleishman 1962; Schmidt and Wrisberg 2008). Understanding that quick direction changes will be more difficult for a larger person helps circumvent frustration and self-deprecation, while understanding what is needed to achieve the quick shifts provides a sense of empowerment. Shifting awareness to forces in the body and acting on the body is one way to begin addressing the issue of connectivity. Let us begin with a quick review of Newton's Laws of Motion (Griffiths 2006; Hall 2003; Hamill and Knutzen 1995; Serway and Faughn 1992).

The Law of Inertia. A body in motion tends to remain in motion at the same speed and moving in a straight line. A body at rest tends to remain at rest unless acted on by a force. Inertia is resistance to action or change. Starting, stopping, and changing directions all require force provided by muscles, so clearly an understanding of inertia is needed in dance technique. Inertia varies with the mass of the object: the larger the person or part, the greater the inertia (Griffiths 2006; Hall 2003; Hamill and Knutzen 1995; Serway and Faughn 1992).

The Law of Acceleration. Acceleration is the result of force divided by mass or $a = F/m$. It is the rate of change in velocity. Changes in the acceleration of the body occur in the same direction as the force that caused it. As the formula indicates, changes in acceleration are directly proportional to force and inversely proportional to the mass of the body. This means that more force is required to accelerate a larger person the same amount as a smaller person (Griffiths 2006; Hall 2003; Hamill and Knutzen 1995; Serway and Faughn 1992). Think of the result of pushing a child and a football player with the same amount of energy. We know intuitively who will move faster.

The Law of Reaction. For every action there is an equal and opposite reaction. This law is extremely important to understand so that it can be manipulated in dance as it applies to all forces, both internal and external. Consider the action of jumping. We push down, and the earth pushing back equally (or the ground reaction force) is what enables us to become airborne. Ground reaction forces are necessary for the take-off in running, changes in direction, and even to establish a solid base from which to do gestural work. We use the Law of Reaction both to overcome inertia and to accelerate movement (Griffiths 2006; Hall 2003; Hamill and Knutzen 1995; Serway and Faughn 1992).

Movement Experience: *Using Newton's Laws Part 1.* Run forward six steps. Stop and change direction quickly to run backward. As suddenly as possible, gallop to the right side. Stop quickly and move to the left. Inertia was at play when standing and initiating the run forward. It is even more apparent when changing direction. Feel how you have to push into the ground to start and stop. The ground pushing back is what provides the force (Law of Reaction). The amount of speed generated is related to the amount of energy invested in the pushing force. The same amount of force will make a smaller person move faster than a larger person (Law of Acceleration). Also consider what optimized the ability to push off and use the internal forces of the muscles most effectively. Connecting the energy of the legs to the torso and arms (and vice versa) allows the body to work as a unit.

Movement Experience: *Using Newton's Laws Part 2.* Facing a partner, join hands. Pull away from your partner, allowing the hips, knees, and ankles to crease, and gently rounding through the spine. Keeping your hips above your feet, counterbalance the weight of your partner. This position does not need to be static, but can move as desired. Enjoy the stretch through the back, and become aware of the connection of the arms to the torso and the legs to the ground. One partner: apply more energy, pulling the other past without releasing hands. Repeat with the other person initiating the pull past (this can be done as an across-the-floor activity).

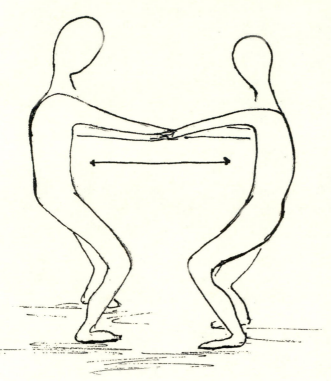

Teaching Tip: Have students analyze how all three of Newton's Laws play into the simple movement sequences above. Identify the forces that were utilized or that needed to be overcome. Students can then work in groups to make their own phrase, exemplifying how these laws are pertinent to dance through their movement choices.

Figure 5.2 Movement Experience: Using Newton's Law Part 2.

Structural Connectivity

"Connectedness refers to the dynamic alignment of the weight-bearing structure, the skeleton, in movement as well as stillness. It allows the flow, the movement impulse, to pass through the body in such a way that complete activation can be realized most efficiently — without unnecessary exertion and stress" (Barteneiff and Lewis 1980, 21). The body and its structural connections are amazingly complex. To gain a holistic view, we need to recognize these connections on different levels. Logically, the connective tissues are instrumental in creating this structural connectivity, as they permeate the human body (Biel 2010; Nordin and Frankel 2001). Among the connective tissues, the skeleton is the base of support and provides the leverage for motion. However, the soft tissues are what determine many of the functional patterns that enable us to move through our lives and the world around us. Ligaments connect the bones to each other, tendons connect muscles to bones, and fascia interpenetrates and surrounds muscles, bones, organs, nerves, blood vessels and other structures (Biel 2010; Nordin and Frankel 2001).

Movement Experience: *Bone-Feeling.* Getting a sense of the bony structure of the body and its parts is helpful in visualizing and accessing structural connectivity. Trace the bones of your feet with your fingers. Really palpate (explore through touch) as many bony landmarks as possible. Start with the medial and lateral malleoli of the ankles and explore the connection to the talus. Go through the full range of motion at this joint. Move down to the tarsals and find the connection of the Achilles tendon at the tuberosity of

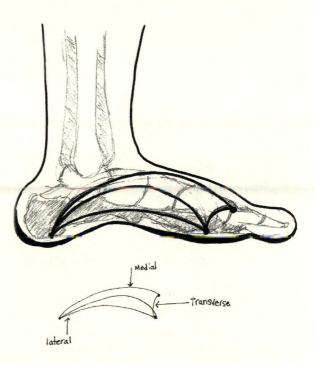

Figure 5.3 The Arches of the Right Foot.

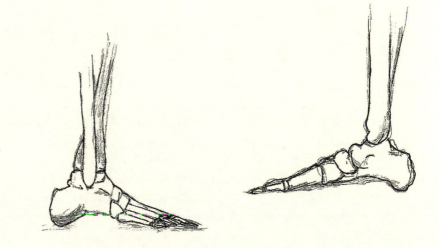

Figure 5.4 The Architecture of the Foot.

the calcaneous. Massage in between the metatarsals and feel the three arches (medial and lateral longitudinal and transverse). Place both feet together and see how the arches combine to make a cavern. Move down to the toes and palpate the two phalanges of the big toe and the three phalanges of the lateral four digits. Pull out gently on each toe with a circular action, providing traction or elongating and creating space between each of the phalanges. When finished, stand up and feel the weight of the body being transferred into the floor through the bones of the feet.

Fascia is a continuous, three-dimensional network of tissue that is distributed throughout the body: from head to toe, from front to back, from interior to exterior (Biel 2010; Carola, Harley, and Noback 1992; Clippinger 2007; Nordin and Frankel 2001; Rolf 1989). It is responsible for maintaining structural integrity, for providing support and protection, and for absorbing shock. It can be categorized as superficial, deep, and visceral. As it covers the body structures on all levels, it is instrumental in disseminating forces throughout the body (Biel 2010; Carola, Harley, and Noback 1992; Clippinger 2007; Juhan 1998; Nordin and Frankel 2001; Rolf 1989).

Teaching Tip: While on the topic of connective tissues and structural integrity, it is important to remember that an inverse relationship exists between stability and mobility. Dancers tend to think that more mobility is always better, but increased mobility means decreased stability. Every body is different in its structural stability, or the "tightness" of its connections. Some of this can be safely altered through stretching, but changing the structural integrity has consequences and trade-offs. For example, stretching ligaments will decrease the stability of a joint, and additional muscular effort will need to be exerted to maintain positioning and joint integrity (Clippinger 2007; Nordin and Frankel 2001). Again, knowledge is a tool of empowerment and will assist both dancers and teachers with safe and effective training practices.

Functional Connectivity

Because of its structural connections, the body is one kinetic chain. This statement merely means that movement of one part affects the rest (Clippinger 2007, 29). As we have discussed, this has implications for alignment, because spot fixing, or correcting the placement of just one piece, will alter forces acting on the remainder of the body. It also has implications for how we respond to forces being applied in movement. For example, when we push off the floor, the ground reaction forces will (can) ripple throughout the body, not just stay isolated to the foot or even the leg. Recognition of this is necessary for total body integration and coordinated and efficient action.

Movement Experience: *Functional Connectivity.* Try doing an inversion (handstand), either with the assistance of a partner or against a wall. While upside-down, think of really pushing into the floor with the hands and creating one long line from hands to feet. Feel how this action connects through the entire body. Be careful not to look up — remember that the head and neck are part of the spinal alignment. Changing the orientation of the body by supporting on the arms can be helpful in experiencing total body connectivity.

Developmental Patterns

Developmental patterns reflect the interplay between reflexes and the structural and functional connectivity of the body. This sequential and progressive growth of movement ability or coordination evolves in humans from birth through the process of learning to walk, and these patterns remain a basis for all movement learned from that point on (Bainbridge-Cohen 1993; Fiorentino 1981; Hackney 1998; Haywood and Getchell 2009; Mills and Bainbridge-Cohen 1990). Traditionally, in somatic thinking the optimal integration of the whole body necessitates mastering and progressing through these various patterns, or movement skills, in order. Current scientific research negates this belief. For example, children that do not crawl do not necessarily have difficulties later in life (Gabbard 2008; Haywood and Getchell 2009). However, major unresolved gaps in the developmental progression or distortion of an existing pattern will probably be evident in movement skills. Frequently, this may also have implications for functioning in other areas of life, such as cognitive or emotional development, as any hindrance to full experience has ramifications beyond motor control. Fortunately, anecdotal evidence also shows that any missing links in the developmental progression can be restored at any point in time with the proper guidance (Hackney 1998; Mills and Bainbridge-Cohen 1990).

Developmental patterns begin to be established in utero or prenatally. Different classification systems are used, but on the base level, prevertebral and vertebral patterns correspond with our evolutionary heritage. The prevertebral level in humans consists of nonlocomotor, internal patterns sometimes referred to as *cellular movement*, or *pulsing motility* (Bainbridge-Cohen 1993). This is the ebb and flow of the life force present from the time of conception, involving a centerless motion of the whole being. While not a learned pattern, this energy flowing through the body is considered to be central to awareness, comfort, and ease. Cells are the building blocks of life, so we need to start there (Hanna 1979; Juhan 1998). Each cell can be visualized as is its own miniature ecosystem, responding and adapting to the environment around it — moving and connecting with adjacent cells via energy and through the fluid environment. These cells work together to form tissues, organs, systems, and finally, the whole being. Thinking about movement on the smallest level can help us sense this subtle energy as it relates to the whole being. This concept and the following activity are drawn from Body-Mind Centering work (Bainbridge-Cohen 1993; Fiorentino 1981; Hartley 1995; Mills and Bainbridge-Cohen 1990).

Movement Experience: *Partner Cellular Touch.* In partners, one person find a comfortable position lying on the floor. Other partner: rub your hands together briskly to create warmth. Feel the energy emanating from them. Gently place your hands on your partner, noticing the shape of the part contacted. Sense the boundaries of skin touching skin, and then gradually bring awareness to the millions of fluid-filled cells beneath your hands. Move your hands to a new place and notice the response of the tissues. Is there a sense of the skin moving toward the touch? Resisting? Staying the same or unresponsive? Ask your partner to "touch back" without moving. Is there any change? Talk to your partner about both of your experiences, and then change roles.

Prevertebral *radial symmetry* is established by the connection of the baby to the mother via the umbilicus. This connection evolves into the ability to reach out from and come back to the center (Bainbridge-Cohen 1993; Hackney 1998; Mills and Bainbridge-Cohen 1990). Reflexes for flexion (bending in) and extension (lengthening out) enable the body to move fully through this range. After birth the pattern continues to develop, as infants gradually extend out from the fetal position to explore and interact with the surrounding environment. This is the basis of moving from the center, or the core, of the body.

Movement Experience: *Wake-up and Stretch Naval Radiation.* Relaxing on the floor, bring awareness to your breath. Notice the subtle contraction and expansion that occurs with each breath, feeling how this connects to the center of your being. Gradually begin to explore how this expansion and contraction, or condensing and expanding, originating from the center can extend into other parts of the body. Imagine you are just waking up, and it is your morning stretch. Allow this growing and shrinking from the center to mobilize and energize your whole body. Without engaging in a sense of directionality, let the action change your position and orientation. Come to a resting place and notice if there is any change in your sense of center or the energy flowing through to the ends of the limbs.

Vertebrate movement patterns move the body through space. The most basic of these, *Spinal Patterns*, are at the core of the body and the self, as they reflect the organization of the central nervous system, the digestive tract, and our vertical orientation. This midline focus actually begins as prevertebral mouthing, as the food tube runs through the center of the body. This primitive reflex continues to develop into vertebrate patterns, influenced by the human existence that is focused around the vertical axis. From the initial undirected or most basic movement exhibited immediately after birth (radial symmetry), an infant gradually begins to develop spinal patterns as he or she begins looking up and leading the body's movement into space from the eyes and the head (Fiorentino 1981; Haywood and Getchell 2009). This coordination can be clearly seen in animals. Consider the cat stalking its prey and how the head and eyes lead and coordinate the movement. Richly endowed with proprioceptors, the vestibular apparatus, and other organs contributing to the kinesthetic sense, the neck

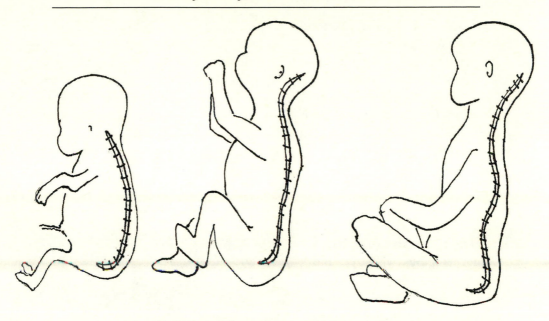

Figure 5.5 The Development of Spinal Curves.

and head are crucial to balance, alignment, and locomotion (Feldenkrais 2005; Haywood and Getchell 2009; Rose and Christina 2006).

As humans, we are challenged by our vertical alignment, as we must balance the weight of the heavy head on top of the spine. To make this possible, we see several evolutionary adjustments. Infants are born with a C curve in the spine. This primary curve is what we see in the fetal position, and it remains throughout life in the form of the thoracic and sacral curves (Carola, Harley, and Noback 1992). As the baby begins to interact with the world, looking up, pushing up from a prone position, and eventually sitting, the cervical vertebrae develop a secondary curve in the opposite direction (Carola, Harley, and Noback 1992). This curve brings the spine under the head to balance its weight. As the child progresses from sitting to crawling to standing, the lumbar vertebrae also develop a secondary curve (Carola, Harley, and Noback 1992). This curve shifts the spine and pelvis into alignment below the rib cage and head.

After the spinal patterns, a series of coordinations begin to emerge through the need and desire to locomote. *Homologous Patterning* works on differentiation between the upper and lower body. Both arms and/or legs move together in pushing and pulling actions (Bainbridge-Cohen 1993; Fiorentino 1981; Hackney 1998; Haywood and Getchell 2009; Mills and Bainbridge-Cohen 1990). A child rocking on all fours in preparation for crawling is demonstrating this kind of upper-lower connectivity. This progresses to *Homolateral Patterning*, which connects the upper and lower units via the right and the left halves of the body (Bainbridge-Cohen 1993; Fiorentino

1981; Hackney 1998; Haywood and Getchell 2009; Mills and Bainbridge-Cohen 1990). Extending the right leg and arm simultaneously is an example. An en chaînés turn in ballet is a dance movement engaging homolateral patterning. In contrast, *Contralateral Patterning* connects the upper and lower via diagonal connections through the body. This is the basis of the opposition we use in walking. Contralateral actions build upon the upper-lower and right-left connections already established to provide for three-dimensional movement in space (Bainbridge-Cohen 1993; Fiorentino 1981; Hackney 1998; Haywood and Getchell 2009; Mills and Bainbridge-Cohen 1990).

Different somatic practices address the concept of connectivity in different ways, so it can be helpful to be aware of the underlying developmental patterns. Consider spinal patterns: In the Alexander Technique, primary control is the guiding principle, where the head leads the body into space. The relationship of the head, neck, and spine, when organized and not restricted, is believed to help achieve whole body coordination and freedom (Alexander 1932, 1969). This principle can be compared to the principle of head-tail connectivity in Laban Movement Analysis/Bartenieff Fundamentals and Body-Mind Centering, or the Line-of-Movement to lengthen the central axis of the trunk upward in Ideokinesis (Hackney 1998; Swiegard 1974). Radial symmetry, or moving from the core of the body, is the foundation of much Pilates work, with its emphasis on the Powerhouse (Silver 2000). This same basic principle is at play in core-distal connectivity in Laban Movement Analysis/Bartenieff Fundamentals and Body-Mind Centering. As we have seen, breath is a connector of the body and a focus of all somatic techniques. Categorizing connectivity in a different way, we can look at and explore the

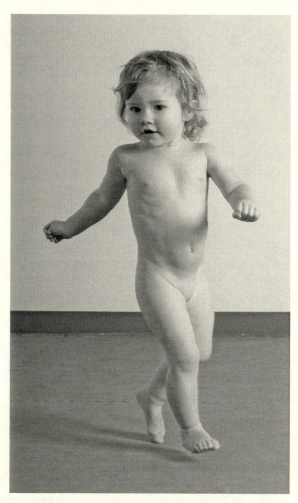

Figure 5.6 Contralateral Pattern (Evi Brodie; photograph by Marcella Hackbardt).

ability to connect internally, externally, and to others. More specific kinds of connectivity can then be applied to each instance, regardless of the somatic-specific terminology utilized.

Teaching Tip: As a class, make a list of different ways of connecting or thinking about connecting. Write on the blackboard or a large piece of paper and post in the classroom to continue adding to, or better yet, write on the mirror with a dry-erase marker. It is fun and almost shocking to blasphemize the traditional use of the mirror like this.

Internal Connectivity

The first tier or level of connectivity that must be established is internal. On this basic level, we can really experience the structural connections within the body. While it is impossible to eliminate external stimuli or forces, reducing their importance to a movement situation can assist dancers with establishing this baseline awareness. This means that forces arising from the body, and the body's response to these forces are of primary concern. The specific kinds of connectivity encountered can be discussed and revisited later, but the initial focus on internal action and reaction can be more general. The following floor exploration is based on developmental movement principles and it is designed to focus attention on internal connectivity. It can also be used to warm-up and prepare the body for later movement. Pay attention to both passive and active forces at play.

Movement Experience: *Radial Symmetry and Flexion/Extension on the Floor.* Find a spot on the floor and lie down. Take a moment to sense and feel your connections to the ground. Do a brief scan from your head to your toes, noting which parts of you have more contact with the floor and which parts are perhaps held away from the floor. In your mind's eye can you visualize the six lines of your body on the floor (see Figure 5.7, The Six Lines). These are the lines of energy extending from your head to your tail and through your two arms and two legs. Once this image is clear in your mind's eye begin to notice your breathing. How are you breathing? Where is your breathing centered? Your chest? Abdomen? To begin, explore how you can bring the ends of your self toward the center of your self. This exploration can be as simple as flexing and extending the proximal joints (shoulders and hips). See how easy you can make it for yourself. Bring your awareness to how you are moving your whole self in this movement. Try alternating between whole body flexion/extension (bending/straightening) and half of the body. Bend and lengthen the right side of the body, then the whole body again, then the left side exploring homolateral connectivity and radial symmetry consecutively. Now see if you can move this pattern (whole body flexing/extending, then right side, then whole body, then left side) to actually change your place in space, as through rolling.

Teaching Tip: There are a few key things to remind students of throughout this warm-up: (1) as always, do not try too hard — there is nothing to achieve, so be easy in your movements; (2) as you are moving, even if not directed to do so, try and bring your attention back as often as you can to feeling your internal connectivity as it is in the moment; and (3) you will be sequencing through some of the developmental patterns, but in your own way — these should not be something "put on," where you do what you think it should be. Strive to do what originates from within your unique experience and based on your interpretation of the directions.

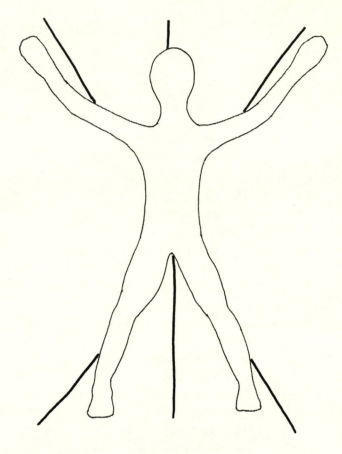

Figure 5.7 Six Cardinal Lines.

Connecting to the Environment

The next level of connectivity involves connecting to the environment. In many situations, the most immediate (and arguably most important) contact is with the floor, but other scenarios certainly arise in dance. Thinking back to Newton's Laws of Motion, the Law of Reaction is crucial to recognize here, either intuitively or specifically. An essential concept for any connectivity exploration is that focusing on our relationship to the ground can increase our sense of internal connectivity. In return, that internal connectivity must be engaged in order for ground reaction forces to be utilized optimally.

Movement Experience: *Grounding Push and Pull.* Lying on the floor, revisit the connectivity within the body and into the ground activity from the introduction. Play with alternately pushing and pulling your self, initiating from either the head or tail. Be specific about the choices being made. Isolate pushing with one foot, the other, then both. Repeat with the hands, and then explore combinations of upper and lower extremities (homologous connectivity). Experiment with different orientations — side lying, all fours, or supine. Begin to explore how this push and pull movement you are doing can actually move you through space, now noting if you are using a cross-body (contralateral) or a same-side (homolateral) connection to do so. Explore both. See if you can push and shift weight from one hand to one foot crosslaterally. Then allow the whole body to sink and extend into the floor and roll to the supine (face up) position.

Next try connecting this pattern to the previous radial symmetry pattern you developed (refer to Movement Experience: Radial Symmetry and Flexion/Extension on the Floor). Flex and extend your whole body to roll from supine to prone, then begin to push and pull alternating between the head and the tail. Connect the whole sequence together so it is more like a set warm-up. Take a moment to think through the progression from the beginning, making sure that the last movement finishes supine so the sequence can begin again. Perform the sequence in your own time. Rest and take note of how you are lying on the floor now. Can you visualize clearly the six lines of your whole self on the floor? What do you notice about your internal and external connections to yourself and to the floor now? How are they the same or different from when you began this warm-up exploration?

Teaching Tip: Teachers can use this as a set phrase they themselves develop and share, or they can have students do their own phrases at the beginning of class. Another option is cycling through the class, having each member create and teach his or her own sequence throughout a term or a series of classes. The purpose of this movement exercise is to illuminate three ideas: (1) developmental movement patterns can be used as a template for crafting sequences that enhance internal connectivity and grounding; (2) providing the time and setting for students to move themselves from themselves, rather than "putting on" someone else's material when going to class or rehearsal often helps them to feel more connected internally and into the ground; and (3) focusing attention on connectivity and the relationship to the ground establishes a foundation for being more connected internally. What you may discover is that students have difficulty or varying comfort levels with different parts of explorations like this. Because the actions in these activities are based on developmental movement patterns that help organize the body for efficient action, problem spots can be revealing of sequences or patterns that are over- or underutilized in their movement repertoire.

Pushing and pulling have been emphasized as the means for generating force from the ground, but attention should also be paid to the associated acts of reaching and yielding. A reach into the space precedes a pull, and the body must yield in order for a push to be effective (Bainbridge-Cohen 1993; Hackney 1998; Mills and Bainbridge-Cohen 1990). Yielding is perhaps the more complex to understand, as it is less visible than an actual reach. For our purposes, yield can be defined as giving way under force or pressure. This description does not imply being limp, but rather allowing the internal connections of the body to absorb (and sometimes store) the energy provided by the push (Hackney 1998, 90). This concept is important to understand, as we apply it similarly in the floor work, standing, and partnering movement experiences.

The Transition to Standing

Standing up challenges connections by changing our relationship to gravity. Somatic practices frequently utilize the floor to enhance body organization and establish frames of reference, but we are often moving upright in the world and in dance. Therefore, we need to find methods for creating transfer between being connected on the floor and being connected when standing. By attending to different aspects of the same action, students can experiment with various ways of connecting or different ways of approaching the same connectivity concept.

Movement Experience: *Standing Connectivity.* Try a simple sequence of bending the legs and then stretching while simultaneously lifting one foot. Go back to the plié, and repeat, lifting the other leg. This movement may also be done with the eyes closed. Gradually begin lifting the leg higher, focusing on a soft crease at the hip. When com-

Figure 5.8 Standing Connectivity Series 1a (Balinda Craig-Quijada; photograph by Marcella Hackbardt).

114

Figure 5.9 Standing Connectivity Series 1b (Balinda Craig-Quijada; photograph by Marcella Hackbardt).

fortable with this action, extend the leg behind after achieving the full crease in front. The upper body can move forward as the leg extends behind, so the back remains long. From this position, bring the leg back to the crease. The support leg should bend and then extend as the leg goes back and again as it returns to the crease, so there is a swing to the motion. As a final challenge, allow the upper body to lower further, eventually taking the weight into the hands. Return via the crease as before, being careful to bend the support leg as it reassumes weight. Rest.

Begin playing with shifting your attention to different ways of connecting: (1) repeat the sequence thinking about connecting into the ground, letting energy radiate up from both the hands and the feet—emphasize the sense of push; (2) rest, and then repeat with focus on the head-tail relationship; and (3) repeat with emphasis on staying in the sagittal plane, working with true flexion/extension and avoiding

Figure 5.10 Standing Connectivity Series 1c (Balinda Craig-Quijada; photograph by Marcella Hackbardt).

rotation and abduction/adduction. Take a moment to share with a neighbor which intention worked best for you. Were there any new connectivity principles that were highlighted by this activity? Add to the list of connectivity posted or written on the mirror.

Figure 5.11 Standing Connectivity Series 1d (Balinda Craig-Quijada; photograph by Marcella Hackbardt).

Locomotion

It is important to train dancers' ability to connect internally and to the environment when moving through the space, in addition to when doing stationary work. A dancer may appear and feel strong and "connected" when at the barre or doing a technical phrase in the center only to loose this integration in the throes of a full-out dancing phrase. When attention is distracted by the excitement of moving through space and adding more artistic elements, the integrity of the movement may easily fall by the wayside.

There are many methods for enhancing connectivity during locomotion. For instance, we can direct attention to the trajectory of movement sequencing through the body (the force dissemination), or we can attend to our sensory modalities, such as visual focus while moving through the space. Taking a developmental movement pattern into upright locomotion not only assists with the transfer from floor to standing, it can also highlight for the student how a fundamental movement is the underlying support for more complex moving that travels through space. The goal is to be able to trust that internal connectivity supports us in moving so that attention can be directed to our relationship to others and the environment through our sensory apparatuses (eyes, ears, and proprioceptors). Practice using a closed kinetic chain provides dancers with an opportunity to sense the sequencing and dissemination of force production within their own bodies and out into the environment differently.

Open and Closed Kinetic Chains

Open kinetic chain. In an open kinetic chain action, one end, or the extremity, is free to move. Typically an open kinetic chain refers to gestural, or nonweight bearing, movements. The focus is generally more isolated to that body part, and internal connectivity is of primary importance (Clippinger 2007, 29).

Closed kinetic chains. In these activities, the extremity is weight bearing and is not able to move freely. Both ends are grounded. Often closed kinetic chain actions work multiple muscle groups and joints simultaneously rather than concentrating on just one (Clippinger 2007, 29). Due to the weight-bearing nature, more stabilization is required. Consider the plank or push-up position (Iyengar 1979). The arms and legs are bearing weight so they cannot move in an unrestricted manner. The core muscles of the body must contract isometrically to stabilize the torso in this position, and it becomes even more difficult as the arms bend. Using a closed kinetic chain like

Figure 5.12 Closed Kinetic Chain Movement Experience.

the plank can help dancers become aware of connectivity possibilities within the body as well as strengthening the necessary core muscles.

Teaching Tip: Many times lack of core support is not a matter of strengthening the abdominals, or at least not the superficial ones. It is not unusual to see athletes with "six-pack" abdominals that cannot roll up through their vertebrae sequentially or move from the center of the body. Sometimes strengthening the transversus abdominus, deep to the superficial abdominals, is needed (Fitzmaurice 2003). More often, going back to the developmental pattern of naval radiation and working on simple actions where the center coordinates movement of the limbs will be revealing of habits.

Movement Experience: *Closed Kinetic Chain Activity to Locomotion.* Find a place at the wall. Lying on your back, put your feet on it (the wall) as if to stand. Bring your whole body close enough to the wall so that you can bend and straighten your legs. Find a place for both of your arms that will allow you to use them to push

Figure 5.13 Open Kinetic Chain Variation Movement Experience (Kora Radella; photograph by Marcella Hackbardt).

and pull (usually above the shoulders on either side of the neck). In this situation explore pushing, pulling, and yielding without displacing the hands or the feet. Begin by pushing, pulling, and yielding, initiating the movement from the lower body (feet), and then alternate with the upper body (hands). Utilize homologous connectivity patterns first. You can also try using one leg and one arm on the same side (homolateral) and then try the contralateral coordination (i.e., left foot/right hand and vice versa). Go at your own pace so that you can sense and feel how your internal sense of connectivity is either the same or different from when the floor is used to create the closed chain. How does the connection to the wall alter your sense of your six lines? Rest a moment.

  Movement Experience: *Open Kinetic Chain Variation.* Try pushing with the feet and allowing the body to slide on the floor, displacing the arms. Now push with the arms so the feet move on the wall with the body. Compare this open kinetic chain experience to the closed kinetic chain experience. Now stand up and move through the space, attending primarily to how you can move and are moving through the space by pushing, pulling, and yielding. See if you can play with the amplitude or magnitude of the push, pull, and yield so that it can be very small or very large or somewhere in between. As you are moving, notice the environment around you. Can you stay in touch with your internal sense of connectivity and relate to your environment in some manner? Consider your relation to the floor, the air around you, and objects within the room. Continue moving by pushing, pulling, and yielding while experimenting with your vision. Really see the objects and people around you. How does altering your visual focus and attention influence your perception of both your internal and external connectivity?

  Teaching Tip: This experience brings up an interesting point. Dancers frequently revert to an internal focus when they are attending to internal connectivity, while directing attention to external connections will tend to encourage an external immediate focus (refer to chapter 4 for a discussion of external immediate focus). Going with these affinities may be helpful in accessing awareness of the different ways of connecting initially. However, as dancers become more comfortable with all possibilities for connecting with themselves, the environment, and others, they should be challenged to try marrying contrasting performance focus with the primary means of connecting. For example, a performer may be asked to do floor work that mostly relies on internal connections with an externally projected focus. Or he or she could be asked to work with a partner while maintaining an internal performance focus.

Connecting to Others

  Connecting to others is clearly an extension of connecting to the environment, but we will consider it separately because it raises special considerations. One aspect that should be acknowledged is that introducing others into the environment and the kind of interaction involved influences how open or closed the skill is. A *closed skill* is one in which the conditions for performance are stable and unchanging. An *open skill* is one in which performance conditions or environmental variables are unpredictable. Feedback must be used to adjust responses to the changing situation in the performance moment (Coker 2009; Magill 2007; Schmidt and Wrisberg 2008). Most skills lie on a continuum between totally open and completely closed (Rose and Christina 2006). In dance, performing a solo is a relatively closed skill, but as soon as others are present, it becomes open to some degree. The range from open to closed varies widely from one situation to the next, which has implications for training.

In dance, we can connect with others in many ways, ranging from merely performing in the same defined space to doing contact improvisation. On the one extreme, contact may just be visual, with the performer only needing to be aware of the location or timing of the other dancers on stage. On the other end, all responses are based on contact with the partner, with no set movement planned in advance. Often we require dancers to work within these two extremes and to be able to work effectively in a range of open and closed situations. Dance education should

Figure 5.14 Connecting to Others and the Environment (Kora Radella, left, and Balinda Craig-Quijada; photograph by Marcella Hackbardt).

take this into consideration, training dancers with specificity principles in mind (see Chapter 8).

Movement Experience: *Connecting with Others in an Open Skill.* Take a few moments to think back on your warm-up phrase you created for the Movement Experience: Grounding Push and Pull. Can you find a way to transfer that phrase into a standing sequence that allows you to travel through the room? It does not have to be identical — just the idea of it. Start with whole body flexion/extension, right side, whole body, and then left side. Allow the flexing and extending to move you in space, and then begin to push and pull. See if you can create an approximation of that warm-up phrase. Once you have an outline, move it through the room, noticing how you are connected now. What is your sense of your internal connectivity? What do you need to let go in order to continue to move through the room while allowing your attention to reside in your internal connectivity? Perhaps you need to move more simply, do less.

As you are moving, notice that you are not alone. Be aware of your own connectivity, the environment that you are in, and the people that are moving with you. If you see someone doing a movement you like, feel free to try it yourself. Follow that person for a while, and then go back to your own phrase. Continue to move through the room doing your own phrase, then follow someone else for a bit, and then go back to your own phrase.

There are several things to consider during and after the movement experience. What did your own phrase feel like after doing someone else's? Did some phrases resonate with you better than others? Did you find that you lost yourself at times? What happened to your connectivity when you became aware of others? Was it enough to just focus attention on it? Or did something else need to happen?

There are no single or "right" answers to these questions, and this is the heart of the matter. Connectivity is always present if you are a normal, healthy individual; it is really the quality or appropriateness of where attention is directed and what type(s) of connectivity are engaged that is important. Particularly when performing open skills, if we are allowed to go more or less at our own pace we are better able to navigate our surroundings and tasks while remaining ourselves. This aspect is fundamental to most somatic practices, and training this way in class will help students access their internal connectivity. This ability to attend to both self and other will eventually carry over to situations when less freedom is available, as when dancing to a specified rhythm.

Teaching Tip: Another way to encourage the transfer of connectivity in relation to technique class is to assign the students homework. Have them create a short movement phrase that makes them feel internally connected and grounded. Make it a certain number of counts and a certain number of movements. Then have half the class be the doers. The other half can move from person to person, following the doers. Switch roles. Have students discuss or, better yet, answer some questions in their journals or on a piece of paper prior to discussing their experience with the various phrases. In this manner, students can begin figuring out for themselves what connectivity means on a personal level and what their challenges may be.

The previous movement experience was somewhat open, as students had to negotiate other bodies in the space while creating and performing movement. Staying internally connected probably became more challenging when they were asked to notice and visually connect with the other dancers. When contact is involved, staying internally connected becomes even more difficult, but this connection is vital when there is weight sharing. Lifting a limp body is infinitely more difficult than supporting an energized and responsive partner.

Being grounded and centered in one's own body facilitates positive interaction with others, as well as greater self-awareness. It may be helpful to think of internal, environmental, and partner connectivity as being overlapping and on a continuum. Dancers always need internal connectivity. It is the foundation for connecting in any other manner. Environmental connectivity is usually necessary too — at least the connection to the floor — but beyond this, environmental connectivity can vary based on the demands of the dance. It is like a pyramid, as internal and environmental connectivity are absolutely needed in order to work effectively with a partner.

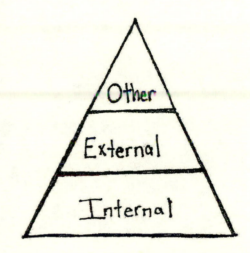

Figure 5.15 Connectivity Triangle.

In a conference workshop on using touch in teaching, Alexander Technique teacher Luc Vanier asked the participants to keep their focus 90 percent on themselves and their own use of their bodies, and only to devote 10 percent of their awareness to their partners (Nettle-Fiol and Vanier 2008). While this may seem self-centered, it points out that in order to be a good partner, one must be self-aware and engaged. When asked to connect with others, whether just by sight or through touch, students frequently get consumed with their partner, losing all internal and environmental sensitivity and connectivity. This type of connection makes it next to impossible to respond to what is being given in an efficient, effective, and intentional manner.

Movement Experience: *Partner Forces.* Give your partner energy through touch. The quality, quantity and source of the contact energy can be varied. Experiment with resisting, yielding or amplifying the forces provided by your partner. Both partners keep an awareness of internal and environmental connections as you work. Next try working with your partner while deliberately *not* connecting internally and

Figure 5.16 Partner Forces Movement Experience (Shaina Cantino and Samantha Beck-erman; photograph by Marcella Hackbardt).

environmentally. Compare these experiences. Half the class can witness while the other half is working, and then switch roles.

Teaching Tip: Have students consider how their response to their partner (resisting, yielding, or amplifying) changes the felt and seen intention of the movement. This choice touches on the role of connectivity in empowering movers and their ability to convey clear intention. Compare your feelings about resisting, yielding, or amplifying in this experience to your earlier responses in the Movement Experience: Partner Cellular Touch (see page 108). Was your initial energetic response to touch the same as your preference for a movement response to a partner?

Connectivity for Empowerment

Somatics, by definition, considers the whole being: body, mind, and spirit in its environment. This topic of connectivity is a place where the environment aspect becomes particularly clear and potent. We have considered the role of sensing the environment, but here we are looking at a holistic approach to acting upon it. Connecting within one's own instrument is only the first step in a longer journey to full awareness and engagement with the surrounding world and people inhabiting it.

Movement Experience: ***Community Building Using a Body Shopping List.*** Teacher: create lists of body parts. For example: two hands, three feet, one head, one elbow, one knee, and one back, or two feet, two knees, three hands, one shoulder, two fingers. Dividing the class into groups of approximately five, give each group a list and the following instructions: You are to work as a group to create a shape. The parts on the list and *only* the parts on the list can be contacting the floor *as a group*, and everybody in the group has to be connected to someone else in the group. Once your group has established its shape, see if you can figure out a smooth transition to arrive at your shape and to detach from it.

Teaching Tip: This activity helps build a sense of community, as it requires group problem solving and comfort with contact and weight sharing. The transition in and out of the shape hopefully establishes that the place arrived at, or the "lift," is not the only important moment. Teachers can give each group a different list (just try to visualize whether or not the list is possible given the number of students in the group), or several groups can be given the same list without knowing it. Use of the same list allows for comparison of how each group solves the identical problem.

Many of the somatic techniques assume that one of the goals is for the individual to develop independence and freedom in movement (Alexander 1932; Bainbridge-Cohen 1993; Bartenieff and Lewis 1980; Feldenkrais 1972, 1985; Hackney 1998; Hanna 1979; Swiegard 1974; Todd 1937). A sense of empowerment is certainly gained through increased awareness and control while engaging in movement of the self in relation to others and to the environment. However, movement experiences in the classroom that facilitate connectivity to the self, other, and environment can also be an inroad to growth and awareness beyond one's self. The goals of the movement experiences in this chapter can be considered metaphors for active and effective engagement as members of society. Growth moves beyond the dance studio when students learn to make internally driven movement choices, when they develop facility with force production and dissemination to convey clear intention, and when they can attend to

Primary Connection	Energy Response	Physical Situation
Self (Internal)	Yield	Floor
Environment	Resist	Standing
Other	Amplify	Traveling

Table 5.1 Creating a Connectivity Smorgasbord.

125

themselves while simultaneously connecting and relating to others and the environment. Ultimately, we are assuming that how one moves is related to how one lives, thinks, and acts in the world. We are working with the premise that dance is not an isolated event in an individual's life that only resides either in the dance classroom or on the stage but rather is core to an individual's life experience.

Movement Experience: *Connectivity Smorgasbord.* Separate the class into groups of around four. Provide time for students to create a short phrase by combining elements from the three categories of primary connection, energy response, and physical situation in different ways (see Table 5.1). Students can think of it as a connectivity smorgasbord, picking and choosing elements and putting them together to create their own meal. For example, movement impulse one could be amplifying a force with focus on internal connectivity while moving through the space. Movement impulse two might be resisting energy from a partner while on the floor. Use the different parameters to create a score.

Teaching Tip: Groups can observe one another and discuss the types of connectivity seen as primary from the audience's perspective. They might also consider the perceived tone or intention of the phrase and how this relates to choices made with regard to the above parameters. Students can then rework their phrase as a group, consciously exaggerating and/or clarifying the perceived tone or intention.

Conclusions

This body of information has many applications for both teachers and students of dance. Students are sometimes overwhelmed with specific alignment corrections from a variety of sources. Addressing basic concepts of connectivity, force production, and its dissemination can provide a foundation for independent application of a

Figure 5.1 "Connectivity" (Karen Snouffer).

variety of methods to self-generate change in movement performance. This approach is empowering as it is internally driven rather than externally applied, thus having the potential to produce stronger technicians and performers. For teachers, being aware of a variety of methods for addressing connectivity can assist with adapting and transferring this major concept of body organization to their own students, teaching style, and material taught. This kind of holistic, rather than reductionist, framework has real implications for injury prevention and rehabilitation as well. A holistic approach that looks at the connections through the body provides more avenues for lasting and real change. Ultimately, knowing what you are doing and how to achieve what you want provides freedom of choice, and freedom of choice is necessary for both personal and interpersonal growth and expression.

6

Intention and Initiation
in Movement

By watching movement of the body, we can see the movement of the mind. The "mind" of a physical form is the moving quality of that form, its inherent intelligence down to a cellular level. — Susan Aposhyan, foreword in Bainbridge-Cohen, 1993, vii

In this chapter we explore philosophies and methods for enhancing clarity of intention and initiation and their importance to subsequent movement. On a microlevel we consider initiation in terms of motor programming, and then on a more macrolevel, how it relates to initiation from specific body parts. As such, the first part of the chapter focuses on intention and the processes influencing movement preparation, while the second part deals with the initiation and follow-through of movement. These ideas are derived from various somatic techniques and are supported by motor learning and development research. Many of the somatic techniques incorporate some form of investigation of intention and initiation, including Body-Mind Centering, Ideokinesis, Laban Movement Analysis and Bartenieff Fundamentals, the Feldenkrais Method (both Awareness Through Movement and Functional Integration), and the Alexander Technique (Alexander 1932; Bainbridge-Cohen 1993; Bartenieff and Lewis 1980; Dowd 1990; Feldenkrais 1972, 1981; Franklin 1996; Hackney 1998; Swiegard 1974; Todd 1937). In all of these somatic methods and in movement science, the intention and initiation of the movement are considered to be crucial in setting up what happens next. In looking at the influence of initiation on our ability to create a desired movement, we assimilate and augment ideas touched upon in previous chapters with regard to motor programming, sensing, and visualization.

Influences on Preparing and Initiating Movement

There are many factors that impact movement preparation and movement initiation. As intention and initiation require cognition, it is helpful to first understand some of the influences on the thought processes related to movement. How we learn and where we are in the learning progression factors into the preparation and initiation of movement, as does how and where we direct our attention. Arousal levels most conducive to learning and directing attention are also important to consider in preparing and initiating movement.

The Progression of Learning

We have seen that learning progresses through different stages or levels. Performers in the early levels of skill acquisition are trying to get the general idea of the movement they want to execute (Fitts and Posner 1967; Gentile 1972). This early (verbal-cognitive) stage is predominantly cognitive in nature in that the order of movements to be performed needs to be both learned and remembered. In the next stage of skill learning (motor), the performer can concentrate on refining their movement execution because more attention is available once learners have the basic idea of what the action entails (Coker 2009). In this intermediate stage, which lasts considerably longer than the first stage of learning, motor skill performance can be progressively fine-tuned through the selection of more effective movement patterns (Nourrit et al. 2003). Performance becomes more consistent, and less attention is needed to remember what to do next in movement terms. This leads into the last stage of skill learning (autonomic), in which many aspects of movement production are relegated to automatic or unconscious motor control. In this advanced stage, the performer has even more attention available for things that come up in the moment or to cope with the situation at hand (Fitts and Posner 1967; Gentile 1972; Magill 2011; Schmidt and Wrisberg 2008). This automation of movement execution is a positive and necessary development for skilled performance, but it also is related to the concept of habit formation and the ability (or lack thereof) to make new choices in movement initiation and follow-through.

Attention

Attention, or how we direct our mind, is a limited resource (Schmidt and Wrisberg 2008) that is related to the stages of learning. As with the ability to respond to kinesthetic feedback, attention can develop with age and experience (Haywood and Getchell 2009). Attention is important in initiating movement, because what we are attending to is going to influence our intention to move. Intention and attention go hand in hand. Linking this to the stages of learning, beginners are probably just attending to the gross movement patterns initially. In the intermediate stage, dancers can start to pay attention to how they are completing those movement patterns, adding in considerations like alignment and dynamic range. At the advanced level, dancers can delegate the basic actions to muscle memory and focus their attention on the people and things in the environment, as well as on their own internal sensations of the movement.

Attention can be described based on where and how we are directing our thinking. Nideffer (1995) outlined a simple model for how to classify attention based on the placement and bandwidth of attentional thought. Attention can be directed or focused inward on the self or outward on the environment (placement of attention). Additionally, one can select either a broad or narrow bandwidth of attention (width of focus). How we can, or choose, to direct our mind is going to affect how we conceive of and initiate movement.

Applying Nideffer's model to dance, let us first examine the internal or external placement of attention. Internal attention means to direct attention inward on the self; for example, noticing how you inhale and exhale. In terms of verbal cues from the instructor, this translates into suggestions like "feel how your toes can spread on the floor in a rise." External attention means concentrating on elements that are external to the self, or outside of the body. For the dancer, external attention refers to being aware of the path of the movement or the directions traveled, the outcome of the movement, the environment (practice or performance space), the other students or performers, sounds or accompaniment, and the audience or teacher. Verbal cues that will shift attention externally refer to the product of movement, space, others, and sound. So, focusing students' attention on the steps to be completed, the direction to travel or face, or relating to the dancers around them will encourage external attention, whereas asking students to attend to their own bodily sensations, sequences of muscles used in moving, or arm positioning while moving will encourage an internal focus of attention.

Substantial research evidence indicates that directing a student's attention externally is more beneficial for both the performance and the learning of skilled movement (Wulf 2007). Traditional sports training suggests that directing the learner's attention internally makes previously automated movement patterns conscious again. The resultant degradation of performance can be explained by the Bliss-Boder Hypothesis (see Chapter 4 for discussion of the Bliss-Boder Hypothesis). As there is little research specific to dance, attentional placement, and verbal teaching cues, it is interesting to consider how these findings might apply to the dance class and somatically based teaching. First, there needs to be clarity as to what is actually meant by directing attention internally. In dance and somatic teaching, verbal cues are often utilized to direct the student's attention internally to bodily sensations, feelings, and organization (Dowd 1990; Feldenkrais 1972; Franklin 1996; Hackney 1998). However, in many of the research studies on sports learning and attention, verbal cueing for internal attention consisted primarily of concentrating on a detailed biomechanical breakdown of how to execute the skill (Wulf 2007). Therefore, it is plausible to assume that it is not the placement of attention on the internal self that results in less skillful performance and learning, but rather *what* we ask the learner to focus on internally that is crucial. In keeping with this theory, it has been suggested that metaphors for movement or movement qualities actually translate into external cues, as they highlight the result rather than being a reductionist analysis of how all the parts coordinate together to produce a movement (Wulf 2007). This would explain the pedagogical effectiveness of directing attention to internal sensation and/or emphasizing movement quality and imagery.

Also relative to the Bliss–Boder Hypothesis, it is noteworthy that reaction time decreases if a performer is focusing attention on the stimulus to move, rather than on the response to be made. Reaction time is the amount of preparation time that exists between the stimulus and when a performer actually moves (Coker 2009; Magill 2011; Schmidt and Wrisberg 2008). This has clear implications for dance. In class, when dancers want to enact change or discover new possibilities and reaction speed is not an issue, thinking about the action to be performed may be preferable. In the performance setting, however, dancers will be better served by attending to cues to move rather than thinking about the steps to come. In this case, not only will using attention effectively decrease reaction time, it will also assist performers with accessing the muscle memory they have worked so hard to develop, freeing attention for the more artistic and expressive elements of their performance (Wulf 2007).

Thinking back to previous chapters, the internal and external placement of attention is related to the different kinds of performance focus and the various levels of connectivity that can be employed. For instance, there is a tendency to use an internal performance focus when attending to internal sensations and working on internal connectivity. This tendency makes sense, as effective performance focus is defined as the eyes revealing or reflecting the kind of attention being employed in a given performance situation. Ideally, however, dancers arrive at a point in their training where they can select any performance focus desired while maintaining both external and internal attention and connectivity. The ultimate goal is to be able to respond to the environment without losing the ability to attend to internal sensation or interfering with the appropriate automated movement responses.

The second category defined by Nideffer is bandwidth, or width of focus. Attention can be narrowed or pinpointed to a small part of the experience or diffused to encompass a general sense of the whole. In Laban Movement Analysis a related effort concept in reference to external attention is having a direct or an indirect relationship to the space. As far as internal attention, one might focus on one specific body part, or on the other end of the bandwidth spectrum, try to gain a more global perspective of the body in that moment (Hackney 1998). Again, neither is better or worse, but to maximize learning and performing potential it is helpful to recognize one's preferences and tendencies and identify what is most effective given the specific situation. The ability to effectively direct attention to bodily and environmental stimuli is related to the arousal level of the performer (Schmidt and Wrisberg 2008).

Arousal

Arousal is important to bring up because it can positively or negatively influence both the width and type of attention available to the performer. Too much arousal has a negative impact on available attention. Think back to the tunnel vision that results from being placed in a situation of extreme stress. The narrowing of the visual field is a reflection of the attentional bandwidth shrinking. Again, we need to recognize that an adaptive survival mechanism will usually not be helpful in a performance setting where thoughtful choices should be made based on artistic interpretation (Schmidt and Wrisberg 2008). Part of this artistry revolves around the ability to perceive and respond to many different environmental cues. In addition, the bandwidth needs to be broad enough to include information from the body as well the environment (Wulf 2007). Conversely, too little arousal can create too broad a focus of attention, which can negatively impact performance as well. Without some heightened physical experience, performers may not pick up on and select the most relevant aspects of the situation to initiate and drive their responses (Wulf 2007). The ensuing lack of specificity, spontaneity, or urgency reflected in the movement initiation can result in flattened dynamics and a sense of complacency.

These observations about optimal arousal levels are reflected in research from the motor learning field and can be related to the type of movement being performed, as well as the performance situation. The Inverted U Hypothesis states that each movement we do has a corresponding optimal level of arousal (Magill 2011; Schmidt and Wrisberg 2008). For example, the ideal level of arousal is quite different for executing a slow adagio movement versus an energetic jumping and turning combination across the floor. In general, activities involving gross movement and power benefit from higher arousal levels, while those requiring more fine control are performed better from a calmer place (Schmidt and Wrisberg 2008).

Intention, Thought before Action

Our intention, or thought, directs how we organize ourselves to move. Intention occurs first and is followed by initiation. The intention to move is an important component of the decision-making process, determining to a large degree the motor program that is put into play. Every time we change our intention or thought, the organization of our bodies changes in response and/or in preparation for accomplishing the action (Coker 2009; Schmidt and Wrisberg 2008). For example, close your eyes for a moment. Think about your right shoulder. Can you see it in your mind? Notice what your eyes are doing while you are thinking. They are probably directed at your right shoulder, because our thoughts organize our actions. You can also try this exercise with a group of people with eyes open. Have one or two members of the group observe the others, verifying what happens during this activity more objectively. The following movement experience illustrates how our thinking directs our moving and was adapted from Feldenkrais (1985) and Vealey and Greenleaf (2006).

Movement Experience: *Moving an Object with the Mind.* Sitting comfortably in a chair, place a locket, pendant, or a key attached to a 10- to 12-inch length of string between the thumb and forefinger of your dominant hand. Place your dominant elbow in front of you on a level surface such as a table or desktop. Without moving your hand, wrist, or arm, begin to think about the pendant/locket/key moving in space. Clarify your thought, mentally restricting the motion to the spatial direction of forward and backward. Continue thinking the directions until you notice the object is moving. For fun, see if you can get the object to move left and right, in circles in both directions, and stop, all without consciously moving your arm. If you are having trouble getting the object to move by thinking alone, coordinate your eyes with your intention (thought).

Teaching Tip: This movement experience can be a valuable tool to get students to realize the influence their thoughts have on their actions. The stopping of the object can also be used to illustrate the concept of inhibition.

Processes Involved in the Preparation and Initiation of Movement

The preceding movement experience reveals how our thought is directly linked to our motor system, which carries out our intention by activating the neuromuscular pattern of the movement we are thinking about. In this case, the intention was subconscious, resulting from thinking about movement without even trying to do it. At other times, we make a conscious choice to move, but the component parts of the movement may still be automatic. Sometimes making the impulse for movement external can give us new information about how we may be anticipating or limiting the responses available to us.

Movement Experience: *Intention and Initiation with Touch.* Begin in child's pose with your arms between the lower and upper leg so that the hands or fingertips can be placed on the ischial tuberosities (sitting bones). Gently push the ischial tuberosities in different directions to determine what you can sense and feel of the trajectory of the movement. Give yourself or your students clear directions to try, such as pushing up toward the ceiling or in the direction of the head. Consider whether you feel the movement traveling all the way up the spine to the head. If not, why not? Is there too much muscular tension throughout the body, even in a repose position? Does the trajectory give you clues as to what you actually do when you are moving? Pay attention to the pattern that unfolds, such as sequencing, held parts, or dominant side. Do you anticipate where the motion will go before you actually feel

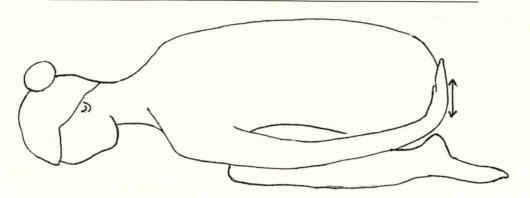

Figure 6.2 Intention and Initiation with Touch Movement Experience.

the impulse for the movement? What about the end of the movement? Do you allow yourself the opportunity to experience the whole motion through the spine or do you stop before the end? What is the end and what is the beginning for you?

These ideas can be explored to give you clues about habitual movement patterns that appear when you are not paying attention to what you really intend to do and move in your body. Having information about our patterns or habits can be helpful in understanding the choices we make in movement (consciously or not) and in recognizing that we also can choose something else once aware of these tendencies.

Movement Experience: *Continuation with a Partner.* In child's pose with your arms along your sides, have a partner gently and lightly (without too much force) push from the ischial tuberosities through the spine toward the head a few times. Notice if the push goes easily toward the head through spine or if it is deflected off to the side or dampened at a particular vertebra. In the same position have your partner outline, through touch of the fingers (gentle and light circles), each vertebra moving from the bottom of the spine toward the head. Repeat the gentle initiation of a push from the ischial tuberosities that sequences through the vertebrae to the head, and notice if it feels different than the first time. Trade roles and go through the whole process again. Take a few moments to share your experiences with your partner. Were there any vertebrae that felt restricted or less receptive to the impulse? Do you have a more complete picture in your mind of your spinal column?

Teaching Tip: Working with a partner can illuminate blank spaces in one's picture of self for both parties. Drawing before and after movement experiences or class can also reveal places that are overrepresented or underrepresented in one's self-image. Additionally, partner work can clarify understanding of directions and directional trajectories in movement.

Stages of Processing Information and Initiating Action

The simple description of how humans organize themselves to move is as follows: sensory (afferent) information enters the central nervous system; it is perceived and identified, and the person then chooses how to respond. Again, this may be a conscious choice or not. If a response is required, the appropriate motor program is selected and an action is produced through the efferent, descending pathways out to the muscles (Coker 2009; Magill 2011; Schmidt and Wrisberg 2008). If the action lasts long enough, intrinsic and extrinsic feedback (see Chapter 3 for a more detailed description) from the environment and the body, as generated by the action, are used to make adjustments by the decision-making centers in the brain.

Intention, or the process of choosing how to respond to a stimulus, is most relevant to the issue of initiation because once the choice to move has been made, or thought, the basic motor program will be set in motion. Motor programs are thought to be general in nature in that they exist for classes of movement that have shared characteristics, such as traveling through space or object manipulation (Schmidt 1975; Shea and Wulf 2005). These motor programs are sets of instructions or templates stored in the memory that code for how to accomplish a type or kind of movement (Coker 2009; Magill 2011; Schmidt and Wrisberg 2008). As such, they can be adapted to the specific situation based on the environment, context, and intrinsic feedback available to the performer. These generalized programs for movement are updated and refined through experience and over time, reflecting the stages of learning. With enough repetition, the neuromuscular pathways that are programmed become established, even entrenched, as the default response to a given stimulus (Coker 2009; Magill 2011; Schmidt and Wrisberg 2008).

Building on our conceptualization of movement processes, after the initial influx of information gets sorted and identified, a plan is picked and then carried out. What we can do afterward depends on the movement we are executing and how long it lasts. Any movement that takes over two hundred milliseconds to complete can be modified after the first forty milliseconds have occurred, based on additional information coming in from the environment and the body itself (Magill 2011). It is a closed-loop system of control. Therefore, movements exhibiting some kind of continuity, for example a sustained gesture, can be adapted and adjusted as they are being performed. However, movements lasting less than forty milliseconds, for example very brisk frappés, can only be adapted on the next attempt. These types of movements use an open-loop system of control (Coker 2009; Magill 2011; Schmidt and Wrisberg 2008). Refer to Chapter 3 for more information on open-and-closed loop motor control.

This information has implications for the initiation of both slow and fast movement. In both cases, we start with the intention to move and initiate it by engaging a motor program. Thus, the appropriateness and clarity of both the intention and the initiation are vital to creating the desired action, and this is especially true for fast movements. If the action is quick, the motor program can only be adapted or adjusted for the next try after the action is completed. These adjustments occur based on knowledge of the results of performance (Magill 2011). If a dancer sees, senses, or is told the frappé was too high the first time, this information is incorporated into the planning for the next attempt. In a slower action, we have the luxury of being able to modify this program as it proceeds.

Whether the action is slow or fast, if the motor program and the initiation of it have become habitual, the following may be happening:

1. We may no longer be making conscious choices about the intention, or what we really want the movement to be, when engaging in the action.
2. We may be desensitized to the feedback coming from the sensory receptors in order to alter the motor program, whether the feedback is coming during or after the completion of the action.
3. Even when aware of feedback, it can still be difficult to alter the motor program and the associated neuromuscular pathways once they have become ingrained.

Habits

Feldenkrais (1981) and Alexander (1932) both spent many hours exploring and discovering their movement patterns and habits of self-use. Through this process they discovered that what they thought they were doing and what they actually were doing were not the same. In later years Feldenkrais went on to state, "If you know what you are doing then you can do what you want" (Feldenkrais 2007, 1).

Habits are neither good nor bad. Habits in movement are the result of selecting particular movement patterns that were appropriate and even necessary at one time. Therefore, it is sometimes beneficial to consider them as fulfilling a specific need for the performer, rather than being a negative consequence of poor training. We all have a large repertoire of habitual movement patterns that are efficient motor programs, as these unconscious patterns free up available attention for responding to other immediate influences or stimuli in the environment.

Human attention is limited in any given movement, and human functioning is complex, so automating movement patterns (meaning delegating parts of our action to an automatic/unconscious place) allows us to do more and be more skillful (Schmidt and Wrisberg 2008). For example, if we had to think about how to walk every time we needed to do it, nothing else would happen for us, let alone dancing. As we become more skillful, more movements and movement patterns become automatic. This change represents the final stage of learning and is the muscle memory we have previously discussed. Not having to think about the habitual act of walking allows the performer to add other layers of movement complexity. The problem lies in having a reliable perception of the habitual action and then in having the option of changing this automatic action if so desired.

Movement Preparation

Taking a closer look at what actually occurs in the time between the intention to move and the initiation of motion can give us some ideas about how to deal with the difficulties in circumventing habits. This period of movement preparation involves selecting a motor program from memory and refining it based on the specific situation. Preparation is made for postural support for the action, for the performance of the limbs in relation to the task, and for the spatial coding and rhythmic patterning involved in the activity (Magill 2007).

The time required to make these preparations (reaction time) varies based on the situation. The parameters most relevant to dance are movement complexity, the number of response choices, the repetition of a movement, attention and alertness, and practice (Magill 2011). We have already seen that directing attention to the cue to move as opposed to the action to be performed will reduce the reaction time. As movement complexity and the number of possible responses to a situation increase, so does the amount of time needed to react (Henry 1961; Henry and Rogers 1960; Schmidt and Wrisberg 2008). With repetition, practice, and increased attention and alertness, the reaction time decreases — the motor program is being refined and the neuromuscular pathways established (Rose and Christina 2006). While establishing the neuromuscular pathways and decreasing response time are good for performance, this phenomenon speaks again to the importance of slowing down to create change. Prolonging the period of movement preparation gives the body and mind time to sense the situation and adapt the motor program in this important phase that lies between intention and initiation.

Inhibition

To bring the impulse or initiation back into a more voluntary and less habitual control, the concept of inhibition becomes key. Inhibition is used and referred to in different ways in various somatic approaches, but it basically entails stopping the automated response to a stimulus at the level of movement preparation. In *Motor Learning: Concepts and Applications,* Magill (1998, 45) notes, "A prepared movement will be initiated and carried out unless there is sufficient time to attend to feedback indicating that the movement should not be made, and to inhibit the movement commands issued to the musculature." In somatic approaches, the emphasis on working slowly and with attention to sensation does just this — it stops the automatic response and allows for fine-tuning of the motor program. This applies to both the initiation of the action and to actually performing the movement slowly enough that it can be a closed-loop situation where adjustments are made throughout the process.

Somatic wisdom recognizes not only the importance of inhibition in changing the sequence of responses, but also that the central nervous system needs new directives to start reprogramming the neuromuscular pathways. There is the need to replace the habitual with something else. In Alexander work, this entails thinking movement (intention), stopping the action (inhibition), and then replacing it with the directions for primary control before engaging in the movement (Vineyard 2007). In some Feldenkrais Awareness Through Movement Lessons, where the second side is only visualized, and in Ideokinesis, which is usually done in the constructive rest position, the action is imagined without moving at all in order to repattern the neuromuscular response (Dowd 1990; Feldenkrais 1972, 1981; Franklin 1996; Swiegard 1974). In Bartenieff Fundamentals and Body-Mind Centering, developmental movement patterns are explored to reveal patterns and preferences and then new choices are encouraged through specific movement initiations (Bainbridge-Cohen 1993; Hackney 1998).

Initiation and Follow-Through

So far in this chapter we have primarily focused on the cognitive and neurological processes related to the intention and initiation of motion, but the topic of intention and initiation can be approached from a body level as well. Making clear and specific choices about where in the body a movement is starting, where it is directed in space, and how we want that movement to sequence is often helpful in discovering new options for accomplishing a given action, as Bartenieff Fundamentals and Body-Mind Centering exemplify above. Because the nervous system needs to be given new directives to replace habitual patterns, it is important that dance classes move away from the product-driven mentality so frequently found. Exploring a variety of beginnings in relation to a desired movement outcome can facilitate the ability to choose different pathways for movements. For example, if you want to move your right arm out to the side you can begin by lifting your shoulder, or your elbow, or your wrist, or your fingertips.

Movement Experience: *Awareness of How to Begin.* Begin this movement exploration lying on the floor with the arms alongside your body and the legs extended on the floor. Take a moment to notice the different kinds of sensory input you are experiencing. Can you identify in your mind the visual, auditory, taste, smell, and kinesthetic (both touch and pressure) sensations you are experiencing? You are going to flex and extend one leg along the floor. Close your eyes and decide which leg you are going to move — the right or the left. Begin moving by sliding or dragging the leg into flexion along the floor; then extend it back to the starting position. Rest.

Where in your body did the movement begin? The foot, the knee, the hip or the belly? Repeat the flexion and extension of the leg a few times in order to clarify for yourself where the movement started. Rest. Repeat the flexing and extending of the leg but play with where the movement begins. For example, move a few times starting from the foot, and then try the knee, the hip, and finally, the abdomen. While resting briefly in between each initiation, take a moment to determine for yourself which initiation patterns feel familiar and which ones feel foreign.

Teaching Tip: Remind students to go slowly and easily. Ask if they can move the leg without engaging extra muscular tension and action in other parts of themselves. If students are having difficulty, ask them to coordinate the movement with their breath. Use of the breath can also be emphasized if they are progressing rapidly through the movement exploration. If you have time, ask students to reverse the breathing so that the inhalation occurs with the flexion and vice versa.

Coordination and Control

In motor development and learning, coordination is defined as "the patterning of body and limb motions relative to the patterning of environmental objects and events" (Magill 2011, 442). As such, movement initiation should be taken into consideration when looking at the development of coordination and control. In human development, movement skill growth and learning progresses from the top down, or from the head to the feet (cephalo-caudal), and from the proximal to the distal, or from the center out to the peripheral edges of the body (Haywood and Getchell 2009). This corresponds with the spinal (head–tail) and naval radiation (core–distal) patterns so essential to efficient movement. Human development also moves from a more general functioning to a more complex, differentiated functioning. For example, rotation of the spine occurs first as a block, where the whole spine turns in space as a single unit. As we move through the developmental stages, we are eventually able to accomplish gradated spinal rotation, or the coordinated, sequential rotation of each individual vertebra (Haywood and Getchell 2009).

Movement Experience: *Initiation from the Core to the Distal.* Close your eyes and begin to explore moving your body and its parts in relation to your breath growing and shrinking. Start slowly and gently. Exert less force. What do you sense and feel as you grow and shrink the whole of yourself on the floor? Can you make it smaller? Larger? In what direction(s) are you growing and shrinking? Front to back? Both sides? Up and down? All three dimensions together? Now notice what you sense and feel as you grow and shrink a part of yourself on the floor. Can you continue growing and shrinking as you move your arm and leg? Both arms? Both legs? Arms and legs together? Head and pelvis? Explore how growing and shrinking can move you. Let your growing and shrinking move you from side to side. Back to front. On to all four limbs. Can you change levels and still grow? And then shrink? Can you move from the floor to standing and then back to the floor again while growing? Shrinking? Can you move through the level changes continuously, sequencing the movement without stopping? What are you sensing and feeling as you grow and shrink while changing levels? What happens when you go slower, faster, make it smaller or larger? Are you still able to grow and shrink? Rest for a moment on your back and notice how you are contacting the floor now. Has anything changed? Notice the differences you feel in yourself now.

The developmental progression of movement skill acquisition carries over to how we learn movement as adults and is related to the stages of learning discussed earlier in this chapter. In our first, or early, attempts to execute a motion, human coordination of the self involves restricting the action to a smaller number of joints, resulting in less specific motion (Turvey 1977). This idea can be seen in the previous example of spinal rotation progressing from moving the spine as a single unit to being able to move the spine using all of the vertebrae. Through practice, differentiation of the individual joints occurs, allowing a more coordinated, articulated movement to take place. It is one of the major principles of movement that when initially learning to do something, the overall experience is of too much movement production (Coker 2009). Refinement needs to occur while learning how to accomplish exactly what one intends. With practice, the intention and initiation become clearer, the motor program becomes more efficient with fewer motor units being recruited to accomplish the given action, and this in turn provides for more differentiation in the joints. The result is more easeful, expressive and clear movement.

Movement Experience: *Body Part Initiation.* Playing with moving different body parts in isolation can provide ideas about the ability to initiate and differentiate movement at the joints. Either alone or manipulating the joints of a partner passively, explore how the parts of the body move. While standing, sitting or lying, go through the major joints/bony aspects of the body and articulate the joints through their range of motion. For example, flex and extend, abduct and adduct, and circumduct the ankle, hip, wrist and shoulder joints. Next, explore the articulations of the hands and feet. Using one or both hands, palpate each foot, then each hand, and explore the amount of available motion in each foot and each hand. Feel the spaces between the bones as well as the bones. Done with a partner, this can be a pleasant way for both individuals to make discoveries about the movement potential at the various joints, holding patterns, and the ability to release and trust.

Teaching Tip: A strategy for working with this exploration in a timely manner is to parse it into explorations of the axial skeleton (the skull, ribcage, and spine) or the appendicular skeleton (the shoulder and pelvic girdles and the limbs). Relationships between end points can be outlined, such as where the legs connect to the pelvis or how the hand relates to the shoulder girdle, to name just a few. Chose what makes sense in relation to class material and initiations you want to highlight. This movement experience can also be done as a whole class session. Moving through the entire body and exploring the range of motion through the bony anatomy is a relaxing change of pace and a lovely way to increase awareness of the movement potential at all the joints.

Practicing Initiation and Intention

In its simplest form, initiation of a movement can begin on a body level from proximal/core, midlimb, or distal parts of the skeleton. Well-developed coordination in dance arises from the ability to begin a movement anywhere in the body. Once the motion starts, dancers should examine how and where the motion sequences, or moves, through the body.

Movement Experience: *Sliding the Arms While Side Lying.* Have students lie on their sides with their arms in front of them, palms together. Reach the top hand beyond the bottom hand, feeling how this action ripples through the body. Return to neutral by moving the hand back into position. Now propel the top arm forward and pull it back, initiating from the center body. Compare these sensations.

Figure 6.3 Sliding the Arms Movement Experience 1a (Julie Brodie; photograph by Marcella Hackbardt).

Figure 6.4 Sliding the Arms Movement Experience 1b (Julie Brodie; photograph by Marcella Hackbardt).

Overview of Movement Sequencing

The initiation of an action can be from more than one part, as in a simultaneous action, or it can be from one part and then travel through the body in different ways. In one scenario, the initiation is carried through the body in a "chain reaction," with each part affecting the next. Or the action might "jump" from one body part to another segment. Take a swing of the body, for example. One way to perform the swing would be to think of both the top of the head and the coccyx dropping and coming together, rebounding, and then returning to vertical at the same time. Another way might be to start from the coccyx, sequencing through the spine so the neck and head are the last to respond, rippling back before dropping. In a third option, the knees might initiate with the head coming next and the spine following the head. There is no right or wrong way to perform a swing; it is a matter of having a clear intention, starting the action from the desired place, and allowing it to follow through in the body with choices being available. In *Making Connections*, Hackney (1998, 219) suggests the following method for analysis: "Simultaneous—do all the active body parts move at once? (i.e., head and both hands make an action at the same time); Successive—does the movement of one body part flow successively into the next adjacent part? (i.e., a succession within one movement phrase: shoulder, elbow, wrist, hand); Sequential — does the movement of one part of the body flow sequentially into other non-adjacent body parts (i.e., a sequence of movement of non-adjacent body parts within one phrase: head, leg, and arm move — one immediately after the other)."

Movement Experience: *Sequencing Initiations.* Playing with different initiations, explore starting movement from various points and see which initiations feel easier and clearer. Begin with the limbs, trying to initiate from the joints. Then play with movements traveling from head to toe, feet to head, and center/core to distal. The connectivity patterns discussed in Chapter 5 need to be established and functional before an initiation can move effectively through the body. As adult movers, we have (hopefully) progressed through all of the stages of skill development, and these developmental patterns can be explored under the umbrella concept of initiation. It can be informative to notice which patterns feel most natural and which are more difficult to access. Continue playing with different initiations, and begin to notice how they connect to the following, larger movement. Change the focus to what happens next. Do the initiation and follow-through tend to be simultaneous, sequential, or successive? Can you initiate a movement that sequences from one end of the body to the other? Can you initiate a movement from two places simultaneously, like the same side hand and foot (body half from the distal ends), or successively from the core/center/naval out through the limbs to the distal ends of the same side hand and foot? Can you initiate a flexion on one side of the body while extending the other side of the body (shortening and lengthening in a more complete body half)? How does it feel to start an action from one part and carry the momentum generated into a non-adjacent part? Maybe initiate a turn from one arm and sequence the follow-through to the opposite leg or into rotation of the head. Try different combinations and notice how you prefer to sequence actions.

Change the context. Continue the above but change your situation. For example, start lying on your back, roll to your side, and then to your stomach. Does the context of where you are in space influence your ability to access a particular initiation and/or sequencing?

Change the quality. Continue experimenting with different initiations and contexts and see how many ways you can change the quality of the initiation and/or subsequent movement. Can you initiate a movement from your big toe lightly, strongly, quickly, or slowly? Take note of the choices that were easier for you, and in which combinations.

Change the level. Continue exploring all of the above but change level. That is, allow the initiation to continue through the body and into the space. Explore the different possibilities of moving from lying to sitting, sitting to standing, standing to moving around the room, and back to lying. Try sequencing these together, as well as taking them in parts.

Teaching Tip: For students with less experience or comfort with improvisation and guided discovery methods of teaching, be simple and specific about what concepts or relationships they are moving and exploring. For instance, compare and contrast initiating from the proximal and the distal one situation at a time. Then progress to a couple of movement qualities and finish with changing levels from lying to standing and back down. It is important not to take on too much at once. Layering the experience and allowing time for feedback helps students feel comfortable and not overwhelmed with choices.

Spatial Intent

In addition to thinking about initiation on a body level, one can approach the concept of initiation spatially. In Laban Movement Analysis terms, "Spatial intent organizes body connections by establishing a clear pathway/goal for the movement" (Hackney 1996, 354–355). Alexander Technique also uses this idea in directing, where the thought is for the "head being up and out, and the back long and wide" (Vineyard 2007). By thinking about points in space (external attention), the body can begin to select the most effective mechanisms for achieving that spatial goal.

Arcing and Spoking

When gesturing, we can make three distinct choices with regard to how the body will interact with the space. The gesture can arc, taking a peripheral path while moving from one spatial destination to the next. The gesture can spoke, moving through the center of the body. Transverse pathways lie in the space between peripheral and central. Defining the spatial pathway can be an effective tool in clarifying initiation and how it follows through in the action, as it combines body and spatial considerations (Hackney 1998).

Movement Experience: *Peripheral versus Central Paths, Spoke versus Arc.* Begin with gesturing one arm in the direction and level of your choice. Note the relationship of the hand to the shoulder. Move the arm into a new place in space, and notice the path it took. Repeat this several times, allowing the rest of the body to move and respond to the gestures. Now limit the exploration to peripheral paths in space for a minute. Experiment with small and large ranges or degrees of arcing in all three planes: sagittal (wheel), frontal (door) and horizontal (transverse). Of course transverse paths can also be used, and it is fine if the arms move through center as a transition, but keep the focus on the peripheral path at first — its beginning and ending points and the path between them. Notice whether the arms lead the body or the body leads the arms.

Now begin to notice the transitions through center as well. When do they tend to occur naturally? Shift your exploration to these central, or spoking, paths. Again, notice the beginning and ending directions and the path through center. Where does the movement tend to initiate? Do the fingers usually lead? Play with different initiations — from the elbow, or the body.

Begin arcing and spoking the legs in space now. See how this experience differs from the arms. Change levels and notice the difference in range when the body does not have to stabilize against the pull of gravity. Notice how, even then, the legs have less mobility than the arms. Vary the timing. Try a swinging action, and notice the timing of the arc. Again, vary the initiation — try a central path led by the body and a central path led by the foot. Try a peripheral path led by the body and then led by the foot. Compare the experiences.

Now intermix arcing and spoking through the space with both arms and legs. Vary the timing, the level, and the flow of the movement. Bring the improvisation to a rest. Do you have any comments about the experience? Make any discoveries?

Teaching Tip: A future class could focus on transverse paths moving obliquely in the space between the periphery and the center, but for clarity it is helpful to concentrate on fully understanding and embodying peripheral and central paths first. To follow up on this movement experience, teachers might take a set phrase of movement and direct students' attention to which aspects are arc-like and which ones are spoke-like. For example, in sun salutation the opening movement of bringing the arms from the sides of the body to overhead is arc-like while the movement of the arms pushing into upward facing dog is spoke-like. Incorporating this kind of analysis throughout class can clarify spatial pathways and reveal preferences. This approach, or method of analysis, can also be applied in relation to the concept of phrasing.

Figure 6.5 Sun Salutation: Arcing Movement Example.

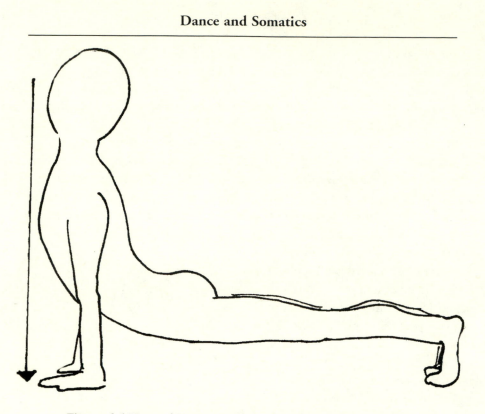

Figure 6.6 Upward Facing Dog: Spoking Movement Example.

Phrasing

The phrasing of an action is another important consideration for the follow-through, along with the concepts of sequencing and spatial intent. How a movement is initiated will determine the overall phrasing. A movement can start with force that dwindles, as in a toss, or as sometimes occurs with the accent at the beginning of a port de bras. Other movements build in power to the moment of completion, as in a punch, or a frappé. Still other actions may be even in the phrasing throughout the movement, as is typical of much Butoh dance or a dévellopé. The intent right from the start of the movement will determine the phrasing of the rest of the action. These kinds of phrasing are sometimes referred to as impulsive, impactive, and even (Hackney 1998).

Movement Experience: *Breath Phrasing.* Bringing attention to the breath, begin with an easy, continuous rhythm. Allow the movement of the breath to be sent through the body. Next explore an impactive breath rhythm, where the breath begins to escape and then ends with power and force (Hackney 1998). Allow the movement of the body to reflect this breath phrasing. Think of a punch supported by a kiai (battle cry or yell), as in the martial arts. Continue this exploration with impulsive phrasing of the breath, which starts with strength and then tapers off (Hackney 1998). Begin with the breath again, and then allow the body to follow. This activity can be fun and informative to continue to explore with a partner. Once these breath and movement rhythms have been established, take them into a "conversation" with another person. How can you, or how do you want to, respond to an impactful statement from someone? What about an impulsive statement? How can you break from continuous exchanges? From here, dancers can be asked to make specific choices regarding breath and phrasing with a set combination.

Preferences in Patterns of Movement

The Somatic Principle of initiation illuminates movement preferences as well as movement habits. Preferences and habits in movement are not always the same things. Movement preferences are patterns of movement we choose over other patterns of movement. Preferences in movement can be influenced by movement habits, structure of the body, the task to accomplish, and personal experience. Consider this scenario: Knee drops (one of the Basic Six movement patterns in the Bartenieff Fundamentals) are often taught so the knees tilt to the right while coordinating the head movement to the left (Bartenieff and Lewis 1980). In an Awareness Through Movement Lesson, the knees tilt to the right but without the corresponding head motion (Feldenkrais 1972). A student having a lot of experience with BF before being exposed to this ATM lesson found that every time she tilted the knees to the right her head was going left, although that was not the direction given by the instructor. She discovered as she was doing the lesson that she could tilt her knees to the right with or without the accompanying head motion once she became aware of what she was doing, but that she preferred to coordinate her head moving left with the action because it felt good. Turning her head was a preference, not a habit, as there was choice involved.

When first attempting a movement, people will automatically activate a preferred pattern they have been using for similar actions. New and different patterns will emerge if they continue to practice and as they become more successful with the new movement (Magill 1998, 37). This idea makes sense based on our knowledge of motor programs and how they are refined. The preference is a starting point, and in a functional situation, the preference can be adapted or replaced with more efficient patterns. As artists, we need to think about this option a little differently than athletes. If we are defaulting to our preferred ways of moving in creating or performing dance, it may be closing us off to other expressive options. Because there is no right or wrong in creating original dance movement, choreographers and dancers may not be compelled to move beyond this initial, preferred response. As always, awareness is the root of the solution, and initiation can be an effective way to discover and explore options beyond our tendencies.

Movement Experience: *Body Part Start.* Go in partners. One person call out body parts for your partner to explore as the initiation point (or the instructor can

Figure 6.7 Initiation with a Partner Movement Experience (Kora Radella, left, and Balinda Craig-Quijada; photograph by Marcella Hackbardt).

call out parts for the whole class). Vary the timing between naming parts so that sometimes there is ample time for exploration and sometimes one initiation comes directly upon another. Observe without judgment, looking for preferences with regard to initiation (location in body and space, pathways, sequencing, and phrasing). Share as both doer and observer, and then trade roles. As a variation, one person provide the impetus for movement by touching your partner gently. Vary the initiation points, timing, and body parts you use to make contact. The act of touching can become your own little dance. Partner being touched: allow the contact to initiate motion in that body segment. You can exaggerate the follow-through to some degree, but try to stay true to the actual impulse from your partner to move. Share experiences as initiator and recipient of the initiations and then switch roles.

The Special Case of Contemporary Modern Dance

Ballet and classic modern dance both adhere to the importance of dancers achieving specific shapes with their bodies, or conforming to an ideal image. Post-modern artists of the 1960s are identified as the generation that questioned this ideal (along with other parameters) associated with "technique" (Brown, Mindlin, and Woodford 1997, 123). One of the beliefs of contemporary modern dance, or release-based technique, for lack of a better word, is the idea that specificity in movement initiation and sequencing should be prioritized over form. This value system is based on the premise that movement will play out slightly differently in different bodies when the intention and initiation point are emphasized. Each dancer can achieve freedom and ease because he or she is allowed to focus on the initiation and sequencing, rather than the final form. By the same token, efficient dynamic alignment will allow this sequencing of the initiation to move through the body organically and somewhat predictably (Batson 2008, 146). As Wendell Beavers (2008, 130) observed, "Funny things occur with this way of working; like our history is our future and the more things differentiate the more they integrate. This latter experience is proving very useful in this time of flying apart, of disunity, of multiplicity of techniques and views of dance. It seems important to keep letting things differentiate and consider that the difference between disintegrate and differentiate is only one of state of mind."

Because of the freedom from form, in a sense, a big emphasis is placed on the connections that allow the initiation to sequence. Energy going out away from the body also needs to come back in, conforming to the Law of Reaction. The limbs may fling, but with connection to the body. Dancers' training needs to include specificity of initiation, sequencing, and spatial intent, and an understanding of how these aspects of movement relate to the ability to be aware of and to engage the connections inherent in the body's structure. Without the ability to release unnecessary tension and holding, the initiation and how it follows through in the body cannot occur organically.

Movement Experience: *Initiation from Different Layers of the Body.* Starting on one side of the room, travel from this side to the other in low level. Students can move across in groups of five or six, depending on class size. Think of initiating movement on a skeletal level, focusing on the joints and how they provide for the movement of the bones. The movement may feel particularly relaxed, weighted, and free when working with this intention. On the way back, place the intention on moving from the muscle tissue of the body. This level may give the movement a more viscous, connected, and strong feeling. On the third pass, focus on moving from the outer layer, or the skin. The movement may take on a new lightness and sense of external sensitivity. This series can be repeated in middle and high level.

Conclusions

Dancers may need reminders to keep making choices in their movement, rather than just going on auto-pilot. This need can be particularly true for movement that

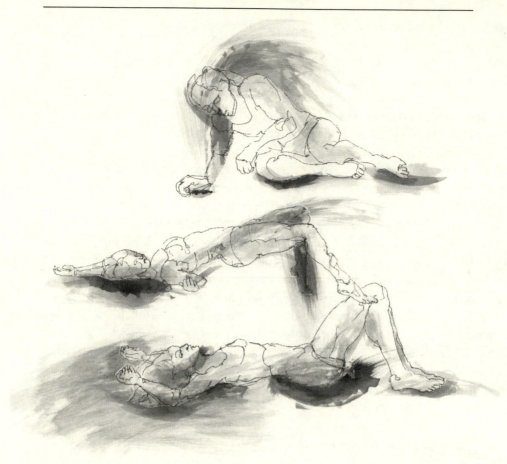

Figure 6.1 "Intention and Initiation" (Karen Snouffer).

is performed repeatedly, as in a dance work that is in rehearsal for many months. Making the clear decision "I am going up," for example, will read very differently than just letting the movement happen to you. As one of the pioneers of modern dance, Martha Graham (Brown, Mindlin, and Woodford 1997, 52–53) has been quoted as saying, "The reality of the dance is its truth to our inner life. Therein lies its power to move and communicate experience." This quote gets at the essence of intention and initiation and its importance in dance. What we think and feel is reflected in our bodies. In an art in which the body is the instrument of expression, dancers must be specific and clear in what they are intending and where and how that movement begins in order to communicate an honest physical statement. In this way, initiation and intention lie at the heart of the mind-body connection.

Developing a Practice
of One's Own

*Learning is the process by which we vary our responses to information based on
the context of each situation.*— *Bainbridge-Cohen, 1993, 5*

As a student or teacher of dance and/or an aspiring performer, you might be
asking yourself why you need to read this chapter as you already spend a considerable
amount of time and energy practicing and performing your craft. It is true that both
dance teachers and students spend a large quantity of time in class, rehearsal, and
performance. It is equally true that one of the underlying goals of the somatic techniques is to create change in an individual's movement repertoire, and creating change
in movement responses takes time, just as learning different dance techniques like
ballet, modern, or jazz takes time. Additionally, the conditions for achieving this type
of change in movement response require a different kind of approach than what is
typically used in dance technique classes. One of these conditions is creating a context
for learning in which the process and experience of moving is of primary concern,
rather than the outcome of mastering technique and executing dance combinations.
Another condition is the attention and responsibility placed upon the individual for
participating in the process of creating change. For example, most of the somatic
techniques engender an environment in which it is not how high your leg can go in
the air, but rather, whether you fully experience what you intend in moving your leg
in the air (Alexander 1932; Bartenieff and Lewis 1980; Hackney 1998; Hanna 1993;
Hartley 1995; Feldenkrais 1972; Swiegard 1974; Todd 1937). The emphasis is on learning, and in particular, self-learning rather than continually striving for an abstract
aesthetic goal. Working in this reflective manner requires a slower pace that is not
always suitable for technique class.

Another underlying assumption in the somatic techniques is that the alterations
we are trying to evoke involve habitual movement choices and patterns (Alexander
1932; Hackney 1998; Hartley 1995; Feldenkrais 1972; Swiegard 1974; Todd 1937).
Because habits are primarily under unconscious control, they are difficult to reset; the
habitual response will occur before we even consider another possibility. In this way
all habits (such as habits of eating, communication, posture, alignment, and thought)
are similar and share commonalities such as being resistant to change, requiring a

Figure 7.2 Benefits of a Self-Practice (Julie Brodie in "Mired," choreographed by Julie Brodie; photograph by Marcella Hackbardt).

variety of new conditions in order to support the desired change, producing a sense of awkwardness when the new response is compared to the previous habit, and needing continual attention in order to supplant the old pattern with the new pattern (Alexander 1932, 1969; Alon 1996; Hackney 1998; Feldenkrais 2005; Todd 1937).

Most of the somatic techniques as practiced today presuppose a self or reflective practice in which the person takes responsibility for his or her growth and takes the time to develop skills at an individual pace. In the Feldenkrais Method, students improve their skills in both Awareness Through Movement and Functional Integration lessons by working on their own in addition to doing structured classes. In Laban Movement Analysis/Bartenieff Fundamentals one is encouraged to develop a practice of one's own, applying the elements of body, effort, shape, and space to their movement. Alexander students also spend time expanding awareness and applying directives as a way of practicing on their own without the aid of the teacher. Traditionally, self-practice in addition to group instruction has been an integral component for students studying both martial arts and yoga (Iyengar 2005; Yang 2005). Students of dance can draw from this model to reap the benefits of devoting time and attention to their specific requirements in a self-practice.

Benefits of Developing One's Own Practice

Self-practice can take many forms and fill different needs. In developing your own practice, it may be helpful to consider what you most want and need to change. This change may involve addressing an inefficient movement pattern in order to rehabilitate or prevent injury or to enhance performance. The change may be to explore new movement options, encouraging the creative process and versatility as a mover. The change may be to better prepare the body and the mind for class or performance, taking form as a warm-up or pre-performance ritual. While these practices serve very different purposes, they all center around the idea of taking time for yourself to work at your own pace on what you need.

There are numerous benefits to developing a practice of one's own for both the teacher and student of dance, with one major asset being the potential for integrating and applying the Somatic Principles presented in this book to and for oneself. Think of it as homework. In contemporary educational theory, homework is just that — the integration and application through practice of what was learned in class (Gardner 1993b). As teachers of dance, we know that in training dancers some of what needs to occur for their individual growth and advancement has to happen outside of class. If we are concerned about core strength in our students, we provide them with practice routines to do at home; if they need to work on their flexibility, we suggest stretching exercises to do before and after class (Kassing 1992). There simply is not enough time for technique class to do and be everything for everyone. As a student of dance, you know that practice outside of class can assist you with challenging aspects of technique, such as the combination that you cannot quite get right or improving the lightness of your landing in a jump. This same approach can be applied to the Somatic Principles used in this book. If what you want to change is related to a habitual way of moving, working on breathing, sensing, connecting, or initiating outside of class is one way to approach this type of movement re-education that requires time and practice to evoke. However, the primary emphasis of this chapter is on developing a practice outside of class that is more than just spot fixing problems with technique or movement habits; it is about actualizing and expanding conditions for change that the learner can self-support over time.

Another benefit of a self-practice is that it can allow the dance student to experience moving without comparing himself or herself to others or to an aesthetic ideal. Making time to move in a nonjudgmental environment can be an effective tool for creating change. Most of the somatic techniques operate under a system of less external feedback in relation to an aesthetic ideal than the typical technique class offers (Alexander 1969; Alon 1996; Bartenieff and Lewis 1980; Hackney 1998; Hartley 1995; Franklin 1996; Todd 1937). For some students, just having the opportunity to move without that restriction can open up more movement potential than was previously experienced. Additionally, a self-practice can help dancers learn how to reduce the internal dialogue or self-talk of self-criticism, which can also improve movement performance and creativity (Gallwey1976; Lidor and Singer 2000).

Figure 7.3 A Self-Practice (Shaina Cantino; photograph by Marcella Hackbardt).

What to Include in a Self-Practice and Why

Self-practices can range from being highly organized to being fairly unstructured and spontaneous. However, it is useful to have some order and regularity to your practice if you are concerned with seeing specific improvements or being able to identify the results of your work. Using a reference movement at the beginning and end of each practice (similar to a pre- and posttest in research experiments) can be beneficial. For example, doing a body scan at the beginning and end of your practice and noting changes in how your body contacts the floor or doing leg swings before and after and noting the difference in ease and quality can be your assessment of how your practice went and what was useful to you. These frames of reference (see Chapter 3) provide before and after snapshots of your self-practice that are useful as both feedback and motivation.

A self-practice should contain a combination of whole body movement patterns and a refinement of those movement patterns as revealed through differentiation of the involved parts. Work on the parts should then be integrated back into the whole body movement patterns. This methodology is in keeping with the way in which we develop and learn movement. It also honors the fact that we are a functional whole, a concept that has arisen repeatedly throughout this text. Determining where a problem or weakness really begins is a complicated process and frequently requires looking beyond the obvious manifestation (Alon 1996; Feldenkrais 1981). For example, the source of knee pain may be the alignment of the tarsus, which may be off as a result of inefficient pelvic placement. Once the root of the issue is determined and addressed, the changes need to be reintegrated into the whole. So in the previous example, once a more appropriate pelvic alignment is discovered, attention must be brought back to how this change alters weight distribution through the legs and into the feet, and also how it affects alignment up through the spine to the skull. If the self-practice is more creatively oriented, looking at whole body movement preferences may reveal some patterns or movement options that are underutilized. After isolating and becoming familiar with these particular elements, time should be spent integrating these more foreign ways of working back into the known movement patterns.

Movement Experience: *Discovering Preferences in Movement Patterns.* This exploration draws on ideas from Laban Movement Analysis and Authentic Movement. It is intended to increase self-awareness of movement preferences and can be included in a technique, improvisation, or composition class setting. Partner up with someone and decide who will witness and who will dance first. First dancer: begin to improvise and continue moving for five minutes. Try not to be self-conscious — just dance the way you like to dance. Partner witnessing: observe carefully, taking notes or drawing if you desire. Provide detailed feedback at the end of the time, and then switch roles.

Teaching Tip: Five minutes is a long time to improvise. The idea is that even if a student starts out self-conscious, with fatigue he or she will revert to their preferences in movement. After sharing with partners the activity can be expanded in several ways: (1) students can go back and create a set phrase that exemplifies what they tend to do in movement; (2) they can also explore and create, demonstrating what they do not typically do in movement; (3) these phrases can be combined; and/or (4) they can create a phrase based on what they observed of their peer's movement preferences.

Deciding What to Change and Avoiding Spot Fixes

A dance teacher at a university was watching her students do a plié combination and noticed that many were not working with the full range of knee, hip, and ankle flexion. There was a sense of tension to the movement, and some were lifting their heels off the floor at the bottom of the demi plié. Initial encouragement to use the full plié resulted in temporary improvement, however, on the very next combination and then throughout class, she continually had to remind students. Knowing what to correct and how to correct it is not always a straightforward process, as this familiar class situation illustrates. It frequently goes beyond recognizing the importance of kinetic chains as in the earlier knee pain and pelvic alignment example. In bringing about change, the whole psychophysical being must be taken into consideration. Even when receiving augmented (teacher supplied) feedback, corrections will not last if the underlying problems are not addressed (Coker 2009; Schmidt and Wrisberg 2008). Identifying possible reasons for why something is happening can be helpful in deciding whether to correct it directly or to go at it from a more global perspective, looking beyond just the part-whole issue on a body level (Coker 2009; Schmidt and Wrisberg 2008). This approach is just as true in developing a self-practice as it is in correcting students during technique class. From either the students' or the teacher's perspective, several possible reasons can be identified for the plié being foreshortened in our previous example. Overall increased stress or tension in the students could be contributing to the issue and also to not being aware of the holding pattern. Other factors could include fatigue, imitation of a less than adequate demonstration by the teacher, feeling overwhelmed by class material or a class environment that is unsupportive, or less optimal functioning somewhere else in the body such as the torso and spine (Coker 2009; Magill 2011; Schmidt and Wrisberg 2008).

In a self-practice, one has to learn how to navigate corrections and adjustments of movement patterns without augmented feedback and without an external standard to strive to achieve. There is nobody else to instruct, correct, or motivate. This absence can be unsettling initially for dancers who are used to working in a group setting with someone else responsible for directing activity and giving feedback (Mosston and Ashworth 2002). To add to this, in dance technique classes, teachers and students have an aesthetic ideal of how movements should look on the human form. In somatic disciplines this is not necessarily the case. The aesthetic is usually of what is natural, organic, and fitting for the individual (Bainbridge-Cohen 1993; Feldenkrais 1972; Hackney 1998; Swiegard 1974; Todd 1937). While this is ultimately freeing and helpful in discovering new movement options, it can initially be problematic for dancers. Moving without comparing oneself to an aesthetic ideal that often embraces beauty can feel foreign and even pointless. For these students it can be tempting to approach working with the Somatic Principles in the same manner, which can lead to spot fixing or adjusting a part to conform to an idealized image. While altering this mentality may be challenging, teachers can make students aware of these value judgments and tendencies. Modeling through the inclusion of movement experiences in class, covering or turning away from the mirror, and directing attention to how movement feels rather than looks may prove helpful.

Movement Exploration: *Discovering Your Adjustments.* Try this movement experience to learn more about your underlying assumptions about movement correction. Lying on the floor, take a moment to scan your body (see Chapter 3 Movement Experience: Scanning the Body for complete body-scan directions). Notice whether you are able to lie on the floor and be still or if you adjust or correct your body positioning. Roll to your side, get up, walk around the room, and go back to lying on the floor. Continue the body-scan activity from before. Notice if you are able to remain still in whatever new configuration you are lying in on the floor. Repeat a few more times, and notice whether you perceive there to be a right or "correct" way to lie on the floor. Do you have to adjust your parts in relation to this right way of positioning yourself, or can you let go of this ideal and rest as you end up without fixing anything?

Tools for Creating a Self-Practice: Expanding Frames of Reference

Some other tools can be employed in a self-practice to help circumvent this desire to correct or "fix." In many cases it can be effective to think of a self-practice as a laboratory, playing around with all the possible combinations or ways of doing an action until you learn something more or figure out what works best for you. In motor learning terms, this process is called expanding the frame of reference (Coker 2009). For example, exploring how many ways you can solve a movement problem, like initiating flexion of the leg at the hip, creates new possibilities for the learner. Every time we attempt a movement in a slightly different manner, we are allowing ourselves an opportunity to develop a deeper and broader frame of reference for that action. Having these options helps us discover and decide what is more correct or efficient for each given situation. Rather than physically practicing the identical movement repeatedly, the somatic techniques often ask the individual to explore nuances and variety within a given movement (Feldenkrais 1984; Hackney 1998; Hartley 1995).

157

This tactic can be incorporated into a self-practice, reducing the need to evaluate whether you are doing a movement "right" or "wrong" and giving you permission to discover if you can do it differently. Expanding the frame of reference can also be useful in comparing the actual to the intended movement, as it provides the opportunity to use movement to extremes (see Chapter 3). For example, when placing one's feet in a parallel position, it may be easier to find the desired position by moving the feet closer and farther apart a few times until one is able to feel the appropriate relationship between the foot and hip. One can also do the same thing lying on the floor with the feet on the wall as if it were the floor. Then stand up and experience what it feels like to place the fleet directly below the ischial tuberosities (sitting bones).

Movement Experience: *Comparing Actual and Internal Self-Image.* Sit on a piece of paper and make a pencil mark where your ischial tuberosities contact the floor. Look at the distance between the two marks and see if it is what you expected or not. Now stand on the marks, feeling how the feet are placed directly in line with the sitting bones.

Novelty

Novelty is part of the process of expanding the frame of reference, and it also fits with the concept of using variety to increase kinesthetic sensitivity. As such, it is a powerful tool for creating change in movement response. A novel movement is one that has not been done before, or a familiar movement performed in a different or unfamiliar configuration (Schmidt and Wrisberg 2008). The advantage of using novelty is that it capitalizes on what is called the power law of practice. The power law of practice states that the greatest amount of improvement in the execution of a previously unexperienced movement occurs after just a few practice attempts. After this, there will be a leveling off of progress or a plateau (Coker 2009; Schmidt and Wrisberg 2008).

In the Feldenkrais Method, novelty is integral to broadening the spectrum of available movement responses or expanding the frame of reference. Feldenkrais wrote on many occasions that every individual should have more than two solutions for every movement problem (Feldenkrais 1981, 1984, 2005). His reasoning was that having two choices was really the movement equivalent of only being able to say yes and no. He postulated that to increase freedom in movement, an individual needed to be able to make the movement equivalent of yes and no (or on and off) plus two more options (Alon 1996; Feldenkrais 1981, 2005). One method for discovering novel movement solutions employed by many somatic techniques is adapting the context in which the movement happens. Shifting spatial orientation is one of the most frequently used methods for changing the context and creating novelty, and can include turning to face a new direction or doing the movement to the other side (Franklin, 1996;

Hackney 1998; Todd 1937). As we have seen, many somatic techniques also utilize moving on the floor, thereby resetting one's habitual relationship to gravity (Bartenieff and Lewis 1980; Feldenkrais 1972; Hartley 1995; Swiegard 1974).

Accessing the Right-Brain Mode of Thinking

As we have already acknowledged, working alone in the studio is foreign to many dance students, as dance is usually a communal experience. It can be intimidating, even paralyzing to go into an empty studio to try to develop a self-practice (Tharp 2003). Regardless of the type of self-practice being developed (or put into use), dancers need to learn to move away from a verbal, analytical, judgmental mode of thinking in order to create and perform most effectively. This shift takes time to achieve for many people, but with regular practice it can occur more consistently and quickly. Most of us can relate to going into the studio to create and feeling as though nothing of value results for the longest time. At some point, if you stick with it long enough, you experience a moment when things start to "click." You become immersed in the process and the exploration; time ceases to be relevant, distractions are unimportant, and a sense of alert, yet calm, confidence surrounds you.

In brain lateralization theory, this way of processing is associated with shifting to a thinking mode in which the right hemisphere of the brain is dominant. The brain is divided into two hemispheres that are connected via the corpus collosum (Kandel, Schwartz, and Jessell 1991). The left hemisphere of the brain is associated with verbal, analytical, and sequential functioning, while the right hemisphere is associated with visual, perceptual, and simultaneous operations (Edwards 1999, xvii; Kandel, Schwartz, and Jessell 1991). While we all utilize the whole brain, the left side of the brain tends to dominate for many of us because of the significance of language in our lives. By learning to down-play this proclivity to default to the analytical side for certain tasks, we can take advantage of the other, more intuitive parts of the brain that are sometimes overpowered by language.

In her book, *Drawing on the Right Side of the Brain,* Betty Edwards (1999) examines right brain processing in terms of visual art, primarily, and suggests methods for being more aware of and able to control making this shift. Much of this shift revolves around seeing without labeling to circumvent the language centers of the brain. As Edwards states, "In order to gain access to the subdominant visual, perceptual R mode of the brain, it is necessary to present the brain with a job that the verbal, analytic L mode will turn down" (xx). As such, she provides exercises like drawing a figure upside down or using images that shift perception between positive and negative space. Karen Snouffer, one of the artists for this text, uses tools to enhance this shift with her students as well. One technique she employs involves having students hold an object in their lap, feeling the outline of it with their nondominant hand. Without trying to "figure out" what the object is, students then do a contour drawing of what they are feeling, using their dominant drawing hand. The idea is to imagine the pencil is tracing the object in one continuous line (Snouffer 2011).

While we cannot dance upside down or replicate complex movement sequences by feeling the contour of another dancer, the right brain theory and its applications in visual art do suggest that we consider ways of accessing and optimizing this mode of thinking in dance. Reflecting back to other topics in this book, we have actually touched on this many times because of the inherent overlap between mind and body in dance and somatic work. Brain lateralization can be related to the concept of the Bliss-Boder Hypothesis, focal versus ambient vision, quieting the voice of Self 1 that sits in judgment of Self 2, and finding ways to be present in the moment.

Other possibilities exist for maximizing right brain contributions in dance classes, including the strategic use of language in teaching. We have occasionally used ballet and modern vocabulary in this text because one of the benefits of language is its ability to quickly describe and identify actions when visuals are not present. As teachers, we may want to avoid this benefit as much as possible. The minute we identify an action with a verbal label, students will tend to move to their association with that term and cease really seeing (and feeling) the movement. If a student is struggling with a jump and the teacher says, "It's like a pas de chat," the student may have more success with quickly achieving some version of the action, but may well stop seeing what makes it different from a pas de chat.

Feldenkrais wrote about this language issue as well. He discussed the disadvantage that labeling presents to problem solving and creating. He felt that, as a society, we tend to look at a complex situation and seek some term to describe it as a way of understanding it. This reaction goes back to the tendency for the left brain to dominate. The problem, then, is that we may stop recognizing the complexities and resort to the status-quo solution. For example, by labeling a stroke victim as just that, we can forget to look at the specific needs and abilities of the person (Feldenkrais 1981, 32).

We can also encourage the shift to right brain thinking in other ways. Flashing (Movement Experience: Flash Phrase for Learning and Programming Movement in Chapter 4) is one example. By encouraging really seeing and not labeling, talking about, or analyzing the movement, we are essentially taking a similar approach to contour or upside-down drawing. "Seeing is a primary source of sensory data that sparks the imaginative process. Any individual who is working creatively is not concerned so much with labeling as becoming aware of the form and spatial relationships, the inner structure as well as the outer shape of an object, and in sensing the qualities that pervade the experience" (Hawkins 1991, 21). This quote suggests another classroom technique for accessing the right brain — using the concepts of positive and negative space. Just as perceptions of figures can change when viewing visual art, we can look at the space occupied and not occupied by the physical body in the performing arts.

Movement Experience: *Positive/Negative Space Sculptures.* Go with a partner. One person be the "sculptor" and mold your partner (piece of clay) into a shape. Really attend to the position of the limbs in relation to each other and to the body. See the shape as it stands in the space. When everyone is pleased with his or her sculpture, take a walk through the "art gallery," and admire each others' creations. Each sculptor select a new piece of art (not your own creation). Take some time to look at this work, and start attending to the space around the shape. Find some aspect of this space that calls to you, and shape your body to it, thus emphasizing the negative space. Original "clay pieces," unmold yourselves, while original "sculptors" stay frozen. This second group can now go for a gallery walk and repeat the same process. Trio version: One person: assume a still position. Second person: examine the negative space around him or her and shapes your body to it. Third person: repeat this with the new, more complex shape created by persons one and two. All three take a moment to sense the shape, then person one detach and remold to the shape that remains with person two and three. Keep repeating this process. As it becomes easier and more fluid to see and respond to the negative space, start thinking about the transitional movements. Try to make the detaching and reattaching a conscious part of the visual picture, so the movement between positions is just as important as the positions themselves.

Dominant Side of the Body

We all have a dominant side or a preference for using one side of the body over the other. This goes beyond handedness to include the eyes and legs (Edwards 1999, 42; Kandel, Schwartz, and Jessell 1991). Dominance is

Figure 7.4 Positive/Negative Space Sculptures.

related to, but distinct from, brain lateralization. It can be an observable manifestation of brain organization because the right side of the brain controls the left side of the body (and vice versa) through the neural connections between brain and body that cross over (decussate). Someone who prefers working with the right side is expressing left hemispheric dominance in terms of motor control, but it does not mean a right-handed person has to revert to left mode thinking predominantly.

Movement Experience: *Finding Your Dominant Side.* Sit in a chair comfortably, and close your eyes. Get up and take a step. Sit back down again, and repeat a few more times. Did you step out on the same leg each time? If so, this is your dominant leg. Which leg do you use to step onto a curb? When you go up or down stairs, which leg do you step with first? These are all means of finding your dominant leg. To find your dominant eye, stand some eight to ten feet away from an object. Extend your arm in front of you with your hand in a thumbs-up position and centered so that your thumb obscures the object. Close one eye while still looking at the object beyond your thumb. Repeat using the other eye. Compare the visual image, noticing which eye closing resulted in less movement of the object. Was it the right or the left eye? Your dominant eye is the one for which the image shifted less. To find your dominant hand for moving, consider beyond the hand you write with because writing does not always coincide with dominance. Which hand do you use to get a cup out of the cupboard, or which one picks up objects, unloads the dishwasher or opens the door?

Dominance of a side of the body occurs when we have information coming in from two sources, such as the paired eyes, ears, hands, or feet. The brain processes information in this situation from one side at a time, much like the convergence of a two-lane highway into a single lane road. This means that information from the dominant eye precedes information from the nondominant eye into the brain. It is another example of automating responses; the central nervous system prioritizes one side over the other at some point in development to make the decision-making process more efficient (Coker 2009; Magill 2011; Schmidt and Wrisberg 2008).

Teaching Tip: Movement vocabulary or material is routinely taught favoring the right side. This is true for Kenpo Karate and other movement forms as well as dance. In Kenpo, techniques are taught with "the strong side forward," which is modeled as being the right side. This practice presents a disadvantage to left-handers initially, although in the long run they probably wind up being more even and less lateralized than right-handed practitioners. Take a minute and think through your typical lesson plan and identify the number of dance phrases where you have your students begin on the right side. Do you know how many students in your class are left-side dominant? Do you give equal time to translating and performing combinations on the left? Given the preceding information, consider whether you are providing enough opportunities for your left-side-dominant students.

Research indicates that the transfer of movement from the dominant side to the nondominant side is stronger and more efficient (Coker 2009; Schmidt and Wisberg 2008). Feldenkrais sessions take full advantage of this research, as students are instructed to perform the lesson on whichever side they wish. About one-third of the time, the other side is done through visualization alone, and students are amazed to discover no difference between the two sides at the end (Feldenkrais 1972). Sometimes it is even better on the visualized side! The left-dominant dance student is continually being presented with movement material that he or she learns first on the nondominant side and then transfers to the dominant side. Simply starting combinations on the left side rather than the right sometimes can be beneficial and more equitable for all students. In doing this, your right-side dominant students will also be given opportunities to become more proficient with their nondominant side.

These ideas about lateralization and dominance are presented here because recognizing one's own and one's students' tendencies and preferences may be helpful in guiding the development of a self-practice. Incorporating some of these techniques in classes to bring awareness to sidedness and the right brain mode of thinking will hopefully carry over and assist students with their own process alone in the studio. As we move into the next section, the connections that can be drawn between learning styles and the tendency to engage in right or left brain modes of processing will become clear. Given the trend in education for inclusion and honoring diverse learning styles, we should remember that relatively simple solutions, like reversing phrases and using road-maps, are available. The goal is ultimately to honor the fact that the whole brain is working at all times in everyone and to find ways to prepare and develop all of our students for both the intuitive and the more analytical aspects of the training process.

Road Maps or Navigation Tools for the Journey

What follows are three methods or road maps for guiding the process of creating, developing, and experiencing a self-practice. These road maps are an effective way to get started and were developed out of the authors' experiences with dance training, motor learning and development principles, and somatic practices. A road map for the journey is a useful metaphor for the experience that one undergoes in devising a self-practice. Having a template or structure for the process assists in making it happen. The road map is a good place to begin, but the actual experience or journey will be individual, and adaptations may need to be made to the plan as it develops and is put into play. You can try working with all three road maps to discover which one is most appropriate for your process at this point in time, at this point in your life, and given your specific needs and desires for change.

Learning Styles

Since the purpose of both a self-practice and the somatic techniques in general is to learn something new, learning styles and factors that impact learning need to be considered. As teachers we work with a variety of students who have diverse learning styles. Students can learn from any method presented but have a preferred way in which they learn best (Coker 1995, 2009; Dunn and Dunn 1975; Dunn and Dunn 1993; Dunn, Dunn, and Price 1989; Gardner 1993a). Commonly referenced learning styles are analytical, global, or a combination of the two (Coker 2009; Dunn et al. 1982). Analytical learners will prefer to learn new information one step at a time. They would rather have information presented in a chronological and orderly manner, moving through smaller pieces of related new information before going on to the next piece to be learned. Global learners prefer to learn new information by getting an overview of the big picture before going into details. They would rather get the "lay of the land" before tackling pieces of new information. Global learners also tend to prefer to explore different avenues before settling down to the task at hand (Coker 2009; Dunn et al. 1982; Dunn, Dunn, and Price 1989).

Other factors related to learning styles include how the students deal with the environment in which they are learning, the content being taught, and preferences for types of sensory input. Analytical learners prefer fewer distractions, tending to concentrate on one thing at a time, while global learners can accommodate distractions and attend to different pieces of information more readily (Coker 2009; Dunn, Dunn, and Price 1989). We should recognize that for any individual, their learning style may shift with time and experience, and the learning style employed may be discipline specific. It is not uncommon for a student to have different learning styles depending on the content being presented (Coker 2009). Others may adopt a relatively consistent learning style regardless of the discipline. Most learners prefer some aspects of both the analytical and the global learning styles (Coker 2009). Another aspect of learning style to consider is the student's preferred mode for taking in new information. Students tend to respond best to a specific set of sensory input, whether visual, auditory, kinesthetic, or a combination of the three (Coker 2009; Gardener 1993b). Consider exploring an expanded frame of reference with the Movement Experience: Comparing Actual and Internal Self-Image (p. 158) to find the parallel position of the feet. While the variation of going wider and narrower with the feet will probably be effective for the kinesthetic learner, drawing and seeing the actual width of an ideal parallel position may assist the visual learner more. A teacher explaining parallel might work best for the auditory learner.

The road maps that follow are goal setting, themes, and a constraints model; any of the three can be the scaffolding for a self-practice that uses the Somatic Principles to enact change in some specific dance arena. The goal-setting road map may be best suited for a combination learner, engaging some aspects of both global and analytical learning styles. Recognizing the larger, overall goals requires a more global approach, while identifying the more specific steps toward achieving these goals shifts the process to a more analytical approach. The global learner may be better served using a theme road map, where concentration centers on the exploration of and discovery through general concepts. The analytical learner might prefer the constraints map, with its logical analysis of all variables influencing the desired change.

A teacher can approach the road maps in several ways. Before assigning a road map as homework or class work, students can complete a brief learning styles inventory. You can use the one provided (see Table 7.1 at the end of this chapter), you can reference other existing inventories (there are many online), or you can develop your own based on the ideas provided. After some information has been collected on the individual's learning style, students can be directed to the appropriate road map. Another method is to have students try out all three road maps for the first part of their self-practice development and then stick with the one they prefer. Lastly, students can use all three maps to develop three different self-practices and then decide for themselves which self-practice is most beneficial and effective.

In any of the three road maps, a good way to get started is to ask students to generate a list of what they want to learn more about, work on, or transform. Perhaps a student is continually being reminded to adjust his or her pelvic tilt, or he or she has struggled with their ability to shift levels, moving in and out of the floor easily. Maybe some are interested in reducing performance anxiety, or they want to develop the ability to create movement that radiates expressivity through the arms. Perhaps they want to address an old injury that plagues them. Students should be encouraged to think about all aspects of the dance experience to avoid focusing solely on technical skills.

An important next step is for students to examine why this change is meaningful for them. What is motivating the student to focus on this particular aspect of his or her movement? Spending a little time reflecting on what would be gained if this particular change were accomplished can give students an idea of what they value in it and if they are truly interested in concentrating on it. Sometimes we create goals for ourselves that are based on what we believe others want for us or from us, rather than what we truly desire for ourselves. At first glance this may seem to be veering off topic, but it is a relevant aspect of the change process that is inherent in somatic techniques and necessary for developing an effective self-practice. The ability to create change is greatly influenced by the motivation of the individual to integrate and implement the new behavior. Research has suggested that when the individual values or believes the change is meaningful or important for them, he or she is more successful at integrating the new behavior. This finding goes along with the idea that learners absorb corrections best when they ask for or really want them (Magill 2011; Schmidt and Wrisberg 2008). To summarize the questions presented in the previous section:

1. Generate a list of what you want to learn more about, focus on, or change.
2. Examine why this change is meaningful for you.
   a. What is motivating you to focus on this particular aspect of your movement?
   b. What would you gain if this particular change were accomplished?
   c. What do you value about this type of change?

Road Map #1: Goal Setting

Setting goals can be a tool in developing a practice, creating support for the change process itself. Goal setting is one method for placing attention on what we are doing and how that compares to what we are intending to do (refer to chapter 6 for more information on intention). Identifying and labeling the goals to be accomplished in terms of outcome goals, performance goals, and process goals can be useful in planning what needs to happen along the journey to creating change. Because the larger-scale goals will take longer, breaking them down into component parts that are more easily attainable can help avoid frustration. Outcome goals are the end result, or long-range goals. Performance goals are shorter-term goals that involve improving discrete skills needed to achieve the outcome goal. Process goals relate to the specific technical or artistic requirements of executing the performance goal movement skills and are more immediate in scope (Coker 2009; Schmidt and Wrisberg 2008; Taylor and Taylor 1995).

The first step in setting goals is to identify an outcome goal — a general, global, or overarching goal, perhaps derived from or inspired by the list the student made. Some examples of general goals for the student of dance could be: I would like to be more expressive during performance situations; I would like to be more skillful at auditioning; I would like to be more fluid or relaxed during technique class. After identifying a general goal, reexamine it and see if it can be framed more accurately and specifically in the present tense. The previous examples could be restated as performance goals: I would like to experience my expressivity more often during performances by really seeing and engaging with the other performers; I would like to pick up phrases faster in auditions: I would like to experience dance class as less effortful more frequently than I am now.

The next step in the goal setting process is to identify specific changes that can be realistically accomplished. For example, the last goal can be narrowed down to: I feel tense during barre work and would like to experience more ease in my head and neck. These specific changes, or process goals, can be viewed as the foundation that supports attainment of the outcome or general goal. It is here that the Somatic Principles can be applied. Say, for example, a student's outcome goal is to be a great jumper. A performance goal might then be to be able to do a split leap. Achieving this entails ascertaining issues relevant to this movement and growth overall, or process goals. This particular student may discover that he or she needs to work on release in the hamstrings and the ability to maximize ground reaction forces. As such, self-practice could include carefully designed stretching and relaxation exercises using the breath, plus connectivity-based movement experiences to work on using the feet and legs to propel the body through space, combined with visualization activities. In this manner, students can expand and explore component skills more holistically, rather than just repeating the split leap over and over, but they will hopefully still be working on creating a desired change.

Teaching Tip: Teachers may want and need to provide some support or advising in the goal-setting process. It is often more difficult for students to come to appropriate and desirable goals than might be expected. Teachers may want to ask students to include an artistic goal in addition to a specific technical goal in developing their self-practice in order to best manage goal setting for the intended purpose of overall growth. Frequently, students will initially gravitate to very specific concrete or technical goals rather than considering the importance of the global use of the body or artistic goals (Kassing 1992, 59). The split leap would be a good example, or wanting to be able to do a triple pirouette. Even with technical goals like these, with guidance, students can recognize that "tricks" are not the only measure of dance ability. Encouraging students to work on the issues related to turning or the ability to do a split leap (i.e., balance, release in the neck to improve spotting, coordination, flexibility) can improve their dancing in many ways, and not just with reference to certain movements. It is important to emphasize the *how* and not just the *what* no matter what kind of goal is being established. Table 7.2 at the end of the chapter may be helpful in organizing the goal-setting process.

Another aspect of the goal-setting process is to check in regularly to acknowledge the changes that have been made and to refine and reevaluate goals. Often times we do not know all the steps that need to occur along the way in order for new behavior to emerge and be sustained. It can also be difficult for students to recognize their own growth because it is gradual, and they are too invested to be objective. Clarification and re-evaluation is an important part of the process. It is in this stage that one can begin to identify clearer images of the new movement pattern, which, in turn, facilitates integration and use of the new pattern (Hackney 1998, 24–26). It is important to remember that if it is truly change, one cannot know exactly how it will play out. What we know is what we are familiar with, and conversely, what is unfamiliar is unknown at this point in time (Alexander 1932; Feldenkrais 1972; Gallwey 1976; Hackney 1998). Acknowledging this idea can help students avoid "end-gaining," or being too product-oriented, and encourage them to invest in the process of discovering real change. Teachers can help by meeting with students at various points in the semester, providing feedback about progress, and assisting them in refining their goals and/or self-practice.

Road Map #2: Creating or Adopting Themes for a Self-Practice

Many of the somatic techniques have themes of study embedded within them. For example, in Laban Movement Analysis/Bartenieff Fundamentals there are the themes of inner and outer, exertion and recuperation, function and expression, and stability and mobility (Hackney 1998). In the Alexander Technique, themes include the concept of primary control and the use of the primary and secondary curves in movement (Alexander 1932, 1969). In Body-Mind Centering there is the theme of moving from a physiological system through sensing and feeling, and in Feldenkrais there are the themes of independence, self-image, and differentiation and integration (Bainbridge-Cohen 1993; Feldenkrais 1981,1985). We have presented the themes of breathing, sensing, connecting and initiating through the course of this book.

Themes like these can be fodder for creating a self-practice. After examining their lists and identifying which movement patterns, issues, or ideas interest them and why, students drawn to this method should consider what larger themes may be underlying more specific comments or desires. These may be themes adopted from established somatic techniques or their own theme they create. This approach starts in a similar way to the goal-setting map, but rather than identifying specific goals and ways to achieve them, students go out to a macrolevel first. They can begin with spending time doing movement experiences around their theme, discovering more about it, and then refining the self-practice based on what they learn.

Because this type of self-practice starts more open-ended and tends to be less specific and linear than goal setting, it may appeal to the global learner more than goal setting. The self-practice can approach the theme from many different vantage points to see what is most helpful. Take the example of wanting to create movement that radiates expressivity through to the ends of the limbs. As much as you try when choreographing to "do this," you are still finding this expressivity lacking in your movement. In a themed approach, you might first select explorations related to expressivity and energy flow. You could begin with the Laban Movement Analysis theme of function and expression and take some time to reflect on your movement responses outside of class. Recognizing triggers for the issue, or situations that inhibit your expressivity may ultimately be the most helpful step in overcoming the problem. Remember, awareness is the first step toward change. You might consider initiation as a starting place for explorations to determine if you are fully accessing the proximal, midlimb, and distal joints. Perhaps spending time on core-distal explorations would be helpful, or breathing and vocalizing while improvising. Movement experiences like these could be augmented with a set sequence you develop that helps you find this flow of energy to the ends of the limbs. This routine could cycle back into an improvisation score that focuses on gestures. The possibilities are endless and will be determined by the individual through the development and evolution of his or her self-practice.

Road Map #3: Constraints Model of Shaping Behavior through the Environment, Task, and Individual

Considering that most of our movement organization occurs in relation to ourselves, the task we want to do, and the environment in which it is performed, it makes sense to examine another approach for making changes in behavior. The constraints model developed by Newell (1986) was originally published in a paper for motor development. In subsequent years, his model has been taken up by a variety of disciplines within the field of kinesiology, including motor control, motor learning, and sport psychology. In his paper, Newell outlines a few basic constructs about how human behavior and movement patterns are shaped by our physiological and anatomical structure, our internal motivation, attention, and mental traits and personality. He calls these components the constraints acting on the individual. Movement organization and patterns will also be affected by the constraints presented by the task and

Figure 7.5 Turning Preference Example (Shaina Cantino; photograph by Marcella Hackbardt).

the environment. An example may clarify how both the dance student and teacher can use the constraints model to navigate a course of change in movement patterns. When doing pirouettes, a dancer is able to accomplish three or four turns on her right but only two on her left. Using the constraints model, we can outline a few things that might be contributing to this technical difference. Starting with the structural constraint, the dancer can spend some time alone or with the teacher to discover if this preference for turning right is just during pirouettes and other technical turns or if she generally turns more easily to the right, even with her feet stationary. The latter would suggest at least two possibilities as to the difference in turning: (1) a structural predisposition, perhaps due to scoliosis or (2) a functional predisposition, perhaps resulting from a habitual self-use organized around standing on the right leg. Because she turns more times to the right than to the left, her approach to doing pirouettes on each side is also going to be different. It will influence her relationship to pirouettes in particular and to turning in general. Her motivation could be different as a result, and so will her anxiety and arousal levels for each side. The task itself can be considered, looking at whether the turning preference is there for all turns or just this particular kind of pirouette. The environment could also be considered, such as whether or not the difference in turning ability is exaggerated in a performance situation. If so, is it the lighting, performance pressure, or the surface creating the problem? Based on the results of this analysis, a self-practice can evolve that reflects the relevant constraints to turning left.

The same road map might be used to create a preperformance ritual reflecting one's own individual constraints, the piece to be performed, and the environment in which the performance occurs. A dancer can evaluate the performance experience in terms of the physical demands of the piece (task) in relation to his or her own body. In addition to physical issues including demands for range of motion, strength, and stamina, the performer can look at fatigue/stress levels and mental constraints, such as optimal arousal and attention levels. Environmental considerations might include looking at the performance space, the temperature, and even the consistency of fellow dancers. Again, there is no one recipe — the whole point is that the practice will be different and tailored to each individual, but as an example a preperformance ritual could look something like the following progression:

1. Lying on the floor, come into oneself to release muscular tension and mental anxiety using the Somatic Principles of breathing and sensing.
2. Mentally go over parts of the piece or the whole piece with visualization techniques discussed in Chapter 4.
3. Starting on the floor, sense where the body is in the moment, and what it will need to perform optimally. Do some connectivity movement experiences to address individual structural constraints such as range of motion and core support activation based on the physical demands of the piece.

4. This might progress into an exploration of developmental movement sequences, followed by some grounding movements. This could include changing levels from lying to standing, back to lying, and/or weight shifting and propulsion actions. Balancing/counter-balancing and working with eyes closed can help center and bring awareness to kinesthetic input.

5. This could be followed by moving in the space any way desired, or putting on some music that is energizing and/or reflects the quality of the piece to be performed.

6. The self-practice could conclude with either a lively, energetic release of excess energy and tension or lying on the floor and resting and breathing fully.

All of the preceding parts of the preperformance ritual should be adapted to reflect the actual performer, the piece to be performed, and the performance space.

Teaching Tip: Students can be encouraged to think outside of the box in developing a self-practice. Another type of self-practice might be developed utilizing an alternative training method. This might be for rehabilitative purposes, for corrective or preventive conditioning, for maintaining training, or even just to provide variety to the daily routine. For example, a dancer might create his or her own pool ballet class. Because working in the water changes the resistance to movement and provides a greater sense of buoyancy, it reverses the muscular action for dance movements. This can be helpful in balancing muscular strength and flexibility around the joints and for increasing sensitivity to how actions can be performed on land (Hamill and Knutzen 1995). Water resistance when performing a port de bra, for instance, can give students a new qualitative sense of the shaping of the arms. When doing a dégagé in the water, it is much more difficult to close into the standing position. This level of difficulty helps reinforce the importance of this part of the action and will help to strengthen the hip adductor muscles that may be less developed than the abductors. This kind of a class is also beneficial in an injury situation, as the water takes much of the weight off of the joints, and it can be used to maintain conditioning through the off-season.

Teachers can model alternative training classes to jump-start students' self-practice ideas. These classes also can provide a welcome change of pace for students who are burned out toward the end of the semester. Other kinds of alternative classes could entail doing floor-barre or a physio-ball class, where technical work is adapted to be performed with the ball.

Transfer: Taking It Back into Technique Class

The last step in developing a practice is to apply what you have learned in your self-practice to other situations, thereby creating conditions for integration. In motor learning, this step is called transfer. Transfer is when knowledge of a previously learned skill can be used to further performance of another distinct skill (Coker 2009; Magill 2011; Schmidt and Wrisberg 2008). Transfer can be of two types, near or far, which describes the relationship of the learned material to the new material. Near transfer applies when the situations are similar, and far transfer is when the relationship is distant, making it more difficult to integrate the skill set (Coker 2009; Magill 2011; Rose and Christina 2006; Schmidt and Wrisberg 2008). If you are incorporating the Somatic Principles from this book into your self-practice, then the relationship of your self-practice to technique class is probably somewhere in the middle of the near-far continuum, as the principles in this text are related to the foundations of movement execution rather than practicing specific phrases of dance technique.

One method for increasing integration is to get to class a few minutes early and lie comfortably on the floor with your eyes closed. Mentally, go through your self-practice in relation to class and its typical structure. Imagine moments in class when you can consider the changes you want to make and implement them. So if your self-practice, or part of it, is concentrating on the breath, consider when in class you can pause for even a moment and think about your breathing. Is there time in the class to repeat a combination with the emphasis on your breathing? If you are using this book on your own without the guidance of a teacher, it may be helpful to speak with your instructor about what you are working on so he or she can understand your approach to the class. Ideally the teacher of the class is assisting students with setting the themes and directions for their self-practices and subsequently can include moments in class to highlight the transfer of the self-practice topics to the technique class. In this manner, the student is learning how it all comes together with the guidance of his or her teacher.

Teachers can help with other ideas and strategies for integration. Carrying the self-practice concepts beyond the class and the practice time can contribute to the transfer process. Students can be encouraged to attend to changes in their everyday actions, as it is frequently in these simple activities that transfer can occur most readily (Fortin and Girard 2005). After class it is equally important to reflect on what did and did not work in terms of transfer to more complex dance technique. Students may not know all the answers, but taking the time to acknowledge where they are and where they are headed is part of the process of transfer. Journaling, discussing, and reflecting on the class experience are beneficial to the process of transfer. Research on the integration of somatic work into dance technique has revealed that "the process of putting experience into written or spoken words leads to deeper analysis of difficulties and to their possible solutions. These methods of classroom data collection could aid both teacher and student in reflecting on each other's actions within the dance class" (Fortin and Girard 2005, 131). To help assess transfer when teachers and students are working with similar principles in and out of class, an example of a midterm self-reflection assignment is provided at the end of the chapter (see Table 7.3).

Conclusions

It is ironic, but a habitual practice is what is needed in order to address changing habits or even just to discover new movement options. Twyla Tharp (2003) speaks of this in her book *The Creative Habit* with reference to the need for a regular routine to facilitate creativity. Other research has shown that the preperformance routine is "some plan, procedure, or ritual that facilitates learning and performance and gives

Select the most appropriate answer. When learning new things you:	
1	2
Prefer Alone or One on One	Prefer Group
Prefer Formal Setting	Prefer Casual Setting
Prefer Structure and Guidance	Prefer Less Structure and Guidance
Prefer No Distractions	Prefer Distractions
Prefer No External Noise	Prefer External Noise
Prefer No Breaks	Prefer Breaks
Prefer Bright Lights	Prefer Soft Lights
Prefer No Drink or Food Breaks	Prefer Drink or Food Breaks
Tally how many items you selected from columns one and two. More items from column one indicate a preference for an analytical learning style while more items from column two suggest a preference for a global learning style.	

Table 7.1 Modified Learning Styles Inventory.

	Outcome Goal Long-term, general goal	Performance Goal Skill needed for outcome	Process Goal Quality of Movement Skill
Technical Goal			
Artistic Goal			

Table 7.2 Goal-Setting Process.

Name_____   **Date:**

Please complete this assignment, and bring it with you to discuss and submit at your midterm conference.

Themes for the class so far have included the concepts of:

- Breath
    - Including applications to falls and swings
- Kinesthetic Sensing
    - Including the use of body scans
- Visual Sensing
    - Including applications to types of performance focus
- Connectivity
    - Including application to rolling, under and over-curves, inversions, and partnering
- Initiation
    - Considering location, phrasing, and sequencing

1. Reflect on these themes and what they mean to you, both in theory and in application. In other words, explain each concept and discuss your ability to access this way of working in movement. Which of these do you consider to be strengths? Which are harder for you to do or understand? In what situations are particular themes helpful? Which themes are already incorporated in your movement vocabulary?

2. How do these themes relate to your self-practice? Do you experience these themes differently in class than when working on your own?

3. Do you have any specific goals for the rest of the semester? How do you plan to achieve them?

4. What would help you to achieve your desired results? Can I help?

5. Please reflect and comment on your experiences in class so far. This may include: a) Questions you may have had in class and/or about class; b) Parts of class which you find most challenging and/or enjoy the most; c) Aspects of your dancing that you are most pleased with this semester; d) Discoveries you have made; e) Things you would like to address in class; f) General comments.

performers control over their motor, emotional and cognitive behaviors. The most effective preperformance routines are usually employed with a high degree of consistency" (Lidor and Singer 2000, 34). The benefits of consistent, self-directed exploration and application of the Somatic Principles holds true for any kind of self-practice, whether its function is technical or artistic growth, pre- or post-class or performance. Participation in a regular self-practice driven by Somatic Principles can also broaden the scope of what a dancer considers his or her self-practice to be. Students often start applying what they are learning to everyday life activities and pedestrian movement. This can lead to the

Figure 7.1 "A Practice of One's Own" (Karen Snouffer).

realization that, just as the whole self is invested in a movement experience, one's whole life shapes one's movement potential, not just dance class. As such, a self-practice can lead to a deeper immersion in Somatic Principles, and dancers who delve more deeply may profit in their artistic and creative performance careers.

Opposite: Table 7.3 Midterm Self-Reflection Assignment.

8

Specific Applications to Technique

For the dancer, technique is a harness that provides the necessary control to fly and spin, allowing the dancer to rebound in and out of the earth with unseen wings.—Erkert 2003, 4

Introduction

In this chapter, we examine more specific applications of dance science and the Somatic Principles to dance technique. We begin with a more general discussion of conditioning and training principles and look at how this information relates to dance training with a somatic backbone. We then consider specific components of dance technique. Rather than starting with the Somatic Principle and applying it to the teaching of class, we begin with specific dance skills and discuss different ways to address them using this body of somatic and/or scientific information. This format is included as a way of incorporating additional ideas and building upon concepts previously presented, and so that teachers can easily reference techniques for teaching particular skills.

Conditioning for Dancers

The basic fitness considerations are similar for any movement activity, although the specific demands of dance do distinguish its physical conditioning needs somewhat from sports or exercise programs. Any conditioning program has four fundamental objectives: (1) strength; (2) flexibility (accessing full joint range of motion and muscular flexibility); (3) muscular endurance; and (4) cardiorespiratory endurance (Brooks and Fahey 1985; Clippinger-Robertson 1988; Welsh 2009). According to Sally Sevey Fitt (1996, 388), with its aesthetic considerations dance adds the following: alignment, neuromuscular coordination, and relaxation.

All of these conditioning categories adhere to the training principles to be discussed next, and technique classes vary in their emphasis on each of these objectives (Fitt 1996; Franklin 2004; Welsh 2009). In general, dance classes will always place attention on neuromuscular coordination, but there is not enough time to train in

176

all the other areas (Clippinger 2007; Fitt 1996; Franklin 2004; Welsh 2009). Take cardiorespiratory endurance, for example. This system is rarely taxed in the classroom, because dance combinations tend to be shorter than three minutes (the point at which aerobic metabolism starts to activate), and there is frequently quite a bit of starting and stopping to teach new material, give feedback, work on corrections, and switch groups (Brooks and Fahey 1985; Mareib 1992). However, dancers may routinely be expected to perform in pieces lasting ten minutes or more. Class (and often even rehearsal) will not physically prepare the dancer with the stamina required to perform at a high level for this length of time, so cardiorespiratory conditioning outside of technique class is needed.

Weaving somatic work, or the Somatic Principles, into the classroom helps address the dance-specific objectives. Designing classes that concentrate on breathing, sensing, connecting and initiating will incorporate the components of alignment, neuromuscular coordination, and relaxation. Hopefully self-practices using the Somatic Principles will reinforce these dance-specific needs even further. This reinforcement is particularly important, because outside-of-class training for issues of strength, flexibility, and endurance will probably not be working specifically to increase capacity in alignment, neuromuscular coordination, or relaxation.

With some creativity, and just through awareness of the different demands being placed on dancers and what class is tending to emphasize, teachers can help physically prepare their students in some of the traditional conditioning parameters. Floor work can incorporate some strength training and range of motion work, improvisations can last longer than three minutes, and a cool down can include time for stretching, for example. This kind of analysis of the dancers' needs and what class is providing can actually be inspiration for teachers wanting to explore new territory; however, dance class still cannot fill all conditioning needs. This void is inevitable, and artistic considerations need to take priority over physical conditioning in the dance classroom. Artistic exploration should never be sacrificed for a workout.

Teaching Tip: It can be frustrating for teacher and student alike when a misunderstanding occurs about the goals of technique class (Kassing 1992). It is not unusual to encounter the student mentality that it is only a good class if there is a lot of sweat and hard muscular work involved. However, sometimes this is not what students really need, and teachers may have loftier, more artistic goals. On the other hand, teachers should recognize that dancers find pleasure in being physically challenged and moving through space, and not just fine-tuning the sensory-motor systems. Finding a middle ground can be helpful at this point in training, where some conditioning is incorporated into combinations, along with somatically based patterning and more traditional dance movement. A discussion about the desired goal of dancing through such combinations, and not just getting a workout, can challenge dancers to find the artistry while still allowing them the kinesthetic pleasure of moving fully.

Movement Experience: *Aerobic Dance Phrase.* As we just noted, dance is generally not aerobic. For variety, create a phrase that is simple and can easily be repeated on alternating sides. Including some arm movements (especially above the region of the heart, shoulders, and head) and level changes will help to increase the heart rate. Have dancers repeat the phrase for at least three minutes. Give them feedback on form throughout, especially as the dancers start to fatigue. Discuss their experience with this movement experience.

Training Principles

In considering how to incorporate somatic work into dance classes, it is important to remember that the principles of training apply here as they do with any type of conditioning and movement training. In addressing some of the training principles, however, dancers may need to be encouraged to be moderate in their approach. In all training, whether working toward achieving a specific skill or to increase the capacity of a system, it is important to keep in mind that process is more important than product. Dancers can tend to be anxious for results, but it is the attention to process that defines and creates true artistry in movement, or in Alexander terms, prioritizing the "means whereby" versus "end-gaining" (Alexander 1969; Bell 1996; Nettl-Fiol 2006).

Adaptation. This principle states that in order for increases in capacity to occur, the living system must be stressed (Brooks and Fahey 1985; Carola, Harley, and Noback 1992; Mareib 1992; Welsh 2009). In order to develop strength, for example, the muscles must be pushed to do more work than they are accustomed. We are all familiar with the saying "no pain, no gain." While this saying is based on the principle of adaptation, dancers can tend to push too hard. Pain is the body's warning signal and should always be heeded (Arnheim 1980; Clippinger 2007; Watkins and Clarkson 1990). Adaptation will occur when a system is challenged; it does not necessitate injury. This applies to stretching, as well as to strength; a muscle should be lengthened to the point where tension is felt, but it does not produce pain (Watkins and Clarkson 1990, 37).

Dancers should also be reminded that adaptation can occur in terms of the neuromuscular patterning that provides for power and efficiency in movement (Carola, Harley, and Noback 1992; Mareib 1992). One way that the body can produce more power is by becoming more adept at recruiting the motor units in each muscle (Brooks and Fahey 1985; Mareib 1992). The muscles themselves do not necessarily need to hypertrophy, or get bigger (Carola, Harley, and Noback 1992). Along this line of thought, it may be helpful for dancers with a propensity to overwork to reconsider how they are defining efficiency. In our culture, we tend to think of efficiency in terms of time, or getting as much work done as quickly as possible. Easeful movement occurs when only as much effort is exerted as is needed to execute the given action

(Kandel, Schwartz, and Jessell 1991). Through the process of proper training and adaptation, the body and the neuromuscular system can find and pattern the most economical way to do a movement (Kandel, Schwartz, and Jessell 1991). Redefining the concepts of adaptation and efficiency to emphasize ease rather than speed or base-line power may be helpful to dancers who tend to overwork or carry extra tension.

Reversibility. If a capacity is not used, it will diminish (Welsh 2009). Again, we know the saying "use it or lose it." In terms of somatic work, any repatterning or growth needs to be consistently reinforced, especially initially. It is a cruel fact, but we tend to lose fastest in the areas that come least naturally to us (Brooks and Fahey 1985). As technique classes tend to keep progressing forward with new material, a self-practice and/or transferring somatic growth into everyday movement are ways to prevent backsliding with discoveries. Teachers can assist by reiterating ideas, layering the new onto the old as they move through the semester. Some teachers may also need to be reassured that repeating material for more than one class and even building material over multiple weeks are pedagogically sound decisions.

Specificity. Changes in capacity are very specific to the manner of training (Henry 1968). This concept is seen in the need to work on the Somatic Principles when standing as well as on the floor. Adaptations will not transfer to other situations if they are only worked with one orientation to gravity (Coker 2009; Henry 1968; Magill 2011; Schmidt and Wrisberg 2008). This principle should also be considered when working slowly. While going slow is beneficial when it comes to finding new ways of moving or being, the changes need to be practiced in "real time" too (Coker 2009; Magill 2011; Schmidt and Wrisberg 2008).

Another example of specificity can be seen in the kinds of flexibility dancers can develop. Dancers may work to achieve enormous passive flexibility but not have the strength to either move through this full range on their own volition or to control the action when it is achieved through the use of momentum. Functional flexibility is the ability of a dancer to move through and control the range of motion at a given joint. Research has indicated that the larger the difference between the functional and the passive ranges of motion, the greater the risk of injury (Alter 2004; Watkins and Clarkson 1990). To be most effective, stretching should be specific and focus on this functional range, or generate both flexibility and the strength to support it.

MOVEMENT EXPERIENCE: FUNCTIONAL VERSUS
PASSIVE RANGE OF MOTION

1. Exploring the Passive Range of Motion. Go in partners. First person to be stretched: place your back against the wall or a barre. Partner: lift this person's leg in front of them to the end point of their range. Be careful to watch for compensations or displacements in alignment, such as hip-hiking. Ask for feedback if you are unsure how far to stretch your partner. In this situation, the individual makes no contribution to generating the stretching force (there is no voluntary muscular effort). The motion is created by an outside agent, such as a partner, equipment, or gravity.

2. Passive-Active Range of Motion. Starting in the same manner, lift the leg of the person being stretched through the full range. Dancer being stretched: attempt to hold the leg at this end point. The initial stretch is by an outside force, and then the individual holds the position with an isometric contraction. The leg can be lowered with control, utilizing eccentric contraction of the hip flexors.

3. Active-Assisted Stretching through the Range of Motion. Person being stretched: lift your leg with no assistance. Go as far as possible, concentrically contracting the hip flexors. Both partners watch for compensations, so that correct alignment is maintained. Partner: at the end point, assist with lifting the leg through the remaining range of motion. There is an initial active contraction of the agonist muscle group, and then the partner completes the range of motion passively.

4. Active Stretching through the Range of Motion. In this version, stretching is done through the use of the opposing (antagonist) muscles only. Person stretching: lift your leg forward as far as possible, with a concentric contraction of the hip flexors.

Figure 8.2 Functional versus Passive Range of Motion Movement Experience.

The hip extensors (or antagonists) will lengthen with the aid of reciprocal inhibition. Reciprocal inhibition is the reflexive action that provides for synchronized contraction and relaxation of muscles around a joint. As one muscle group contracts, the opposing group is inhibited to reduce resistance to the action. The leg can be held isometrically and then lowered through a controlled, eccentric contraction of the hip flexors.

Teaching Tip: Passive stretching will develop passive flexibility, while introducing active components will target functional flexibility. These active components will help strengthen weak agonists and aid in establishing the neuromuscular patterning needed for coordinated motion. In general, passive stretching may be indicated when the elasticity of the muscles is the primary restriction of flexibility or if the agonist is too weak to move the limb at all. Active stretches are usually preferred when the weakness of the agonist is the primary restriction of achieving full functional range (Alter 2004; Henry 1968; Voss, Ionta and Myers 1985).

The previous movement experience uses a partner, but a dancer can achieve the same results by lifting the leg with his or her own hand. Partner stretching benefits from the positive aspects of teamwork, such as motivation, feedback, and support from peers. However, both partners need to know what they are doing and must be sensitive to the safety, needs, and tolerance of the other person.

Progressive overload. In seeking adaptation, the stress placed on a system needs to be increased gradually. If too much is attempted too quickly, compensations can occur or injuries can be sustained (Franklin 2004, 6). Instructors and students should be aware of signs of fatigue, such as muscular weakness, shortness of breath, and delayed responses. Attempting to change too much too quickly can also overwhelm students, leading to frustration, tension, and even resistance to change. As teachers, we want to "give" as much as we can to our students, but we need to recognize each student's capacity to absorb and assimilate before adding new information, suggestions, and corrections. This statement holds true for somatic concepts as well as technical material. Once desired adaptations have occurred, less overload is necessary to maintain that performance level (Watkins and Clarkson 1990; Westcott 1996).

Compensation. In training for increased capacity or even to repattern alignment or basic coordination, the body may adjust to the new demands by misaligning and placing the load on stronger muscles. Maintaining alignment and working the desired muscles can be best achieved through awareness and careful progressive overload (Clippinger 2007; Fitt 1996; Swiegard 1974; Todd 1937; Watkins and Clarkson 1990; Welsh 2009).

The Pilates system provides a good example of the training principles applied in a somatic context. In Pilates, emphasis is placed on maximizing core strength (Silver 2000). The exercises are designed to stress the system and build strength and endurance, thus adhering to the principle of adaptation (Silver 2000). However, in developing his system, Joseph Pilates recognized that adaptation could be achieved with fewer repetitions, encouraging awareness and a less robotic approach to training the body (Franklin 2004; Westcott 1996). He also designed his exercises in stages, so that each one has variations based on strength and skill. In this manner, progressive overload is achieved, and compensation avoided. In terms of specificity, Pilates utilizes both floor work and standing exercises to access the benefits of stabilizing on the ground, while also acknowledging the need to transfer newfound ways of moving to standing (Silver 2000).

Balance and the Elusive Center

It is common to hear directives about "the center" in technique classes, regardless of the dance style. However well intended (and essentially correct), dancers may be confused about comments like "Hold (or lift) your center to stay balanced on your leg!" or "Move your arms from your center." These directives are really getting at two related, but distinct, physiological constructs. The first is referring to the center of gravity and how it relates to balance, while the second is getting at core-distal connectivity issues. In fact, the terminology seems to be shifting somewhat, with "core" replacing "center" in the teaching vocabulary. Regardless of the word employed, it is important that students understand both what the center or core is and how it relates to balance. We will return to the importance of connectivity in balancing, but it may help students if it is clear what they are being asked to do, so let us first define the center of gravity and its role in balance (and movement).

The center of gravity is the point around which the body's mass and weight are equally balanced or distributed in all directions (Hamill and Knutzen 1995). The exact location in each dancer's body varies, depending on build and the position his or her body is assuming. If a dancer has a very muscular upper body, for instance, his or her center of gravity will tend to be higher, as more weight is carried higher in the body. For this reason, men tend to have a higher center of gravity than women, who tend to carry more weight in the hips and thighs (Hamill and Knutzen 1995; Nordin and Frankel 2001). If a dancer leans to the right, the center of gravity will shift to the right and additional muscular effort and/or counterbalancing will need to occur to stay over the base of support. The center of gravity can also be thought of as the intersection of the three cardinal planes, or the meeting point for the cardinal sagittal, transverse, and frontal planes. The cardinal planes are those bisecting the body equally based on mass (Biel 2010; Carola, Harley, and Noback 1992). While there is variation from person to person, the center of gravity is located approximately in the middle of the pelvis at the level of the upper sacrum or the navel (Hamill and Knutzen 1995).

In order to balance, the center of gravity must be over the base of support (Hamill and Knutzen 1995; Woolacott and Shumway-Cook 1989). When the center is directly over the base, we can think of it as a *stable balance*. This is sometimes referred to as static balance, but as the body is never truly motionless, we prefer the term stable (Gabbard 2008; Haywood 1993). In dance, we frequently shift the center toward the edge of the base, as this prepares us for movement in that direction or to aborb forces coming from the opposite direction. This is called *off-set balance* (Fitt 1996, 24). It is important to remember that stability is at the cost of mobility, and both are desired at different times in dance sequences. Once the center moves past the base, the dancer is "falling," and a new base must be established, whether by catching the weight in a step or with some other body part such as the hands. This is called *dynamic balance* (Gabbard 2008; Haywood 1993; Thomas and Nelson 1990).

Movement Experience: *Standing Stability and Mobility*. Standing with the feet in parallel position and with the eyes closed, feel the small adjustments the body is making to maintain the upright position. Notice the connection from the heels, all the way through the spine, up through the head. Initiate a small rocking action at the ankles, keeping the rest of the body long and connected. Gradually increase the size of the rocking, being sure the body moves in one piece rather than in a disjointed fashion. Keep increasing the size until the rocking becomes so large you have to take a step to prevent falling. Repeat several times and in different directions. Gradually decrease the magnitude until you are just barely moving back and forth around the vertical axis. Discuss stable, off-set, and dynamic balance in relation to this activity.

You can maximize stability in several ways: (1) make the base larger; (2) center the weight over the base; (3) lower the center of gravity; (4) increase the mass (Goldie, Bach, and Evans 1989; Hamill and Knutzen 1995; Haywood and Getchell 2009). Obviously it is not possible to instantaneously increase the mass of a given dancer, but the other factors can be manipulated to help performers improve their balance. For example, widening the stance and finding a neutral, centered alignment will make balancing easier (Haywood and Getchell 2009). Likewise, sinking into a plié will make a dancer more stable. Knowledge of these parameters may also help dancers with understanding the difficulties they may face in a given movement. For example, a dancer with very small feet may have a harder time balancing than one with larger feet, or a heavier performer may be more stable but have a harder time with initiating motion. Being on relevé is more difficult than being in plié. Self-acceptance, and not unnecessarily berating oneself, is vital to dancing with confidence. Dancing with confidence is crucial to taking chances and fulfilling one's artistic potential.

Movement Experience: *Partner Stability and Mobility*. Go with a partner. Stand normally while your partner tries to push you off balance. Now stand like a football player (low, wide, and centered) while your partner pushes. Switch roles and compare experiences.

The relationship of the center of gravity to the base of support is important to be aware of when in a neutral position, but dancers also need to keep in mind that the location of "center" shifts with every change of position because the distribution of weight changes (Hamill and Knutzen 1995). Therefore, dancers must either shift another body part to counterbalance this change or contract an opposing muscle group to maintain balance (Hamill and Knutzen 1995; Nordin and Frankel 2001). While it need not always be conscious, an ability to manipulate the center of gravity plays into every movement.

Movement Experience: *Counterbalancing.* Standing on one leg, shift the gesture leg into different directions. Notice how the arms and body respond. Then focus on shifting the torso and notice what happens in the limbs, including the standing leg. Discuss the adjustments of the other limbs or the contraction of muscles observed or felt during the activity.

Teaching Tip. This activity highlights the importance of being fluid with the idea of balance and becoming comfortable with the feeling of being off balance. Generally speaking, we harbor a cultural bias against being off balance. Consider the words we use to indicate the act of falling, such as "faltering" or "stumbling." Likewise, a negative connotation is associated with descriptive phrases like being "off center" or "unbalanced." As dancers and teachers, we need to encourage and embrace being off balance in order to go with the body's intuitive adjustments, rather than holding against them, and so that we can ride the energy provided by the physical forces acting on the body.

Alignment. On the most basic level, alignment refers to the relationship of body parts to one another. Our relatively mobile (and unstable) upright alignment is not mechanically balanced. There is constant activity in the "anti-gravity," or extensor muscles of the body to keep us from collapsing forward with the pull of gravity (Feldenkrais 1985; Hamill and Knutzen 1995; Nordin and Frankel 2001; Todd 1937). This underlying baseline of muscular tone is necessary, even with the most ideal alignment. If any body parts are shifted away from our best approximation of the vertical, it will necessitate holding of muscles and/or shifting of other parts (Hamill and Knutzen 1995; Nordin and Frankel 2001; Rolf 1989; Todd 1937). Because the body acts as a kinetic chain, movement of one body part will often result in compensatory movement elsewhere (Hackney 1998). It is counterbalancing on the most basic level. Therefore, standing and balancing with the bodily weight segments stacked up and aligned over the base of support is most efficient, as it requires the least amount of muscular effort (Nordin and Frankel 2001; Rolf 1989; Todd 1937). This is the major reason that both dance and somatics place so much emphasis on alignment and the center of gravity.

Movement Experience: *Standing Alignment.* This exploration is an extension of Movement Experience: Standing Stability and Mobility (see page 183). Take a moment to lie on the floor and note which parts of you are completely resting on the ground and which parts are held away from the ground. Come to standing on both feet in your normal stance. Which parts of your feet are pressing more strongly into the ground? How far forward is your nose in relation to your feet, your navel, and your sternum? Begin to shift your weight forward onto the toes of your feet and then back toward your heels. Try to make the motion of weight shifting smooth and even. Notice the difference between how much displacement you make forward versus backward. Continue shifting your weight, but initiate the movement from the top of your head. Imagine that you have a pencil attached to your head, pointing toward the ceiling, and that there is a piece of paper touching it. Through the action of moving, you make a corresponding line on the piece of paper. Do that a few times, making the line on the paper smooth and approximately the same length in the forward and backward directions. Now initiate the movement from different places in your body like the hips, the knees, and the ankles. See if you can allow the head to remain where it is in space, staying behind the rest of the body. Then let it come along as a result of the movement while you initiate from these different parts. Rest a moment. Notice the pattern of weight distribution in your feet again. Is the relationship of your nose to your feet, navel, and sternum the same as when you began?

Try this all again, but this time move side to side, shifting your weight first over the right foot and then the left. Do you travel the same distance over each leg? Use the pencil image again while shifting slowly from side to side. Is the line straight? Is it the same length from the center to both sides, or is one side longer than the other? Rest and notice the changes that have occurred in your standing posture after this variation.

Begin to circle your weight clockwise on your feet, shifting your weight forward then sideward, backward, other side, and then to the front. Attempt to make a smooth and round circle. Think again about the piece of paper above your head, and see if you can imagine that you are drawing a circle while your weight is shifting circularly on your feet. Go counterclockwise a few times too. Stop and notice the changes in your standing posture after doing these small movements. If time allows, repeat all of the above with one leg crossed over the other (oscillate forward and backward, side to side, and circle both ways while experimenting with initiating from the head, the ankles, and the hips). Continue thinking about drawing smooth pictures of the corresponding lines and circles. When you have finished, stand easily on both feet and notice what has changed in you. Lie on the floor again, and notice what is different after doing these small movements.

Teaching Tip: The previous movement experience can be split up and done at the beginning or end of class on different days. Alternately, one could do a portion of it in class and then assign the variations as homework via a handout or a recording of the instructions. Have students walk around during the rest periods to relieve strain and reduce effort, and ask them to make the oscillations smaller or larger depending on what you see. The point is not to work hard, but to move enough and in such a way that they have time to notice a natural coordination emerge of standing more through the skeleton and less through the musculature of the body. When weight is borne more through the central axis of the skeleton, less muscular effort and work is required from the muscles and central nervous system (Hamill and Knutzen 1995;

Nordin and Frankel 2001). This movement exploration is just one example of how seemingly small, easy movements done with awareness and attention can provide greater understanding of how to stand and move with heightened ease and coordination.

The importance of efficient alignment becomes even more apparent when considering the relationship between stabile and dynamic alignment. Any alignment issues present when standing still (stable alignment) become magnified when moving through space (dynamic alignment). The neuromuscular patterns and counterbalancing present in stillness provide the backdrop for motion; they do not disappear with motion. Ideally, dancers have a blank slate for their movement, not a canvas that already has background coloring (Nordin and Frankel 2001; Rolf 1989; Todd 1937).

The following is an example of how the four fundamental principles can be incorporated in class to address alignment and/or balance. Note the overlap between principles and how they support one another. Breath is related to relaxation, and relaxation is related to the ability to sense and adjust. Both breath and sensing can assist with connecting internally and to the environment to maximize alignment and stability. The initiation of movement will not sequence effectively and efficiently without the connectivity implicit in a healthy dynamic alignment. Again, finding the appropriate inroad for individual dancers is frequently the challenge.

Breath. Reminding dancers to breathe fully will often help lower the center of gravity and improve stability. Chest breathing results in holding the weight "up" in addition to creating unnecessary tension (Calais-Germaine 2005; Hamill and Knutzen 1995; Nordin and Frankel 2001). Being more relaxed will enable dancers to make necessary alignment adjustments to maintain balance. Breath can also be used to help dancers access their core muscles, enhancing connectivity and the ability to sense where "center" is and needs to be in relation to the base of support for optimal balance (Franklin 2004).

Sensing. Encouraging an appropriate amount of muscular tone, or tension, can help enable dancers to sense and adjust based on kinesthetic input. If the body is rigid, it becomes difficult to enact the small adjustments needed to find a more ideal alignment or to maintain balance (Feldenkrais 1985). In addition, sensing the environment (for example, attending to the support foot connecting to the floor) can assist with finding the connectivity that can in turn aid with alignment and balance issues. Finally, bringing attention to sensory input can effectually occupy the conscious mind. Trying too hard to balance or adjust alignment can be counterproductive if it results in unnecessary tension or interferes with innate balance reflexes (Rose and Christina 2006).

Connectivity. Really sensing the foot (or other supporting part) pushing against the floor helps establish connections between the lower and upper body. This connection encourages the body segments to "stack up" in an efficient alignment so that the center is over the base (Laws 2002; Nordin and Frankel 2001). Connecting to the center and allowing the energy to radiate out in space can also be very helpful in balancing as well as in organizing the placement of body segments. Sensing the energy emanating from the center and out through the limbs is one method for finding the appropriate amount of tone so that the body is neither limp, nor tense or locked (Laws 2002).

Initiation. Clarity of initiation is crucial to dynamic alignment. If a given movement starts from a place in the body that does not support the follow-through or line of action, it will not sequence as successfully. A common example might be going into an arch. If a dancer is thinking of initiating in the ribs or low back, the length in the spine will probably be compromised as the pelvis counterbalances forward. Starting from the eyes and thinking of the head going up and back will give the action length and support from the core muscles of the body. Another image for initiating the arch is to think of the spine as a length of chain being elongated link by link, thus emphasizing the connection from head to feet (Clippinger 2007; Hamill and Knutzen 1995; Laws 2002; Nordin and Frankel 2001).

LOCOMOTION AND PHRASE WORK

The four fundamental principles might be applied to class combinations and movements traveling through space as follows.

Breath. The physical exertion of moving the body in space requires additional oxygen. Dancers need to be breathing as fully and as easily as possible in order to supply the muscles with the oxygen needed and to expel the carbon dioxide being generated (Brooks and Fahey 1985; Mareib 1992). While this may seem obvious, dancers frequently hold their breath in challenging sequences. Bringing awareness to the breath can be helpful in this regard, in addition to helping enlist the core connectivity needed for successful propulsion through the space (Hackney 1998). The phrasing of a sequence can also be explored through the breath. Having the ability to choose whether to perform a phrase in an even, impactive, or impulsive manner contributes to the artistic statement (Hackney 1998).

Sensing. Recapitulation of themes from the Performance Focus section of Chapter 4 suggests the importance of sensing in locomotion. An internal sensitivity is the foundation for appropriate body organizing, lending itself to the ability to move through the space. Layered on top of this is the necessity for sensing and responding to stimuli in the environment in order to navigate through the surroundings (Haywood and Getchell 2009). Dancers can address these needs by exploring a soft, internal focus early in class, and then attempting to keep this inner awareness while also being aware of the environment and others in the space.

Connectivity. The internal sensitivity mentioned above needs to include a clear awareness of internal connectivity. This should expand to an awareness of external connections to the environment and how that affects the body in motion. Any time the body is moving in space, it can be particularly helpful to remind students of the Laws of Motion discussed in Chapter 5. Effective locomotion requires an understanding of and ability to manipulate inertia, acceleration, and reaction forces (Hamill and Knutzen 1995; Nordin and Frankel 2001). Simple reminders of the floor pushing back when they push down, or the need to invest energy to overcome inertia or create acceleration may work for students.

Initiation. The momentum generated in phrase work and traveling movement is crucial to the concept of initiation and follow-through. Momentum = mass × velocity. Momentum can therefore be related to the quantity of motion. The law of Conservation of Momentum states that without resistance, momentum stays the same. Having an awareness of this can help dancers continue or transfer motion from one body part to another and from one movement to the next so that as little energy is wasted as possible (Hamill and Knutzen 1995; Laws 2002; Nordin and Frankel 2001).

Again, clarity in replicating movement is dependant upon clarity of initiation. In addition to the location of the initiation, if dancers are aware of phrasing and sequencing when moving in space it will enhance their movement accuracy. A proclivity for one type of sequencing or phrasing over another is indicative of movement preferences and sometimes habitual patterning (Hackney 1998). Working on movement experiences and combinations that include initiation from various points, different phrasings, and with successive, sequential, and simultaneous follow-through in the body may increase sensitivity to these components of movement. Taking time to identify, differentiate, and integrate these elements into one's movement vocabulary is crucial to the ability to embody them in locomotor and phrase work, when individual preference will tend to override the intended execution.

Movement Experience: *Simultaneous and Sequential Spinal Dance.* On all fours explore arching and rounding the spine. Begin with simultaneous initiation from the head and the tail. Then initiate from the tail and sequence through the spine, one vertebra at a time. Finally, try initiating from the head. Compare these experiences.

Teaching Tip: This exploration can progress into a standing warm-up for the back. This can begin with a roll-down initiated from the head and a roll-up starting from the tail. Then contrast this with releasing the knees and rounding the spine over with a simultaneous action at both the head and the tail. While hanging over, stretch the knees and lengthen the spine. Then recover by releasing the knees and bringing the head and the tail back up over the feet simultaneously.

Under and over curves. Under and over curves are the basis of many traveling movements, yet they are surprisingly complex and sophisticated to perform. Students are often troubled with finding a gradual change in level during the weight transfer. Application of the Somatic Principles as in the following movement experience can potentially be helpful. When placed at the start of the class, this exploration will begin the warm-up process while also bringing attention to the various ways under and over curves can be performed.

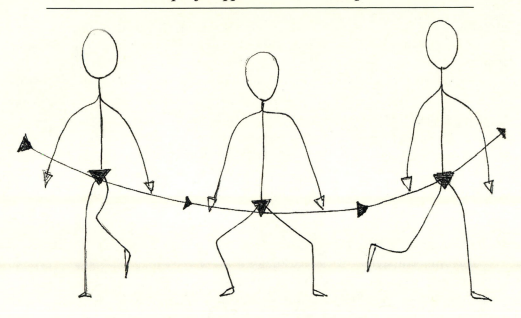

Figure 8.3 U-Shaped Pelvic Under Curve.

Movement Experience: *Under and Over Curves.* Find your own space in the room and face any direction. On your own time, begin exploring under curves in different directions, with different phrasing, in different sizes. Bring your attention to the breath to help find the suspension points. Now try attending to how your feet connect to the floor and propel you through the space. Also notice the arc the pelvis creates, and access your internal connectivity so that the upper body moves with the action of the pelvis and legs. Then play with shifting awareness to the initiation, thinking about really pushing off from the supporting leg to change your perception of the action. Repeat all of this with over curves.

Next try doing the under and over curves with a partner to increase your sensation of the path the pelvis is taking. One person: stand behind the other, and place your hands on your partner's hips. Move through the space together, emphasizing the u shape the pelvis makes in under curves, the n shape in over curves. Change roles. Separate, and repeat the over and under-curves imagining yourself in glow-in-the dark underwear. Visualize the trace-forms created by your pelvis if you were doing the under and over curves in the dark.

The Special Case of Turning

Turning can present challenges to the most experienced performer. Many dancers identify themselves as either being turners or not. Beyond this, most dancers recognize that there are "on" and "off" days for turning. Confidence and consistency are partners in turning. Without confidence in one's turning abilities, it is extremely difficult to be consistent. How, then, can dancers achieve the consistency necessary to develop confidence?

Clearly, turning can be as much of a mental challenge for dancers as a physical challenge. If a dancer is worried about the ability to execute a given turn, chances are reduced that he or she will perform the turn as desired. As we have seen repeatedly, anxiety and trying too hard can create unwanted tension and interfere with the ability to sense and respond in the most productive and efficient fashion. For some dancers, visualization can be an effective way of beginning to address issues in turning. By visualizing the perfect turn, new neuromuscular pathways can begin to form and be strengthened. It can also help to establish a sense of calm and confidence so that the body can work optimally. As with all visualization, being as specific as possible will generally be most effective (Coker 2009).

Teaching Tip: Remember to encourage dancers to try different kinds of images based on their particular issues and preferences. A dancer having problems with grounding while turning might find it helpful to visualize his or her foot as a screw drilling into the floor. A dancer bound up with tension might imagine a top spinning freely and easily. Someone less fanciful but with anxiety or stage fright tendencies might do better with just visualizing himself or herself performing the given turn flawlessly in front of an audience.

Sometimes understanding the physics of turning can be helpful to dancers. It may be a mechanical problem that is finally addressed, another way of occupying the judgmental mind, or some combination of the two. Regardless, understanding these physical components can help teachers give their students something to think about rather than just the fear of turning. The following can be potential concepts to address in turning:

1. The Law of Conservation of Momentum applies. A turn will keep going indefinitely without the interference of an opposing force like friction. The momentum of a turn is equal to the velocity of the turn multiplied by the moment of inertia (Hamill and Knutzen 1995; Laws 2002; Nordin and Frankel 2001).

$$\text{Turning Momentum} = \text{velocity} \times \text{moment of inertia}$$

Moment of Inertia. Body segments that are closer to the vertical axis, or the center of the body, can be moved more easily. The moment of inertia for the whole body is the sum of that for all the constituent parts, and by moving parts toward or away from the center of rotation, the body's moment of inertia can be changed. Because distances are squared in the formula to calculate the moment of inertia, a small change in location of body parts can have a great effect on the velocity of rotation for any given momentum (Hamill and Knutzen 1995; Laws 2002; Nordin and Frankel 2001). Think of a skater; a turn is established with a given amount of energy or momentum. This energy basically stays the same throughout the turn, but as the arms and legs move from a position extended away from the body and pull in toward the center, the moment of inertia decreases. This means the turning velocity will be faster and faster. Dancers turning with their arms too far out will go slower, or they will need to invest more energy in the turn to go as fast as a dancer with a more compact position (Hamill and Knutzen 1995; Nordin and Frankel 2001).

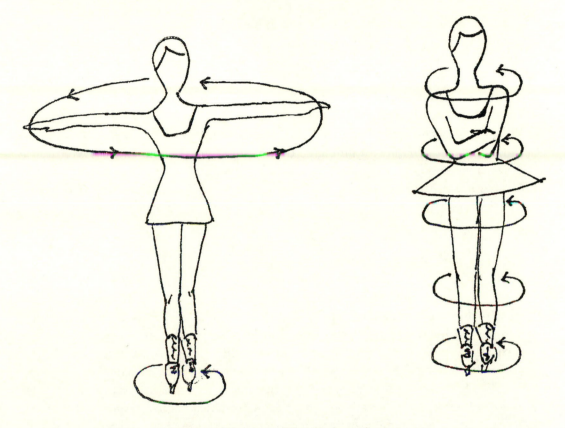

Figure 8.4 Moment of Inertia in a Skater.

2. Newton's Laws of Motion still apply to turning.

acceleration = Force / mass or Force = acceleration × mass

The force to initiate turning must be large enough to overcome the inertia of the whole body and any resistance, such as friction from the floor. To achieve greater acceleration, dancers can increase the muscular force they invest in the push-off for the turn. They can also increase the leverage (or moment arm) by pushing off from wider base (Hamill and Knutzen 1995; Laws 2002; Nordin and Frankel 2001).

Teaching Tip: Using a wider base of support amplifies any given force as it is effectively increasing the length of the lever arm. However, care should be taken when applying this to turns, as frequently force production is not the problem. Often dancers are trying to use too much force to get around, and this can throw the turn off. Also, dancers need to take into consideration that using a larger base means that they will have a greater distance to move the center of gravity when shifting the weight from between two feet to the weight on one foot. Pulling the limbs in may give dancers the speed they want without having to push off harder or using a larger base, both of which can disturb balance in a turn.

The foundational Somatic Principles of breathing, sensing, connecting and initiating can be applied to turning as with alignment and locomotor and phrase work. Certainly breath can help with the increased muscular tension and holding patterns frequently seen in turning. Seeing is crucial to spotting and maintaining orientation. In turns without spotting, dancers need to be sensitive to other kinesthetic input to stay balanced and oriented. Connecting is necessary for the body to move as a unit while turning, and the initiation is important in coordinating the turning action. In ballet turns, for example, the timing of the initiation from the arms and legs is critical. If the upper and lower units of the body are not coordinated in the initiation of the turn, or if one part is not working as effectively as the other, it can throw off balance and timing in the turn.

Floor Work and Inversions

In contemporary dance training and choreography, dancers will inevitably be asked to do floor work and inversions. Somatic approaches to floor work can be woven into the technique class, allowing dancers to reap the benefits of a somatic training perspective, while also developing comfort and skills with floor work as part of the danced vocabulary. The floor really does need to be the dancer's friend!

Much somatic work is done lying down because of the many rewards associated with working in this orientation. Relaxation is promoted because the body does not have to work to stay upright. By the same token, gravity is used to a dancer's advantage in floor work to realign and/or alter muscle contraction. It is easier to isolate deep muscles when the body is relaxed and not struggling for stability. Also for these reasons, floor work is ideal for targeting basic coordinations and training principles like core strength. The floor provides a frame of reference for alignment issues and habitual movement patterns, as contact with the floor provides a concrete means for feeling how the body is being held or is adjusting in motion.

Based on the goals of the technique class, or through backward teaching, dance instructors can assess the physical skills inherent within culminating phrase work and address these component skills through floor work. In this manner, students have the opportunity to augment these specific abilities while deriving all the assets mentioned above. They get accustomed to the floor supporting the body and can work on discrete dance skills that may be done on the floor or adapted to standing later in class.

Throughout floor work, attention can be directed to the breath to relax and focus both the mind and the body and to help engage core connections. Playing with initiations from different body parts tends to work well on the floor, as it can be easier to isolate actions and sense the body connectivity that supports follow-through reactions when not working against gravity. Again, sensing the body in relation to the floor in addition to internal connections is a real benefit of this training option.

Teaching Tip: Transfer to standing always needs to be taken into consideration. Teachers might first try introducing the designated basic coordination or patterning while lying down and with free timing. In this way, dancers can fully explore the concept independently. From this open exploration, the class can move into a more structured floor phrase that relates closer to dance technique. At this point it is a good idea to work on the issue of moving in and out of floor. This transition can start with smaller shifts in and out of positions while lying down and progress to sitting, kneeling, even standing, and then going back down to the earth using this same coordination.

In inversions, the body's standing relationship to gravity is reversed. Instead of the center of gravity being over the feet, it winds up below the feet. Often this involves supporting weight on the hands, but it can also be the head, shoulders, or forearms. Going upside down can be perceived as dangerous, creating anxiety and tension in many people initially. For this reason, relaxation is crucial in inversions. All of the fundamental principles can be utilized in helping to overcome this fear of being inverted. Breath, as always, is crucial in mediating tension levels, including helping to control the heightened physical responses due to input from the sympathetic nervous system (Calais-Germaine 2005; Linklater 2006). The fight or flight response does not serve an adaptive function in inversions; in fact, tensing up can inhibit the righting reflexes that will normally provide for adjustments to land safely on the feet. In addition to breath control, really consciously seeing the surrounding space in stress-evoking situations like this can help calm the sympathetic response (Rose and Christina 2006; Schmidt and Wrisberg 2008).

Inversions are actually a great place to experience the bodily connections in a new way. Closing the kinetic chain through the upper rather than the lower body can bring a new awareness to the upper-lower connections and muscular and postural issues. Encouraging sensitivity to the floor and really pushing with the hands (or other supporting body part) can energize the alignment and will activate the core muscles more strongly. Discussion of the initiation for inversions is frequently helpful for dancers. Most of us associate inversions with gymnastics "tricks" that use an over curve, or throwing action, to help initiate the movement. Depending on the inversion desired, finding an under curve initiation with a gradual shift of the weight to the hands will give the motion an ease and control that will move it away from the realm of tricks. This approach can also ease fears, as the focus becomes the process of transferring weight to the hands, rather than just getting into an upside-down position.

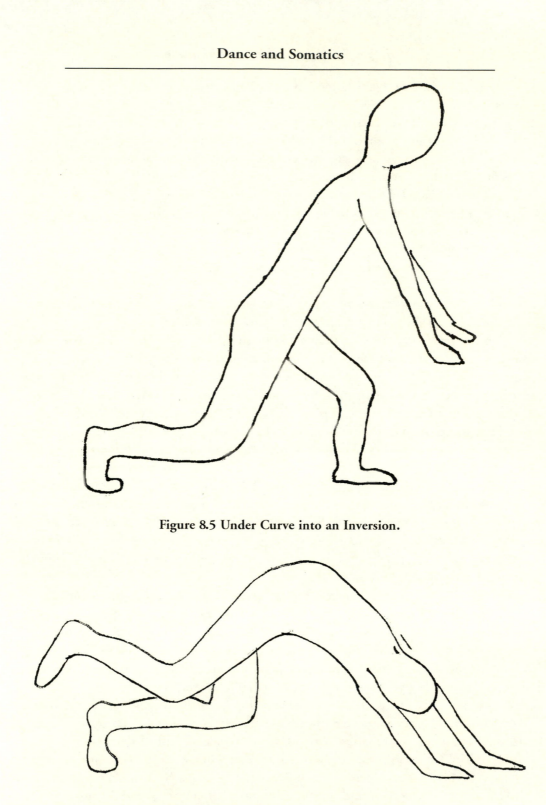

Figure 8.5 Under Curve into an Inversion.

Figure 8.6 Under Curve into an Inversion 1b.

Partner Work

Partner work covers an enormous stylistic range, any one of which could be the topic of its own book. Traditional partnering involves one person lifting or leading the other. On the other end of the spectrum, contact improvisation is a shared immediate experience of sensing, responding, and shaping to one another that can also include lifts. The Somatic Principles can be applied despite stylistic differences in partnering.

Being a good partner requires connecting on the level of self and with the environment in addition to physically connecting to another person (see Chapter 5). It is a tiered system, requiring a solid foundation in order to reach the level of connecting effectively to someone else. Finding the appropriate tension level is a very important component. Being limp makes connecting and transferring energy difficult, while being too rigid detracts from the ability to respond or initiate with sensitivity. Just reminding dancers not to lose themselves in the act of partnering may be helpful. Recall the concept of placing 90 percent of attention on self and 10 percent of attention on the other person from Chapter 5. More specifically, encouraging dancers to focus on their own breath, kinesthetic cues, and connections within their bodies and to the environment can all help with staying "present in the moment," or aware of themselves in addition to their partners and the task at hand.

This being said, partnering is not entirely selfish! A good partner must also be in tune with the other person to feel their timing, impulses for movement, even their comfort level with the joined action. Clarity of initiation is needed to communicate intention, timing, and to move with a partner efficiently and effectively. Particularly in improvisation situations, one partner may tend to always take the lead. Other times you may witness a situation where both dancers seem to have their own agenda, where their energies collide rather than merge. As with any pairing in life, having a balanced and mutual investment usually yields better and more exciting results. Encouraging dancers to really see one another and to take the time to feel what is happening can sometimes help them avoid "end-gaining" or rushing to the product rather than making the process of working together primary. Slowing down is often necessary; there is a tendency to speed up when working with someone else, and at a certain point that can affect the ability to have an honest and full physical response to the energy being given.

Movement Experience: *Body Rolling*. Start with one partner lying prone. The other can sit or kneel beside him/her. Gently place your hands on your partner's back and bring your awareness to his or her breath. After watching his or her breath closely, close your eyes, and become aware of your own breath. After a bit, try to expand your consciousness to absorb both breathing patterns. When you sense that your partner is relaxed, very gently and gradually drape your body over your partner, positioning your abdomen in the hollowed area of your partner's lumbar spine. Attend to how

195

you shift your center of gravity and weight and how your partner responds. Lie there for several minutes, letting your weight settle, and feel the marriage of your breathing. Again, when you sense you are both ready, begin slowly rolling down toward your partner's thighs. Stop before placing any weight on the knees, and reverse direction. Roll back up to the thoracic region, stopping before reaching the area of the neck. Repeat this rolling up and down your partner's body several times. Person who is rolling: check in to be sure there is no tensing or withholding of your body's weight from your partner. Recipient of the rolling: be sure to breathe fully and relax into the floor. Come to rest in the initial draped position, and gradually ease your weight off your partner. It can be helpful for those students who might be unfamiliar with this kind of contact to pair up with someone they are comfortable with until they get acclimated.

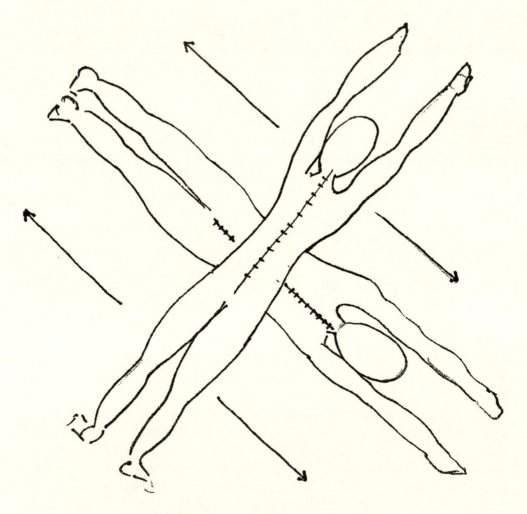

Figure 8.7 Body Rolling Movement Experience.

Awareness of the center of gravity and efficient functional alignment and strength are also needed to be able to bear and give weight effortlessly. Demonstrating and breaking down the mechanics of taking weight can help dancers understand that size is irrelevant in most partnering if it is done correctly. Eradicating this fear or self-judgment for those who deem themselves too big or too small can help in many regards, not the least of which is discovering more appropriate tension levels. It is hard not to tense up if dancers think they are too heavy and will hurt their partner, or if they think they are not strong enough and need to work harder to lift someone. Having students change partners a few times in the previous movement experience can provide a more concrete understanding of this issue.

Teaching Tip: Simple activities and basic information can help dancers learn to transfer their weight (center of gravity) in a gradual and safe manner. It is always a good idea to establish or review the rules before trying partnering explorations: (1) giving the weight gradually, not dropping it onto the person; (2) placing your center over, or as close to your partner's center as possible; (3) bending and lifting from the hips, not the back; and (4) avoiding placing weight on the bony areas.

Movement Experience: *Progressive Partnering.* After applying the above concepts in Movement Experience: Body Rolling, the following experiences can form a nice progressive sequence. Working through each movement experience alone is beneficial, but then they can be strung together to make a phrase that moves across the floor. This can be a "safer" introduction to contact improvisation, as students are learning and working on many of the same principles but in a more structured format.

Body surfing. Approximately six to eight students lie side by side with arms overhead, like sardines in a can. Initially, just work on log rolling, feeling each other and establishing a nice rhythm. Next, person at the back of the line position yourself so you are kneeling perpendicularly to the line, with your arms resting on the first "roller." As the group begins to roll, allow this motion to pull you in, gradually transitioning the weight of your pelvis to the first person. Your arms will already be reaching across your other rolling classmates. The momentum of the rollers will carry you across, as if you are surfing on a big wave, or like groceries being carried on a conveyor belt. This is a perfect place to practice the principles of transferring your weight gradually and finding a balance between tension and relaxation. You will also want to be sure to stay over the torsos of the rollers, avoiding shifting down to the knee or up to the neck areas. As you approach the end of the rolling line, continue reaching beyond the last person to the floor, so that you slide right off of the group. Continue your motion and reorient with the group to begin logrolling so that the new back person in the line can begin surfing.

Body surfing duet. This activity can progress into a variation with a partner. Begin sitting back-to-back, taking time to sense and feel each other. A little "back conversation" can help establish comfort and connection. One partner: slide down to

Figure 8.8 Body Surfing Duet Movement Experience 1a (Julie Brodie, left, and Kora Radella; photograph by Marcella Hackbardt).

Figure 8.9 Body Surfing Duet Movement Experience 1b (Kora Radella, under, and Julie Brodie; photograph by Marcella Hackbardt).

Figure 8.10 Body Surfing Duet Movement Experience 1c (Kora Radella, under, and Julie Brodie; photograph by Marcella Hackbardt).

your side and begin logrolling. Other partner: rotate, so as not to lose body contact, and surf over your partner as in the body surfing movement experience. Find your way into the back-to-back position again, and repeat with the other partner rolling this time. Play with surfing on your back as well as on your stomach. When you are comfortable with the partner surfing, press into your partner from the back-to-back position, finding the balance of pressure between your backs and into the floor so that you can stand without the use of your arms. Change partners, and try it all again with someone else.

Flying and rolling. One partner: assume a position on all four limbs, supporting your back through core engagement. Other partner: gradually transition your pelvis onto the back of your partner and extend your arms and legs out in this position so that you are balanced momentarily, with a sense of "flying." The goal here is to work on a gradual and a safe weight transfer, finding where your center is so that you can balance while also being aware of where you are placing weight on your partner. Balancing in the center of your partner's spine is not the strongest place for them, so care should be taken to position yourself closer to your partner's sacrum. In the extended position, play with the idea of radiating energy out through the limbs without locking or stiffening. From this balance point, fold your upper body, holding

Figure 8.11 Flying and Rolling Movement Experience 1a (Julie Brodie, under, and Kora Radella; photograph by Marcella Hackbardt).

onto your partner's belly and shoulders so that you can do a forward somersault smoothly off of his or her back. After you have completed the roll, transition into an all fours position so that your partner can have a turn with the flying experience.

The hurdle. One partner: stand and crease at the hips, while supporting the weight of your upper body with your hands on your thighs. Be sure that your back is long and at an angle; it does not need to be in a tabletop position. Other partner: place your inside leg on the back of your partner's pelvis (if your right side is facing your partner, lift your right leg, and vice-versa). Use the arm on the same side, helping to transition and shift your weight up and over your partner by pulling on his or her shoulder if needed. Find the suspension point in this hurdle position before sliding off and assuming the hip crease position yourself. Continue this movement across the floor, alternating between supporting and going over.

Figure 8.12 Flying and Rolling Movement Experience 1b (Julie Brodie, top, and Kora Radella; photograph by Marcella Hackbardt).

The death drop. First establish a sense of pull with your partner. With right hands joined, lean away from each other, keeping your spines long. You should be side by side, facing opposite directions. One person: act as the pivot point, spinning in place to circle your partner 180 degrees. Now switch roles, so that the person who made the circular path now becomes the stationary pivot point. Be sure that both of

Figure 8.13 The Hurdle Movement Experience (Julie Brodie, front, and Kora Radella; photograph by Marcella Hackbardt).

you are really committing your weight. If the hand contact were to be lost, you should both fall down.

When both of you feel confident with this spinning, try continuing it down into the floor. Circling person (not the pivot point): tuck your outside leg under to lower

Figure 8.14 Death Drop Movement Experience (Kora Radella, left, and Julie Brodie; photograph by Marcella Hackbardt).

into the floor. This increased lean is the "death drop" moment, as taken from figure skating terminology. The turning momentum will carry you into spinning on your bottom or back, and you can release the hand-hold with your standing partner once you are safely on the floor. Notice how the spinning accelerates if you tuck into a ball, exemplifying the concept of reduced moment of inertia.

Try putting these four movement experiences together in the following sequence: Start with the spinning and death drop. Person who performs the death drop to the floor: assume the position on all fours. Pivot point person: go into flying and rolling. Both partners transition to sit back-to-back. Flyer person: initiate the body surfing roll so that your partner can go over you. Surfer partner: transition to standing with a flat back and hips creased so your partner can hurdle over you. Rejoin hands and repeat, reversing roles.

So far this chapter has discussed conditioning and training principles viewed through a somatic lens and applied to technique. Warming up and cooling down at the beginning and end of class, rehearsal, or performance is also an important part of this process. The following information summarizes key aspect of warming up and cooling down and gives suggestions about how to structure a class or rehearsal with this material in mind. This information is also presented in the form of a handout (see Table 8.1 at end of chapter) that can be printed and distributed to dancers or student choreographers to be referenced as needed.

Warming Up: Preparing to Move

Warming up the body and mind prior to moving provides many benefits. A good warm up can maximize performance and can reduce or even prevent injury. The muscles most frequently pulled or injured are those that are antagonists to strong contractors (Alter 2004; Clippinger 2007; Watkins and Clarkson 1990). These vulnerable muscles also tend to be the anti gravity, or extensor, muscles of the body. For example, a quick, strong quadriceps contraction often pulls the hamstring muscle group if they lengthen too slowly due to being "cold." In extreme situations, initiating strenuous exercise without preparing the body can even cause heart damage due to lack of blood flow (Brooks and Fahey 1985). Although you may feel anxious to start working, remember that warming up is not a waste of time. Dancers will work more safely, be more focused, perform better, and already be familiar with the material if they have a structured warm-up. Remember that people tend to do what feels good to them if left to their own devices. Usually this means what already comes naturally and not what is really needed.

Physiologically a gap of time exists between the onset of activity and the completion of bodily adjustments needed to meet the physical demands of exercise (Brooks and Fahey 1985). Warming up prepares the body for more strenuous exercise, providing time for these adjustments to occur. Specifically, a warm-up should increase the core body temperature and the temperature of the muscles involved in the ensuing physical activity. This will increase the efficiency of muscular contraction by decreasing muscle viscosity and increasing nerve conduction velocity. Warming up also results in a vasodilatation and shunting of blood to the active muscles, which facilitates the influx of oxygen and nutrients to the muscles. This shunting increases enzymatic activity (which makes it easier to extract oxygen from hemoglobin) and leads to a more efficient removal of the by-products of exercise that lead to fatigue and soreness. Warming up also elongates contracted ligaments, fascia, and musculature, and the plastic properties of soft tissue are greater when their temperature is higher. To meet the increased oxygen demand, the respiratory and heart rates will accelerate (Brooks and Fahey 1985; Mareib 1992).

Guidelines for Warming Up

Engaging in approximately thirty minutes of warm-up movement for dance activity is suggested, while ten to fifteen minutes is recommended for other activities (Brooks and Fahey 1985; Fitt 1996; Mareib 1992). Dancers should be thoroughly

---

Guidelines for Warming Up:

1. Approximately 30 minutes warm up for dance activity is recommended, 10-15 minutes for other activities.

2. The body should "break a (light) sweat" and be fully stretched.

3. Go from general to specific movements.

- First get the heart/respiratory rate up and increase the core temp with 5-10 minutes of full body activity.

- Progress to light, general movement of all joints.

- Once perspiring and "feeling warm" move on to stretches.

- Include an activity that stresses core strength and establishes connections in the body.

- Focus on exercises to strengthen and stretch the muscles that will be taxed most in that rehearsal or exercise session.

4. End with movements or combinations from the dance or activity to be performed. This will prepare those muscles and help establish neural patterns.

Remember:

1. Pay attention to alignment and proper technique when executing movements.

2. Stretches should always be held (not bounced) at a point where tension (not pain) is felt. Do stretching when warm for optimal benefits and decreased incidence of injury.

3. Do not push yourself or others beyond their limits. Injuries occur when muscles and individuals are fatigued and less responsive than optimal. **Listen to your body, and encourage others to do the same.**

Above and following page: Table 8.1 Handout for Dancers Leading Classes or Rehearsals.

4. If leading a warm up, be sure that the dancers are familiar with the warm up or that it is simple enough to follow correctly. If using music, keep the volume low enough that others can hear instructions. Repetition is not bad, and participants can concentrate on their bodies better when they know what they are doing.

5. Warming up is not a waste of time. Dancers will work more safely, be more focused, perform better, and already be familiar with the material if they have a good warm up. Remember that people tend to do what "feels good" to them if left to their own devices. Usually this means what already comes naturally and not what is really needed to warm up and prepare for class or rehearsal.

Cooling Down

After strenuous exercise, it is a just as important to end with a cool down. The heart rate, respiratory rate, and circulation should all be permitted to return to non-exercise levels gradually to prevent blood from pooling in the lower extremities. Pooling can cause extreme discomfort, soreness, and faintness.

1. Continue to move for 5-10 minutes following activity until the heart rate and breathing have returned to normal.

2. Stretching after this period will reduce muscle tension.

warmed, stretched, and prepared to participate at full performance level by the end of the warm-up. At the beginning of the warm-up, participants should engage in full body activities like jogging or walking briskly with arm movements. The goal is to increase the heart and respiratory rate and the core body temperature to the point at which a light sweat is broken. Proceed from these more general to more specific movements of all the joints, like isolations, moving easily through the range of motion. Once feeling warm, dancers can begin stretching. It may be helpful to include an activity that stresses core strength and establishes connections in the body. Then move on to exercises to strengthen and stretch the muscles that will be taxed most in that rehearsal, performance, or dance class session. Finish with movements or combinations from the dance or activity to be performed to help establish neural patterns.

Figure 8.1 "Technique" (Karen Snouffer).

Cooling Down at the End of Class

After strenuous exercise, it is a good idea to end with a cool down. The heart rate, respiratory rate, and circulation should all be permitted to return to nonexercise levels gradually to prevent blood from pooling in the lower extremities. Pooling of the blood in the lower extremities can cause discomfort, soreness, and faintness (Brooks and Fahey 1985). Continue to move for five to ten minutes following physical activity until the heart rate and the breathing have returned to normal. Stretching after this period will help reduce muscular tension, and dancers can capitalize on the fact that their muscles are warm and prepared to be optimally lengthened (Alter 2004; Brooks and Fahey 1985; Mareib 1992).

Conclusions

The training and conditioning principles derived from movement science and presented in this chapter do not contradict the somatic approaches presented in this book. Rather, knowledge and understanding of both are needed to effectively train dancers and to recognize what can and should be infused in class, and how best to approach various training issues. As class time is limited, awareness of individual needs may suggest the benefits of accessing supplementary training options outside class that also take these principles into consideration. We hope that applying the scientific concepts to the Somatic Principles and relating both to specific technical demands are helpful in contextualizing this broad range of information. All of the principles, both somatic and scientific, can also provide another avenue of inspiration, in and out of the dance class. They may ignite new interests or provide the impetus for creating unique class material, choreography, and/or self-practices, thereby influencing the manner in which we teach and learn dance.

Conclusion

One of the most exciting things about this time is that we could move beyond technique by understanding how and why it is made. The idea is not to do without technique but to reinvent it over and over again in whatever way the moment requires.—Beavers 2008, 129

In this chapter we share some last thoughts about somatic work and its application to dance training. Current dance trends and dance training practices and their relationship to somatic techniques are touched upon as issues for further and future consideration. The chapter continues with acknowledging the role of our teachers, students, and peers in our quest to better understand what the body of somatic knowledge entails, from where it is derived, and how this led to the development of the Somatic Principles as they are presented in this text. The conclusion of the chapter contains a variety of resources to assist the reader with his or her own journey or exploration of the potential connections between somatics and dance.

Somatic Work in Dance Training

Some final musings about somatic work and its inclusion in dance training today.... While somatic ideology revolves around the concept of finding the best way of working for an individual, the pitfall of "Somatic Platonism" must be avoided. Somatic Platonism, as defined by Don Johnson (1980, 5), involves thinking that there is one idealized body for everyone and that this hypothetical body conforms to a specific image rather than to an idealized function. As the authors of this text, we have both encountered the ethos of an ideal somatic body—that the somatically trained dancer is in some way more valid or pure than the technically trained or that there is some perfect model of the "free body" to attain from somatic training. With age and experience, we have come to recognize that this is actually antithetical to the philosophy of somatic practice. It is just as much an "end-gaining," if you will, as striving for the perfect ballet or modern body. As much as we (and we hope you readers) believe in this body of somatic work, care must be taken not to start to codify its gifts, or it will become something different and limiting in its own way.

Trends in Dance Today

It goes beyond the scope of this book to fully analyze the current dance aesthetic, but it is relevant to mention that the responsibilities placed on dancers have changed in recent years, both technically and creatively. We touched on this in Chapter 6 with the discussion of contemporary modern dance — the aesthetic interest in specificity of initiation and sequencing and the diminished concern with an exact replication of an external form. This does not necessarily hold true for all dance styles, but an enormous demand for technical virtuosity does seem a universal trend. One only has to turn on the television to see dancers flipping upside down, aerials from gymnastics being performed, women lifting men, or dancers' limbs extending far beyond the normal range of motion (even to a dancer's mind!). Perhaps the popularity of dance teams, competitions, and adventure/extreme sports are contributing factors, but regardless, dance looks different today.

In addition to these changes in technical demands, dancers are now frequently asked to contribute creatively in the choreographic process. Many choreographers draw on their dancers substantively in the rehearsal process to help shape and/or generate movement material (Erkert 2003, 14). Most are also interested in working with dancers who contribute a unique style or quality through their performances (Bales and Nettl-Fiol 2008, x). It is our belief that integrating dance science and somatics into their training will help dancers explore, respect, and listen to their bodies, and that it will allow them to utilize the forces acting on their bodies more productively and imaginatively. This, in turn will facilitate dancers' abilities to meet these new technical and creative demands, irrespective of the style of dance being performed.

Current Dance Training Practices

While many aspects of dance training have changed in the last decade or so, in some ways the environment of teacher-student learning, or passing information from one generation to the next through experiential learning, has not changed. Part of our mission with this text is to expand knowledge of the original source for some of the ideas we are seeing in today's dance training culture. We have gone to great lengths in our attempt to reference the basic ideas, to relate them to somatic and scientific thinking, and to recognize current writing and research in the field. However, we have struggled with how best to identify and credit the origin of activities. The movement experiences in this text stemmed from a variety of sources. Some are the result of our original work with the Somatic Principles. Some are our own version of explorations we have found value in doing or teaching through our participation in various dance events. Other movement experiences grew from ideas we have encountered and shared with many teachers and colleagues through our years of experience. It becomes difficult to acknowledge any one person or technique as the source of an activity, so in this concluding chapter we recognize some of the many artists and practitioners we have worked with throughout our careers.

The following people have inspired us in the journey to this book through our direct interactions with them. We have placed their names in specific categories so the reader can seek them out in terms of specialization, but even this seemingly simple act presented its own challenges. Most of these gifted artist/practitioners have broad-ranging experience and influence across disciplines. For these individuals we selected one category in which we deemed their contributions to us most important, and we hope that is satisfactory for them as well. In the realm of **Laban Movement Analysis/Bartenieff Fundamentals**, we thank Melanie Bales, Karen Bradley, Lynn Brooks, John Chanik, Scott Clark, Peggy Hackney, Valerie Preston-Dunlop, Karen Studd and Jacqueline Villamil. In the **Feldenkrais Method**, we thank Larry Goldfarb, Paris Kern, Aliza Stewart and David Zemach Bersin. Influential **Alexander Technique** practitioners include Rebecca Nettl-Fiol, Nancy Romita-Wanich, and Luc Vanier. We recognize fellow **Dancers/Kinesiologists**: Balinda Craig-Quijada, Irene Dowd, Pam Geber, Angie Hauser, Geri Houlihan, Bebe Miller, Kora Radella, Karl Rogers, Jennifer Salk, Molly Shannahan, and Mark Taylor. In the **martial arts** and **yoga**: Steve Hatfield, Al MacLuckie, Terry Ward, Lee Wedlake, Linda Tarnay, and Dr. Yang Yang. One final special acknowledgement goes out to Martha Myers for her contributions in so many of these areas and for her pivotal role in the integration of somatic work into dance technique.

Student Responses to Somatic Principles

We have been inspired not only by our teachers, but also by our students and their enthusiastic responses to this work in classes, workshops, and conferences over the past several years. Sharing some of their thinking about this method of teaching technique, with its infusion of somatic and scientific principles, seemed an appropriate way to conclude. We hope that it will encourage you to try some of these ideas or approaches with your own students. These responses were drawn from midterm and final self-reflection assignments (refer to Table 7.3 in Chapter 7) for modern technique and kinesiology classes and are copied with the permission of the students.

General responses to the concept teaching approach using the Somatic Principles reveal the benefits of this pedagogical choice but also reflect the challenges of applying or layering somatic concepts onto complex technical movement. When asked to reflect upon themes used in classes up to that point in the semester, one student responded in her midterm self-reflection: "Theoretically, the themes we have covered in class represent overall body awareness, mental/physical health, and educational awareness. The themes instill a sense of awareness of what my body is doing on a physiological level. Sometimes placing what I know should happen with my body when doing particular movements is difficult.... It was easier with other actions like over and under-curves because I had experience with those movements before."

Along the same line of thought: "I found this class interesting as it made me stop and think about the micro-adjustments I am constantly making to my movement, and it also forced me to consider that the methods of moving I currently use as my defaults may not be the best for all situations. I'm now tempted to explore new ways of moving in all situations, even merely walking to and from class."

Another student recognized that this body of somatic information has become the lexicon for many styles of modern dance: "As with any art — any discipline, really — dance has a set of tools, and as dancers we have to be fluent with all of these tools, to be familiar with the minute details, the seemingly mundane and microscopic technicalities, in order to achieve specificity, eloquence, and artistry on a more macroscopic level."

Comments on the Four Fundamental Principles

With reference to the four fundamental principles of breathing, sensing, connecting, and initiating and their application in class, we received the feedback below. As might be expected, awareness of each of the principles is frequently mentioned as being primary to the initial experience. Students seemed accepting of the process and trusting that awareness would grow into a fuller ability to access or employ the principle with time and practice.

On breath. The selected responses highlight the primacy of breath to the dancer as an inroad to both change and expressivity.

"Breathing enables you to relax and therefore to really move. This was one of the most difficult things for me this semester. I have noticed that I sometimes stop breathing while I'm dancing which makes my movement stiff. I think there are two reasons for this. First off, I get nervous and tighten up and stop thinking about my breath. Secondly, I think I focus too much on the specific steps I am doing and not enough on the movement as a whole. I would like to work on letting myself relax, and by taking in the whole of the movement I can start using my breath to help my dancing instead of hindering it."

"I have found that a greater awareness of the breath has resulted in free, fuller movement. I have a lot of control over my movement through all of my ballet training, and so it is difficult for me to let my body totally release, relinquishing all control and allowing my movement to originate from the forces of gravity and momentum alone. I have found that by freeing myself from my technique's control, my movement has felt better and fuller in my body."

On sensing. The importance of including exploratory, self-directed activities in technique class that provide time for sensing one's self while moving can be seen in the following student reflections.

"Being able to take the time to do absolutely nothing except be aware of every detail of my body helped me realize what sensations are typical for me and where I hold most of my weight. I found that it was easy to sink my lower body into the floor, but harder to get my shoulders, neck, and head (where I'm often tense) to work into the floor. I like how exploratory activities allow for individuality and how little to no specific instructions were given besides the commands. Because there was this freedom, I wasn't worried about doing anything wrong and was completely absorbed in myself rather than anyone else in the room. (This was a bit of a liberty compared to doing combinations, where awareness of the space and moving as an ensemble is often key.)"

"It was like opening a book and passing page by page through the layers of muscles of my body until I found the "deep level" muscles that get neglected because it's easier to move the surface ones. It felt simultaneously new and old. New because I'm not used to moving with my deeper muscles; old because all these muscles have been here inside me all this time and I recognized them. We just haven't worked on our relationship."

On connecting. Head-tail, upper-lower, and heel–sit bone connections were each the focus of one week of classes before the midterm conferences. There was a large technical range of abilities in the class, but having concepts to concentrate on assisted students at all skill levels find their own challenges within the class material.

"The ideas dealing with connectivity are less intuitive for me — but, if possible, more important given my particular challenges as a dancer. They are all more intimately connected to specific movements of the body and the body's relationship to itself, whereas fall and recovery and the planes of movement deal with the body's relationship to its environment which (for me, at least) requires a less sophisticated and focused sense of the body. I feel I often become fragmented in my dancing — so focused on one particular element or part of my body that I lose touch with other areas. Head-tail, upper-lower, and heel–sit bone connectivity are all directly related to fighting this tendency, making sure that all parts of the body are integrated and working as a whole."

"When I am really concentrating, it allows me to liquefy my body, motivating me to make that smooth connection between the head and tail and creating that snake-like essence seen when rolling. However, I lose that head-tail connection when I strain my neck and look around the classroom to ensure that I'm getting the steps right, which always breaks the connection."

"The upper-lower connection is the ability of the dancer to incorporate both the upper and lower body into movement with congruous expression and timing and physicality. I have a very difficult time incorporating my upper body, especially my arms, into my movement in a connected way. While I am very comfortable with the lower body movement — likely due to soccer — the upper body provides a significant challenge for me. It seems it is an ongoing struggle for me since I have no background in use of my arms, so it is a matter of building the movements into my physical vocabulary bit by bit."

"The upper-lower connectivity part of the class was a concept I had heard before but never understood in the context of my body. I got that there was a connection through the spine between upper and lower halves of my body, but lying on the floor and feeling the connection between the right arm and left leg and visa versa was a whole new experience. It was really interesting to learn about how the human body is connected, and how that can help in understanding and working on the movement pieces."

"My heel–sit bone connection allows me to access the link between the tip of my sit bone running through my hamstrings to my Achilles. This connection is dynamic and gives my movement energy when visualizing the concept. This is a helpful way for me to remember the effect my lower body has on my upper, and how closely connected they truly are, but most importantly it reinforces how economical you can be in the position."

The importance of connecting to the environment as well as to self is evident in this passage: "Awareness in space helps me to feel much more centered in my own being. I feel much more connected to the forces within my body than I have in years past. I am finally starting to understand the interconnections with my body and how they affect each and every movement choice I make. This newfound understanding has helped my rethink my relationships in dance to the important factors of time, space, and tone."

On initiation. The following two selections illuminate the significance of initiation for the individual dancer, and in particular, highlight the relationship between initiation and connectivity issues.

"It has been very interesting discovering through dancing how each part of the body connects and affects other parts of the body. In our warm-up for class we focus a lot of time on forward bending and lateral bending and twisting. These different movements all are centralized at the spine and hips. But each action is initiated from a part of the body."

"On the surface the sequences seemed rather simple, however once I got into them there was a lot to think about. To me it seemed we were almost trying to reach some sort of what I would call a controlled letting go.... It helped to remember to think about what was initiating the movement. All of the turns and sways we did felt like another way to look at this controlled letting go by acknowledging what started the movement, our hand, and then letting our bodies — pelvis, feet, shoulders — react to that. It became clear to me, the idea of feeling how my body is connected and how one movement affects the rest of the body."

The value of including kinesiology concepts, tools like frames of reference, and marrying principles like breath to traditional modern dance themes can be seen in these responses: "During our explorations of various planes of action, I was interested by the idea of restriction. When only allowed to move in the coronal or sagittal plane, I immediately became nervous and unsure of my movement. After a few moments, though, I began to notice the advantage of isolating movement in this fashion. In

Figure C.1 "Monoprint" (Karen Snouffer).

215

focusing my attention on the coronal plane of my body and the movements that can use this plane as a basis of exploration, I discovered new movement possibilities for my body. These movements were small and not particularly interesting, but they were movements I had never done or found in my body before. These explorations are difficult for me because they force me to face the current limitations of my personal movement vocabulary, yet they are valuable for the same reason. In paying attention to the ways in which I already use these planes of the body — and to the way in which they can provide now possibilities and ranges and movement — I see the importance of movement analysis. I can dance wildly and lose myself in that, but if I am not conscious of what my body is doing in those moments, how can I develop and refine the qualities of my movement? This physical awareness is something I struggle with, for I find that the spatial map of my body that exists in my head does not always line up with the realities of my movement."

"I have discovered that modern dance is a lot heavier than the previous dancing I have done. This semester we have spent a lot of time on the floor and working on using the floor to help our movement. I have learned a lot just by letting myself give into the floor and letting my weight go. I have learned that there are definitely differences in where weight can be distributed."

"The mental/physical health theme for me was fall and recovery — there is something very cleansing about doing movements that, just for a second, take my breath away and increase my heart rate. I absolutely loved doing the Doris Humphrey falls; not only were they fairly simple and easy to pick up, but they made me feel better (no matter the day or mood — I always felt a sense of catharsis and emotional release). The same can be said for the applied use of breath and swinging — totally cathartic."

Just as there is no original movement, we want to recognize that the information in this book is not "new." As Twyla Tharp (2003, 22) stated, "Honey, it's all been done before: Nothing's really original. Not Homer or Shakespeare and certainly not you." However, just as with all valid works of art, we hope that our particular approach to understanding, organizing, and presenting material provides readers with different insights into somatic work, the scientific principles that support it, and how both relate to dance training. This student response seems to sum it all up:

"Our bodies are universes, a microcosm of the universe, the macrocosm of our cells. There is so much power embedded in our bodies and yet there are so many people out there that have never established a connection with their physical body. If people only knew that movement is such a powerful gate toward our emotional, psychic, spiritual, and intellectual beings."

A Selection of
Suggested Resources

Readings

THE ALEXANDER TECHNIQUE

Alexander, F. Mathias. 1932. *The Use of the Self.* London: Victor Gollancz.

Alexander, F. Mathias. 1969. *The Resurrection of the Body: The Writings of F.M. Alexander.* Selected and introduced by Edward Maisel with a preface by Raymond A. Dart. New York: University Books.

Nettl-Fiol, Rebecca and Luc Vanier. 2011. *Dance and the Alexander Technique: Exploring the Missing Link.* Urbana: University of Illinois Press.

Gelb, Michael. 1994. *Body Learning.* 2nd ed. New York: Henry and Holt.

Vineyard, Missy. 2007. *How You Stand, How You Move, How You Live: Learning the Alexander Teechnique.* New York: Marlowe.

BODY-MIND CENTERING

Bainbridge-Cohen, Bonnie. 1993. *Sensing, Feeling, and Action.* Northhampton, MA: Contact Editions.

Hartley Linda. 1995. *Wisdom of the Body Moving: An Introduction to Body Mind Centering.* Berkeley, CA.: North Atlantic Books.

FELDENKRAIS METHOD

Alon, Ruthy. 1996. *Mindful Spontaneity: Lessons in the Feldenkrais Method.* Berkeley, CA: North Atlantic Books.

Beringer, Elizabeth. 2010. *Embodied Wisdom: The Collected Papers of Moshe Feldenkrais.* Berkeley: CA: Somatic Resources.

Feldenkrais, Moshe. 1972. *Awareness Through Movement: Health Exercises for Personal Growth.* London: Arkana Books.

Feldenkrais, Moshe. 1981. *The Elusive Obvious.* Capitola, CA: Meta.

Feldenkrais, Moshe. 1985. *The Potent Self: A Guide to Spontaneity.* New York: Harper and Row.

Feldenkrais, Moshe. 2005. *Body and Mature Behavior: A Study of Anxiety, Sex, Gravitation, and Learning.* Berkeley, CA: Frog, Ltd.

IDEOKINESIS

Dowd, Irene. 1990. *Taking Root to Fly: Ten Articles on Functional Anatomy.* 2nd ed. Northampton, MA: Contact Editions.

Franklin, Eric. 1996. *Dynamic Alignment Through Imagery.* Champaign, IL: Human Kinetics.

Sweigard, Lulu. 1974. *Human Movement Potential: Its Ideokinetic Facilitation.* New York: Harper and Row.

Todd, Mabel E. 1937. *The Thinking Body.* New York: Princeton Books.

LABAN MOVEMENT ANALYSIS AND THE BARTENIEFF FUNDAMENTALS

Bartenieff, Irmgard, and Dorrie Lewis. 1980. *Body Movement: Coping with the Environment.* New York: Gordon and Breach.

Hackney, Peggy. 1998. *Making Connections: Total Body Integration through Bartenieff Fundamentals.* New York: Gordon and Breach.

Laban, Rudolf. 1980. Mastery of Movement. London: MacDonald and Evans.

Moore, Carol L., and Kaoru Yamamoto. 1988. *Beyond Words: Movement Observation and Analysis.* New York: Gordon and Breach.

MARTIAL ARTS

Ralston, Peter. 2006. *Zen Body Being.* Berkeley, CA: North Atlantic Books.

Yang, Yang. 2005. *Taijiquan: The Art of Nurturing, The Science of Power.* Champaign, IL: Zhenwu.

YOGA

Iyengar, B .K. S. 1979. *Light on Yoga.* New York: Schocken.

Iyengar, B. K. S. 2005. *Light on Life.* United States of America: Rodale.

A Selection of Suggested Resources

GENERAL SOMATIC READINGS

Hanna, Thomas. 1979. *The Body of Life*. Rochester, VT: Healing Arts Press.

Hanna, Thomas. 1993. *Body of Life: Creating New Pathways for Sensory Awareness and Fluid Movement*. Rochester, VT: Healing Arts Press.

Johnson, Don H. 1995. *Bone, Breath, and Gesture: Practices of Embodiment*. Berkeley, CA: North Atlantic Books.

Juhan, Deane. 1998. *Job's Body: A Handbook for Body Work*. Barrytown, NY: Station Hill Openings.

Keleman, Stanley. 1979. *Somatic Reality: Bodily Experience and Emotional Truth*. Berkeley, CA: Somatic Press.

DANCE PEDAGOGY

Erkert, Jan. 2003. *Harnessing the Wind: The Art of Teaching Modern Dance*. Champaign, IL: Human Kinetics.

H' Doubler, Margaret N. 1957. *Dance: A Creative Art Experience*. Madison: University of Wisconsin Press.

Laws, Kenneth. 2002. *Physics and the Art of Dance: Understanding Movement*. Oxford, England: Oxford University Press.

Bales, Melanie, and Rebecca Nettl-Fiol. 2008. *The Body Eclectic: Evolving Practices in Dance Training*. Urbana: University of Illinois Press.

DANCE SCIENCE AND EXPERIENTIAL ANATOMY

Kapit, Wynn, and Lawrence M. Nelson. 2001. *Anatomy Coloring Book*. 3rd ed. San Francisco: Benjamin Cummings

Biel, Andrew. 2010. *The Trail Guide to the Body: A Hands on Guide to Locating Muscles, Bones, and More*. 4th ed. Boulder, CO: Books of Discovery.

Calais-Germaine, Blandine. 1993. *Anatomy of Movement*. Seattle, WA: Eastland Press.

Calais-Germaine, Blandine. 2003. *The Female Pelvis: Anatomy and Exercises*. Seattle, WA: Eastland Press.

Calais-Germaine, Blandine. 2005. *Anatomy of Breathing*. Seattle, WA: Eastland Press.

Clippinger, Karen. 2007. *Dance Anatomy and Kinesiology: Principles and Exercises for Improving Technique and Avoiding Common Injuries*. Champaign, IL: Human Kinetics.

Fitt, Sally S. 1996. *Dance Kinesiology*. New York: Schirmer Books.

Olsen, Andrea, and Caryn McHose. 1998. *Body Stories: A Guide to Experiential Anatomy*. Berrytown, NY: Station Hill Openings.

Welsh, Tom. 2009. *Conditioning for Dancers*. Gainsville: University of Florida Press.

KINESIOLOGY

Haywood, Kathleen M., and Nancy Getchell. 2009. *Lifespan Motor Development*. 5th ed. Champaign, IL: Human Kinetics.

Magill, Richard A. 2011. *Motor Learning and Control: Concepts and Applications*. 9th ed. New York: McGraw-Hill.

Schmidt, Richard A., and Craig A. Wrisberg. 2008. *Motor Learning and Performance*. 4th ed. Champaign, IL: Human Kinetics.

DVDs

Dowd, Irene. 2002. *Warming Up the Hip Joints: Turnout Dance and Orbits*. Toronto, Canada: National Ballet School.

Hackney, Peggy. 2009. *Discovering Your Expressive Body*. New York: Princeton Books.

Rosenholtz, Stephen. 1988. *The Feldenkrais Method: Basic Lessons in Awareness through Movement*. Series I, Lessons 1–4. San Mateo, CA: Rosewood.

Rosenholtz, Stephen. 1988. *The Feldenkrais Method: Basic Lessons in Awareness through Movement*. Series I, Lessons 5–8. San Mateo, CA: Rosewood.

Salk, Jennifer. 2008–2011. *Experiential Anatomy in Dance Technique: Eight Skeletal Explorations*. Champagn, IL: Human Kinetics.

Salk, Jennifer. 2010. *Experiential Anatomy in Dance Technique*. Champaign, IL: Human Kinetics.

Audio CDs

Beringer, Elizabeth, and David Zemach Bersin. 1999. *Introduction to the Feldenkrais Method*. Volumes 1 & 2. Berkeley, CA: Feldenkrais Resources.

Feldenkrais, Moshe. 1980. *Awareness through Movement: Basic Series*. Berkeley, CA: Feldenkrais Resources

Feldenkrais, Moshe. 2007. *Awareness Through Movement: San Francisco Evening Class Workshop*. Volumes 1–3. Berkeley, CA: Feldenkrais Resources.

Yaron, Gaby. 1990. *Awareness through Movement for Health Professionals, Performing Artists and Athletes*. Berkeley, CA: Feldenkrais Resources.

Zemach Bersin, David, and Mark Reese. 1990. *TMJ Health: Sensory Motor Exercises for Mouth and Jaw Health*. Berkeley, CA: Feldenkrais Resources.

Other Related Readings

Arnheim, Rudolf. 1969. *Visual Thinking*. Berkeley: University of California Press.

Csikszentmihalyi, Mihaly. 1990. *Flow: The Psychology of Optimal Experience*. New York: Harper and Row.

Damasio, Antonio. 1999. *The Feeling of What Happens: Body and Emotion in the Making of Consciousness*. Orlando, FL: Harcourt Books.

Edwards, Betty. 1999. *The New Drawing on the Right Side of the Brain*. New York: Tarcher/Putnam.

Gallwey, Timothy. 1976. *The Inner Game of Tennis*. New York: Random House.

Langer, Ellen. 1989. *Mindfulness*. Cambridge, MA: Perseus Books.

Websites and Contact Information For Different Somatic Techniques

ALEXANDER TECHNIQUE

American Society for the Alexander Technique
P.O. Box 2307
Dayton, OH 45401–2307
Phone: 800–473–0620 or 937–586–3732
Fax: 937–3699
Email: info@amsatonline.org
Website address: www.amsatonline.org

BODY-MIND CENTERING

The School for Body-Mind Centering
P.O. Box 20904
El Sobrante, CA 94820
Phone: 510–243–1500
Email: info@bodymindcentering.com
Website Address: www.bodymindcentering.com

FELDENKRAIS METHOD

Feldenkrais Guild of North America (FGNA)
5436 N. Albina Ave
Portland, OR 97217 800–775–2118
Phone: 503–221–6612
Fax: 503–221–6616
Website address: www.feldenkrais.com

LABAN MOVEMENT ANALYSIS AND BARTENIEFF FUNDAMENTALS

Laban/Bartenieff Institute (LIMS)
520 Eighth Avenue, Suite 304,
New York, NY 10018
Phone: 1–212–643–8888 or 1–212–643–8388
Website Address: www.limsonline.org

OTHER RESOURCES

Integrated Movement Studies (IMS)
  Janice Meaden
  215 Cedar Lane
  Santa Barbara, CA 93108
  Phone: (206) 849–4380
  Fax: (805) 962–0300
  Email:jmeadenims@aol.com
  Website Address: www.imsmovement.com
Ideokinesis
  Website Address: www.ideokinesis.com
The Franklin Method
  Franklin-Methode Institute Hittnauerstrasse 40
  8623 Wetzikon/Switzerland
  Email: info@franklin-methode.ch
  Website Address: www.franklinmethod.com
Moving on Center
  Phone 510–524–5013
  Email:director@movingoncenter.org
  Website Address: www.movingoncenter.com

References

Abernathy, Bruce. 1999. "The Coleman Roberts Griffith Address: Movement Expertise, A Juncture Between Psychology Theory and Practice." *Journal of Applied Sport Psychology*, 11: 126–141.

Alexander, F. Mathias. 1932. *The Use of the Self*. London: Victor Gollancz.

_____. 1969. *The Resurrection of the Body: The Writings of F.M. Alexander*. Selected and introduced by Edward Maisel with a preface by Raymond A. Dart. New York: University Books.

Alon, Ruthy. 1996. *Mindful Spontaneity: Lessons in the Feldenkrais Method*. Berkeley, CA: North Atlantic Books.

Alter, Michael J. 2004. *Science of Flexibility*. 3d ed. Champaign, IL: Human Kinetics.

Aposhyan, Susan. 1993. Foreword to *Sensing, Feeling, and Action: The Experiential Anatomy of Body-Mind Centering*, by Bonnie Bainbridge-Cohen, vii. Northhampton, MA: Contact Editions.

Arnheim, Daniel D. 1980. *Dance Injuries: Their Prevention and Care*. St. Louis, MO: Mosby.

Bainbridge-Cohen, Bonnie. 1993. *Sensing, Feeling, and Action: The Experiential Anatomy of Body-Mind Centering*. Northhampton, MA: Contact Editions.

Bales, Melanie, and Rebecca Nettl-Fiol. 2008. *The Body Eclectic: Evolving Practices in Dance Training*. Urbana: University of Illinois Press.

Baniel, Anat. 2009. *Move into Life: The Nine Essentials for Lifelong Vitality*. New York: Random House.

Bartenieff, Irmgard, and Dorrie Lewis. 1980. *Body Movement: Coping with the Environment*. New York: Gordon and Breach.

Batson, Glenna. 1990. "Dancing Fully, Safely, and Expressively: The Role of the Body Therapies in Dance Training." *Journal of Physical Education, Recreation, and Dance*, 61: 28–31.

_____. 2008. "Teaching Alignment." In *The Body Eclectic*, edited by Melanie Bales and Recca Nettl-Fiol, 134–152. Urbana: University of Illinois Press.

_____, and Ray E. Schwartz. 2007. "Revisiting the Value of Somatic Education in Dance Training through an Inquiry into Practice Schedules." *Journal of Dance Education*, 7(2): 47–56.

Beavers, Wendell. 2008. "Relocating Technique." In *The Body Eclectic*, edited by Melanie Bales and Recca Nettl-Fiol, 126–133. Urbana: University of Illinois Press.

Behnke, Elizabeth. 1995. "Matching." In *Bone, Breath, & Gesture: Practices of Embodiment*, edited by Don H. Johnson, 317–337. Berkeley, CA: North Atlantic Books.

Bell, Jacque Lynn. 1996. "The Alexander Technique for Dancers." In *Dance Kinesiology*, by Sally S. Fitt, 331–335. New York: Schirmer Books.

Biel, Andrew. 2010. *The Trail Guide to the Body: A Hands on Guide to Locating Muscles, Bones, and More*. 4th ed. Boulder, CO: Books of Discovery.

Brodie, Julie A., and Elin E. Lobel. 2004. "Integrating Fundamental Principles Underlying Somatic Practices into the Dance Technique Class." *Journal of Dance Education*, 4(3): 80–88.

_____, and _____. 2008. "More than Just a Mirror Image the Visual System and Other Modes of Learning and Performing Dance." *Journal of Dance Education*, 8(1): 23–31.

Brooks, George A., and Thomas D. Fahey. 1985. *Exercise Physiology: Human Bioenergetics and Its Applications*. New York: MacMillan.

Brown, Jean M., Naomi Mindlin, and Charles H. Woodford. 1997. *The Vision of Modern Dance: In the Words of Its Creators*. 2nd ed. Hightstown, NJ: Princeton Books.

Brown, L. E., B. A. Halpert, and M. A. Goodale. 2005. "Peripheral Vision for Perception and Action." *Experimental Brain Research*, 165: 97–106.

Buchanon, Patricia A., and Beverly D. Ulrich. 2001. "The Feldenkrais Method: A Dynamic Approach to Changing Movement Behavior." *Research Quarterly for Exercise Science and Sport*, 72(4): 315–323.

Calais-Germaine, Blandine. 2003. *The Female Pelvis: Anatomy and Exercises*. Seattle, WA: Eastland Press.

_____. 2005. *Anatomy of Breathing*. Seattle, WA: Eastland Press.

Carola, Robert, John P. Harley, and Charles R. Noback. 1992. *Human Anatomy and Physiology*. 2nd ed. New York: McGraw-Hill.

Choudry, Bikram. 2000. *Bikram's Beginning Yoga Class*. New York: Tarcher.

Clippinger, Karen. 2007. *Dance Anatomy and Kinesiology: Principles and Exercises for Improving Technique and Avoiding Common Injuries*. Champaign, IL: Human Kinetics.

Clippinger-Robertson, Karen. 1988. "Principles of Dance Training." In *Science of Dance Training*, edited by Priscilla Clarkson and Margaret Skrinar, 45–82. Champaign, IL: Human Kinetics.

Coker, Cheryl A. 1995. "Learning Style Consistency across Cognitive and Motor Settings." *Perceptual Motor Skills*, 81; 1023–1026.

_____. 2004. *Motor Learning and Control for Practitioners*. Boston: McGraw-Hill.

_____. 2009. *Motor Learning and Control for Practitioners*. 2nd ed. Scottsdale, AZ: Holcomb Hathaway.

Dowd, Irene. 1990. *Taking Root to Fly: Ten Articles on Functional Anatomy*. 2nd ed. Northampton, MA: Contact Editions.

Dunn, R., D. Cavenaugh, B. Eberle, and R. Zenhausern. 1982. "Hemispheric Preference: The Newest Element of Learning Style." *The American Biology Teacher*, 44(5): 291–294.

Dunn, R., and K. Dunn. 1975. *Educator's Self-Teaching Guide to Individualizing Instructional Programs*. Nyack, NY: Parker.

_____, and _____. 1993. *Teaching Secondary Students Through Their Individual Learning Styles*. Boston: Allyn and Bacon.

_____, _____, and G. Price. 1989. *Learning Styles Inventory*. Lawrence, KS: Price Systems.

Edwards, Betty. 1999. *The New Drawing on the Right Side of the Brain*. New York: Tarcher/Putnam.

Erkert, Jan. 2003. *Harnessing the Wind: The Art of Teaching Modern Dance*. Champaign, IL: Human Kinetics.

Feldenkrais, Moshe. 1972. *Awareness through Movement*. New York: Harper and Row.

_____. 1981. *The Elusive Obvious*. Capitola, CA: Meta.

_____. 1984. *The Master Moves*. Capitola, CA: Meta.

_____. 1985. *The Potent Self: A Guide to Spontaneity*. New York: Harper and Row.

_____. 2005. *Body and Mature Behavior: A Study of Anxiety, Sex, Gravitation, and Learning*. Berkeley, CA: Frog, Ltd.

_____. 2007. *Awareness through Movement: San Francisco Evening Class Workshops*. Vol. 1. Berkeley, CA: Feldenkrais Resources.

_____. 2010a. "Awareness through Movement." In *Embodied Wisdom: The Collected Papers of Moshe Feldenkrais*, edited by Elizabeth Beringer, 69–75. Berkeley: CA: Somatic Resources.

_____. 2010b. "Bodily Expression." In *Embodied Wisdom: The Collected Works of Moshe Feldenkrais*, edited by Elizabeth Beringer, translated by Thomas Hannah, 3–25. Berkeley, CA: North Atlantic Books.

Fiorentino, Mary R. 1981. *A Basis for Sensorimotor Development-Normal and Abnormal*. Springfield, IL: Charles C. Thomas.

Fitt, Sally S. 1996. *Dance Kinesiology*. New York: Schirmer Books.

Fitts, P. M., and M. I. Posner. 1967. *Human Performance*. Belmont, CA: Brooks/Cole.

Fitzmaurice, Catherine. 1997. "Breathing is Meaning." In *Vocal Vision*, edited by Marion Hampton, 1–5. New York: Applause Books.

_____. 2003. "Structured Breathing." *VASTA Newsletter*, 17(1): 1–3.

Fleishman, E. A. 1962. "The Description and Prediction of Perceptual Motor Skill Learning." In *Training Research and Education*, edited by R. Glasser, 137–177. Pittsburgh: University of Pittsburgh.

Floyd, R. T. 2007. *Manual of Structural Kinesiology*. 16th ed. Boston: McGraw-Hill.

Fortin, Sylvie, and Fernande Girard. 2005. "Dancers' Application of the Alexander Technique." *Journal of Dance Education*, 5(4): 125–131.

Fortin, Sylvie, Warwick Long, and Madeleine Lord. 2002. "Three Voices: Researching How Somatic Education Informs Contemporary Dance Technique Classes." *Research in Dance Education*, 3(2): 155–179.

Franklin, Eric. 1996. *Dynamic Alignment through Imagery*. Champaign, IL: Human Kinetics.

_____. 2003. *Pelvic Power for Men and Women: Mind/Body Exercises for Strength, Flexibility, Posture, and Balance*. Hightstown, NJ: Princeton Books.

_____. 2004. *Conditioning for Dance: Training for Peak Performance in All Dance Forms*. Champaign, IL: Human Kinetics.

Gabbard, Carl P. 2008. *Lifelong Motor Development*. 5th ed. San Francisco: Pearson Benjamin Cummings.

Gallwey, Timothy. 1976. *The Inner Game of Tennis*. New York: Random House.

Gardner, Howard. 1993a. *Frames Of Mind: A Theory of Multiple Intelligences*. New York: Basic.

_____. 1993b. *Multiple Intelligences: The Theory in Practice*. New York: Basic.

Gentile, Ann M. 1972. "A Working Model of Skill Acquisition with Application to Teaching." *Quest Monograph*, XVII: 3–23.

Gindler, Elsa. 1995. "Gymnastik for People Whose Lives Are Full of Activity." In *Bone, Breath, & Gesture: Practices of Embodiment,* edited by Don H. Johnson, 5–14. Berkeley, CA: North Atlantic Books.

Goldie, P. A, T. M. Bach, and O. M. Evans. 1989. "Force Platform Measures For Evaluating Postural Control: Reliability and Validity." *Archives of Physical Medicine and Rehabilitation*, 70: 510–517.

Green, Jill. 2002. "Somatic Knowledge: The Body as Content and Methodology in Dance Education." *Journal of Dance Education*, 2(4): 114–118.

Green Gilbert, Anne. 2006. *Brain Compatible Dance Education*. Reston, VA: National Dance Association.

Griffiths, Iwan W. 2006. *Principles of Biomechanics & Motion Analysis*. Baltimore: Lippincott, Williams, and Wilkins.

H' Doubler, Margaret N. 1957. *Dance: A Creative Art Experience*. Madison: University of Wisconsin Press.

Hackney, Peggy. 1998. *Making Connections: Total Body Integration through Bartenieff Fundamentals*. New York: Gordon and Breach.

Hall, Susan J. 2003. *Basic Biomechanics*. 4th ed. New York: McGraw-Hill.

Hamill, Joseph, and Kathleen M. Knutzen. 1995. *Biomechanical Basis of Human Movement*. Media, PA: Williams and Williams.

Hanna, Thomas. 1979. *The Body of Life*. Rochester, VT: Healing Arts Press.

_____. 1993. *Body of Life: Creating New Pathways for Sensory Awareness and Fluid Movement*. Rochester, VT: Healing Arts Press.

Hardy, Lew. 1997. "The Coleman Roberts Griffith Address: Three Myth's About Sport Psychology Consultancy Work." *Journal of Applied Sport Psychology*, 9: 277–294.

Hartley, Linda. 1995. *Wisdom of the Body Moving: An Introduction to Body Mind Centering*. Berkeley, CA: North Atlantic Books.

Hawkins, Alma M. 1991. *Moving from Within: A New Method for Dance Making*. Chicago: A Cappela Books.

Haywood, Kathleen M. 1993. *Lifespan Motor Development*. Champaign, IL: Human Kinetics.

_____, and Nancy Getchell. 2009. *Lifespan Motor Development*. 5th ed. Champaign, IL: Human Kinetics.

Henry, F. M. 1961. "Reaction Time–Movement Time Correlations." *Perceptual and Motor Skills*, 12: 63–66.

_____, and D. E. Rogers. 1960. "Increased Response Latency for Complicated Movements and A 'Memory Drum Theory' of Neuromotor Reaction." *Research Quarterly*, 31: 448–458.

Henry, Franklin M. 1968. "Specificity Versus Generality in Learning Motor Skills." In *Classical Studies on Physical Activity*, edited by R. C. Brown and G. S. Kenyon, 331–340. Engelwood Cliffs, NJ: Prentice-Hall.

Huang, Jane, and Michael Wurmbrand 1990. *The Primordial Breath: An Ancient Chinese Way of Prolonging Life through Breath Control*. Vol. II. Torrance, CA: Original Books.

Iyengar, B. K. S. 1979. *Light on Yoga*. New York: Schocken.

_____. 2005. *Light on Life*. New York: Rodale.

_____. 2010. *Light on Pranayama: The Yogic Art of Breathing*. New York: Crossroad.

Johnson, Don. 1980. "Somatic Platonism." *Somatics*, Autumn: 4–7.

Johnson, Don H. 1995. *Bone, Breath, & Gesture: Practices of Embodiment*. Berkeley, CA: North Atlantic Books.

Jou, Tsung Hwa. 1998. *The Dao of Taijiquan: Way to Rejuvenation,* edited by Lori S. Elias, Sharon Rose, and Loretta Wollering. Warwick, NY: Tai Chi Foundation.

Juhan, Deane. 1998. *Job's Body: A Handbook for Body Work*. Barrytown, NY: Station Hill Openings.

Kamen, Gary. 2001. *Foundations of Exercise Science*. Baltimore: Lippincott Williams and Wilkins.

Kandel, Eric R., James H. Schwartz, and Thomas M. Jessell. 1991. *Principles of Neural Science*. 3d ed. Norwalk, CT: Appleton and Lange.

Kassing, Gayle. 1992. "Performance Contracting and Goal Setting in the Dance Class." *Journal of Health, Physical Education, Recreation, and Dance*, 75: 58–60.

Keleman, Stanley. 1979. *Somatic Reality: Bodily Experience and Emotional Truth*. Berkeley, CA: Somatic Press.

Kimmerle, Marliese, and Paulette Cote-Laurence. 2003. *Teaching Dance Skills: A Motor Learning and Development Approach*. Andover, NJ: J. Michael Ryan.

Koner, Pauline. 1993. *Elements of Performance: A Guide for Performers in Dance, Theatre and Opera*. Chur, Switzerland: Harwood Academic.

Laban, Rudolf. 1980. *Mastery of Movement*. 4th ed. London: McDonald and Evans.

Laws, Kenneth. 2002. *Physics and the Art of Dance:*

Understanding Movement. Oxford, England: Oxford University Press.

Lee, D. N., and E. Aronson. 1974. "Visual Proprioceptive Control of Standing in Human Infants." *Perception and Psychophysics*, 15: 529–532.

Lee, David A. 1980. "Visuo-Motor Coordination in Space-Time." In *Tutorials in Motor Behavior,* edited by George E. Stelmach and J. Requin, 281–285. Amsterdam: North-Holland.

Lee, David N., and E. Aronson. 1974. "Visual Proprioceptive Control of Standing in Human Infants." *Perception and Psychophysics*, 15: 527–532.

Lessinger, Carol. 1996. "Nature of the Feldenkrais Method and Its Value to Dancers." In *Dance Kinesiology,* edited by Sally S. Fitt, 225–331. New York: Schirmer Books.

Liao, Waysun, trans. 1990. *T'ai Chi Classics.* Boston: Shambhala Classics.

Lidor, Ronnie, and Robert N. Singer. 2000. "Teaching Pre-Performance Routines to Beginners." *Journal of Physical Education Health Recreation and Dance*, 71(7): 34–36.

Linklater, Kristin. 2006. *Freeing the Natural Voice: Imagery and Art in the Practice of Voice and Language.* Hollywood, CA: Drama.

Lobel, Elin E., and Julie A. Brodie. 2006a. "Somatics in Dance — Dance in Somatics." *Journal of Dance Education*, 6(3): 69–71.

_____ and _____, eds. 2006b. "Practical Application of Somatic Principles in the Classroom." Special issue, *Journal of Dance Education,* 6(3): 69–100.

Magill, Richard A. 1998. *Motor Learning and Control: Concepts and Applications.* 6th ed. Boston: McGraw-Hill.

_____. 2001. *Motor Learning and Control: Concepts and Applications.* 7th ed. Boston: McGraw-Hill.

_____. 2007. *Motor Learning and Control: Concepts and Applications.* 8th ed. Boston: McGraw-Hill.

_____. 2011. *Motor Learning and Control: Concepts and Applications.* 9th ed. New York: McGraw-Hill.

Mareib, Elaine N. 1992. *Human Anatomy and Physiology.* Redwood City, CA: Benjamin Cummings.

Martin, K. A., S. A. Moritz, and C. R. Hall. 1999. "Imagery Use in Sport: A Literature Review and Applied Model." *The Sport Psychologist*, 13: 245–268.

Mayland, Elaine. 1995. "The Rosen Method." In *Bone, Breath, & Gesture: Practices of Embodiment,* edited by Don H. Johnson, 53–64. Berkeley, CA: North Atlantic Books.

Mills, Marghe, and Bonnie Bainbridge-Cohen.

1990. *Developmental Movement Therapy.* Berkeley, CA: Feldenkrais Resources.

Moore, Carol L., and Kaoru Yamamoto. 1988. *Beyond Words: Movement Observation and Analysis.* New York: Gordon and Breach.

Mosston, Muska, and Sara Ashworth. 2002. *Teaching Physical Education.* 5th ed. San Francisco: Benjamin Cummings.

Myers, Martha. 1983. "Body Therapies and the Modern Dancer." *Dance Magazine*, special pull-out, 1–24.

Nagrin, Daniel. 1997. *The Six Questions: Acting Technique for Dance Performance.* Pittsburgh: University of Pittsburgh.

Nettl-Fiol, Rebecca. 2006. "Alexander Technique and Dance Technique: Applications in the Dance Studio." *Journal of Dance Education*, 6(3): 78–85.

_____. 2008. "Somatics: An Interview with Martha Myers." In *The Body Eclectic: Evolving Practices in Dance Training,* edited by Melanie Bales and Rebecca Nettl-Fiol, 89–100. Urbana: University of Illinois Press.

_____, and Luc Vanier. 2008. "The Rule of Engagement For Change: Using Principles of the Alexander Technique." Workshop presented at the annual conference for the National Dance Education Organization, Towson, MD, June 25–29.

Newell, Karl M. 1986. "Constraints on the Development of Coordination." In *Motor Development in Children: Aspects of Coordination and Control,* edited by M. G. Wade and H. T. A. Whitting, 341–361. Amsterdam: Niijoff.

Nideffer, R. M. 1995. *Focus for Success.* San Diego: Enhanced Performance Services.

Nordin, Margareta, and Victor H. Frankel. 2001. *Basic Biomechanics of the Muskuloskeletal System.* 3d ed. Baltimore: Lippincott, Williams, and Wilkins.

Nourrit, D., D. Delignieres, N. Caillou, T. Deschamps, and B. Lauriot. 2003. "On Discontinuities in Motor Learning: A Longitudinal Study of Complex Skill Aqcuisition on a Ski Simulator." *Journal of Motor Behavior*, 35: 151–170.

Olsen, Andrea, and Caryn McHose. 1998. *BodyStories: A Guide to Experiential Anatomy.* Berrytown, NY: Station Hill Openings.

Ranney, Donald. 1988. "Biomechanics of Dance." In *Science of Dance Training,* edited by Priscilla Clarkson and Margaret Skrinar, 125–144. Champaign, IL: Human Kinetics.

Rolf, Ida P. 1989. *Rolfing: Reestablishing the Natural Alignment and Structural Integration of the*

Human Body for Vitality and Well-Beings. Rochester, VT: Healing Arts.

Rose, Debra J., and Robert W. Christina. 2006. *A Multilevel Approach to the Study of Motor Control and Learning.* 2nd ed. San Francisco: Benjamin Cummings.

Schmidt, Richard A. 1975. "A Schema Theory of Discrete Motor Skill Learning." *Psychological Review,* 82: 225–260.

Schmidt, Richard A., and Craig A. Wrisberg. 2001. *Motor Learning and Performance.* 3d ed. Champaign, IL: Human Kinetics.

_____ and _____. 2004. *Motor Learning and Performance.* 3d ed. Champaign, IL: Human Kinetics.

_____ and _____. 2008. *Motor Learning and Performance.* 4th ed. Champaign, IL: Human Kinetics.

Selye, Hans. 1976. *The Stress of Life.* New York: McGraw-Hill.

Serway, Raymond A., and Jerry S. Faughn. 1992. *College Physics.* 3d ed. Orlando, FL: Harcourt Brace Jovanovich.

Shea, Charles H., and Gabriele Wulf. 2005. "Schema Theory: A Critical Appraisal and Reevaluation." *Journal of Motor Behavior,* 37: 85–101.

Siaw-Voon Sim, Davidine, and David Gaffney. 2002. *Chen Style Taijiquan: The Source of Taiji Boxing.* Berkeley, CA: North Atlantic Books.

Silver, Brooke. 2000. *The Pilates Body.* New York: Broadway Books.

Snouffer, Karen. 2011. Personal communication with author Julie A. Brodie.

Speads, Carola. 1995. "Excerpts from Ways to Better Breathing." In *Bone, Breath, & Gesture: Practices of Embodiment,* edited by Don H. Johnson, 36–49. Berkeley, CA: North Atlantic Books.

Sweigard, Lulu. 1974. *Human Movement Potential: Its Ideokinetic Facilitation.* New York: Harper and Row.

Taylor, Jim, and Ceci Taylor. 1995. *Psychology of Dance.* Champaign, IL: Human Kinetics.

Tharp, Twyla. 2003. *The Creative Habit: Learn It and Use It For Life.* New York: Simon & Schuster.

Thomas, Jerry T., and Jack K. Nelson. 1990. *Research Methods in Physical Activity.* Champaign, IL: Human Kinetics.

Todd, Mabel E. 1937. *The Thinking Body.* New York: Princeton Books.

Tremblay, L., and L. Proteau. 1998. "Specificity of Practice: The Case of Powerlifting." *Research Quarterly for Exercise, Science, and Sport,* 69: 284–289.

Trevarthen, C. B. 1968. "Two Mechanisms of Vision in Primates." *Psychological Research,* 31: 299–337.

Turvey, Michael T. 1977. "Preliminaries to a Theory of Action with Reference to Vision." In *Perceiving, Acting, and Knowing,* edited by Robert Shaw and John Bransford. Hillsdale, NJ: Erlbaum.

Van Tress, Lester. 1976. Personal Communication with author Julie A. Brodie.

Vasiliev, Vladimir, and Meredith Scott. 2006. *Let Every Breath ... Secrets of the Russian Breath Masters.* Toronto, Canada: V. Vasiliev.

Vealey, R. S., and C. A. Greenleaf. 2006. "Seeing is Believing: Understanding and Using Imagery in Sport." In *Applied Sport Psychology: Personal Growth to Peak Performance,* edited by J. Williams, 306–348. New York: McGraw-Hill.

Vincent, L. M. 1978. *The Dancer's Book of Health.* New York: Andrews and McNeel.

Vineyard, Missy. 2007. *How You Stand, How You Move, How You Live: Learning the Alexander Teechnique.* New York: Marlowe.

Voss, Dorothy E., Marjorie K. Ionta, and Beverly J. Myers. 1985. *Proprioceptive Neuromuscular Facilitation: Patterns and Techniques.* 3d ed. Philadephia: Harper and Row.

Watkins, Andrea, and Priscilla M. Clarkson. 1990. *Dancing Longer Dancing Stronger: A Dancer's Guide to Improving Technique and Preventing Injury.* Princeton, NJ: Princeton Books.

Wedlake, Lee. 2000. *Kenpo Karate 101: What The Beginner and the Black Belt Should Know.* Fort Myers, FL: Lee Wedlake's Karate Studio.

_____. 2005. *Kenpo Karate 301: The Intermediate Forms, Short Form Three and Long Form Three.* Fort Myers, FL: Lee Wedlake's Karate Studio.

Welsh, Tom. 2009. *Conditioning for Dancers.* Gainsville: University of Florida Press.

Westcott, Wayne. 1996. *Building Strength and Stamina.* Champaign, IL: Human Kinetics.

Woollacott, Marjorie H., and Anne Shumway-Cook. 1989. *Development of Posture and Gait Across the Lifespan.* Columbia: University of South Carolina Press.

Wulf, Gabrielle. 2007. *Attention and Motor Skill Learning.* Champaign, IL: Human Kinetics.

Yang, Yang. 2005. *Taijiquan: The Art of Nurturing, The Science of Power.* Champaign, IL: Zhenwu.

Index